# Emblems of Quality in Higher Education

## Developing and Sustaining High-Quality Programs

# Emblems of Quality in Higher Education

## Developing and Sustaining High-Quality Programs

**Jennifer Grant Haworth**
Loyola University Chicago

**Clifton F. Conrad**
University of Wisconsin–Madison

**Allyn and Bacon**
Boston • London • Toronto • Sydney • Tokyo • Singapore

*Associate Publisher:* Stephen D. Dragin
*Editorial Assistant:* Susan Hutchinson

Copyright © 1997 by Allyn & Bacon
A Viacom Company
Needham Heights, MA 02194

*Library of Congress Cataloging-in-Publication Data*

Haworth, Jennifer Grant.
    Emblems of quality in higher education : developing and sustaining
  high-quality programs / Jennifer Grant Haworth, Clifton F. Conrad.
       p.    cm.
    Includes bibliographical references and index.
    ISBN 0-205-19546-6
    1. Master of arts degree—United States—Evaluation.
  2. Universities and colleges—United States—Graduate work—
  Evaluation.    3. College teaching—United States—Evaluation.
  I. Conrad, Clifton.    II. Title.
  LB2385.H39   1997
  378.2´4—dc20                                            95-53257
                                                             C I P

Printed in the United States of America

10   9   8   7   6   5   4   3   2   1        00   99   98   97   96

*For Steve Haworth*
*and*
*Lynn, David, Gail, and Tracey Conrad*

# Contents

# List of Illustrations and Tables

# *Preface*

Program quality—how to enhance it and how to evaluate it—has been placed squarely on the contemporary agenda in higher education. Among the reasons for the current interest in program quality, perhaps none is more important than a widely-shared belief that the quality of our nation's colleges and universities is declining. This belief has been recently fueled by a spate of books critical of higher education, including Allan Bloom's *The Closing of the American Mind: How Higher Education Has Failed Democracy and Impoverished the Souls of Today's Students* (1987), Charles Sykes's *Profscam: Professors and the Demise of Higher Education* (1988), Page Smith's *Killing the Spirit* (1990), Dinesh D'Souza's *Illiberal Education* (1991), George Douglas's *Education Without Impact: How Our Universities Fail the Young* (1992), and Martin Anderson's *Imposters in the Temple: American Intellectuals are Destroying Our Universities and Cheating Our Students of Their Future* (1992).

To be sure, there are other compelling explanations for the groundswell of interest in program quality. For one, there is growing public skepticism that our nation's colleges and universities are preparing individuals adequately for the demanding challenges facing the current and future workplace. For another, legislators, bombarded by taxpayer complaints about the rising costs of higher education, are pressuring colleges and universities to become more accountable through quality control initiatives and program review mandates (Conrad and Wilson, 1985). For still another, declining financial support for higher education is forcing many institutions to look critically at their programs to decide which merit continued funding. Finally, a major movement within higher education to improve and assess program quality has led to a deluge of national reports, college and university rankings, strategies for continuous quality improvement, and institutional initiatives targeted at strengthening undergraduate and graduate education in this country.

Program quality is a critical and highly controversial issue in American higher education. Today, more than ever, questions loom large: What is program quality? What contributes to a high-quality program? How can programs be planned and evaluated to ensure that they are of high quality? Given the urgency of these questions—and the lack of agreement on them in the literature and on many college and university campuses—there exists a compelling need to further our understanding of program quality in ways that can help policymakers, administrators, faculty, and students to strengthen and evaluate programs throughout higher education.

## *Purposes and Audience*

The purpose of this book is to present a comprehensive theory of program quality that can be useful to people involved in evaluating and improving academic programs at all degree levels throughout higher education. Our primary audience includes administrators, faculty, and students across all fields of study—from professional fields to the liberal arts and sciences—who are involved in constructing and sustaining high-quality programs. It is our hope that this theory will prompt members of these diverse audiences to revisit their working definitions of a "high-quality program," and to review the criteria upon which they plan and evaluate the quality of academic programs in higher education.

## *Engagement Theory of Program Quality*

In light of our purpose and audience, this book proposes a theory of program quality that we developed over the last several years. The theory is founded upon our definition of high-quality programs as those which contribute to enriching learning experiences for students that have positive effects on their growth and development. It is grounded in the perspectives of 781 people—representing 47 master's programs in 11 fields of study—interviewed as part of a national study of master's education.[1] While anchored in research conducted at the master's level, we advance the theory as potentially instructive and valuable across all degree levels—from the undergraduate through the doctorate. Yet we acknowledge that, as with any theory, further testing of it is important not only at the master's level but at other degree levels as well.

Our theory of program quality is organized around one central idea: student, faculty, and administrative engagement in teaching and learning. That is, high-quality programs are those in which students, faculty, and administrators invest significant time and effort in mutually supportive teaching and learning. Moreover, high-quality programs invite the participation of alumni and employers of program graduates. In short, our engagement theory emphasizes the dual roles that invested participants play in constructing and sustaining programs of high quality.

The theory maintains that in high-quality programs, principal stakeholders—faculty, students, and administrators—invest in five separate clusters of program attributes, each of which contributes to enriching learning experiences for students that positively affect students' growth and development. The five clusters of program attributes are: diverse and engaged participants, participatory cultures, interactive teaching and learning, connected program requirements, and adequate resources. A total of 17 attributes make up the theory as shown:

### An Engagement Theory of Program Quality

*Cluster One: Diverse and Engaged Participants*
  Diverse and Engaged Faculty
  Diverse and Engaged Students
  Engaged Leaders

*Cluster Two: Participatory Cultures*
  Shared Program Direction
  Community of Learners
  Risk-Taking Environment

*Cluster Three: Interactive Teaching and Learning*
  Critical Dialogue
  Integrative Learning
  Mentoring
  Cooperative Peer Learning
  Out-of-Class Activities

*Cluster Four: Connected Program Requirements*
  Planned Breadth and Depth Course Work
  Professional Residency
  Tangible Product

*Cluster Five: Adequate Resources*
  Support for Students
  Support for Faculty
  Support for Basic Infrastructure

### Contributions of Engagement Theory

In broad strokes, the engagement theory advances a new perspective on program quality that builds upon, extends, and deepens current understanding of program quality. More specifically, it makes six major contributions to our understanding of program quality:

**1.** By defining high-quality programs as those that contribute to enriching learning experiences for students in ways that positively affect their growth and development, the theory focuses on a simple but compelling definition: one that emphasizes student learning and development as the primary purpose of the higher learning. In so doing, the theory builds upon an increasingly shared view that the development of student talents and abilities (Astin, 1985) is at the core of higher education.

**2.** The theory highlights the pivotal role that people—primarily faculty, administrators, and students—play in fostering mutually supportive teaching and learning in programs of high quality. By accenting time and energy commitments made by program participants in their own and others' learning, the engagement theory at once builds on and moves beyond conventional understanding of high-quality programs as more narrowly fueled by students—whether through active student learning (Meyers and Jones, 1993), student involvement (Astin, 1977 and 1993), or student effort (Pace, 1980 and 1986)—or by non-human factors such as curriculum requirements and resources.

**3.** The engagement theory marks the first integrated theory of program quality that has been advanced in the literature. Anchored in a substantial amount of empirical research coupled with supporting explanations as to how and why specific program attributes enhance students' learning, the engagement theory systematically identifies and knits together program attributes into a unified theory of program quality.

**4.** The engagement theory brings together a number of attributes of high-quality programs that, in one form or another, have been addressed in disparate literatures but have not been directed at program quality. In so doing, the theory builds on and connects these literatures in ways that contribute to a more comprehensive and holistic perspective on program quality.

**5.** The theory extends and deepens our understanding of program quality by advancing a number of new attributes of high-quality programs. These attributes—such as critical dialogue, integrative learning, and a risk-taking environment—provide new insights into factors that are instrumental in shaping the quality of students' learning experiences and, in turn, their growth and development.

**6.** Viewed as a comprehensive perspective for enriching our understanding of quality, the engagement theory provides the support for a comprehensive framework for developing and sustaining high-quality programs. The framework challenges stakeholders in higher education to reexamine their assumptions and beliefs about program quality while also providing them with a template for assessing and improving the quality of their own program.

## *Overview of the Contents*

This book is divided into ten chapters. Chapter 1 examines contemporary perspectives on program quality in higher education. Anchored in the literature on graduate and undergraduate program quality in higher education, we describe five major views of program quality: Faculty, Resources, Student Quality-and-Effort Curriculum Requirements, and Multidimensional/multilevel. In addition, we identify some limitations of these views and the program quality literature writ large, and indicate how these limitations influenced the development of our theory of program quality.

Chapter 2 discusses how we constructed a theory of program quality. We provide an overview of our research approach and then describe our multicase study design, interview process, and method of data analysis. (Readers interested in an expanded treatment of our method may wish to consult the technical appendix.)

Chapter 3 presents our engagement theory of program quality. After describing its general properties, we provide a chart that summarizes each of the seventeen attributes that comprise the theory.

We elaborate on the engagement theory in Chapters 4 through 8 by devoting a chapter to each of the five clusters of attributes in the theory: diverse and engaged participants, participatory cultures, interactive teaching and learning, connected program requirements, and adequate resources. For each attribute, we examine the actions that stakeholders take to develop and sustain the attribute, describe the ways in which the attribute enhances the overall quality of students' learning experiences, and examine the major effects of the attribute on students' growth and development. By animating these chapters with the voices of people interviewed, we provide readers with empirical documentation in support of the theory and a sense of the immediacy and richness of stakeholders' experiences in high-quality programs. (In this regard, we suggest that readers peruse Chapters 4 through 8 selectively in light of their particular interests.)

Chapter 9 connects theory with practice and proposes a framework to assist faculty, administrators, and others in learning about assessing and improving the quality of undergraduate and graduate programs. Following a critique of traditional approaches to quality assessment, we elaborate on our framework. We conclude the chapter by exploring the potential benefits of the framework for cultivating and strengthening the quality of academic programs.

Finally, Chapter 10 provides a forum to present our major conclusions. We begin by examining overall support from the literature for the engagement theory and then examine support for specific attributes in our theory. We conclude with a discussion of how the theory advances current understanding of program quality.

## *Endnote*

1. We chose to focus our research on program quality at the master's level for three major reasons. First, while much of the recent criticism of higher education has concentrated on the baccalaureate level, there has been growing concern within academe about the quality of master's programs. Many faculty, administrators, and policymakers have questioned the quality of the master's degree—some have labeled it a "second-class degree" or "consolation prize." The rising concern within academe about the quality of master's programs has been fueled in no small part by the unprecedented expansion of master's education in recent years. To wit, the number of master's degrees annually awarded has more than quadrupled in the last several decades, from less than 75,000 in 1960 to more than 337,000 in 1991 (NCES 1991). At the present time, nearly one out of four degrees granted by American colleges and universities is a master's degree.

Second, we studied master's programs because they have become increasingly important to growing numbers of students and employers. As changes in the nature of knowledge, technology, and the economy have affected the American workplace, more and more practicing professionals have enrolled in master's programs to strengthen their skills and update their knowledge (Conrad and Eagan, 1990). Over the past decade, five out of six master's degrees have been awarded in professional fields. In most professional fields, a master's degree is now a prerequisite for career advancement. In a growing number of fields, such as physical therapy, a master's degree has become a prerequisite for entry into the workplace.

Finally, we focused on the master's level because we had access to a comprehensive database for studying program quality at the master's level, one developed as part of a national study of master's education that we conducted under the auspices of the Council of Graduate Schools. While we drew heavily on these data to identify different types of master's programs and sketch a national portrait of master's education in *A Silent Success: Master's Education in the United States* (Conrad, Haworth, and Millar, 1993), we considered program quality only briefly in that study. In short, we had at hand a rich vein of largely unanalyzed interview material on program quality at the master's level. In this book, we draw upon these data to provide the empirical foundation for our engagement theory of quality.

# Acknowledgments

While we assume full responsibility for its contents, this book represents the collective intelligence and commitment of many individuals. Of most importance, we gratefully acknowledge the 781 interviewees who participated in the study. Their generous gifts of time and candor provide the foundation upon which this book is based. We also thank the liaisons who facilitated our research process by identifying and scheduling interviews with stakeholders in each of the forty-seven master's programs in our study. We are indebted to them.

There are many others who also contributed to the realization of this book. Peggy Heim and Frank King of the TIAA-CREF Fund believed in our ideas and secured financial support to underwrite the drafting of the manuscript. The Pew Charitable Trusts, through the sponsorship of the Council of Graduate Schools, provided a generous $400,000 grant to support our fieldwork. As scholars working in the field of higher education, we thank these individuals and organizations for their enduring support of our research.

We also wish to voice our appreciation to several individuals and organizations who unselfishly gave of their time and energy in this project. First, we thank Susan B. Millar and Karen Prager, who, as colleagues on the national study of master's education, conducted many interviews and crafted numerous analytical program summaries that were essential to us in writing this book. Second, we acknowledge Jules LaPidus of the Council of Graduate Schools for his faithful stewardship of our work. During both the national study of master's education and our subsequent efforts to develop a theory of program quality, Jules provided the kind of encouraging, facilitative leadership that underscored his untiring commitment to advancing knowledge and practice in graduate education. Third, we thank Stephen

Dragin, our editor at Allyn and Bacon, for his unflagging and enthusiastic shepherding of our work. His strong appreciation for scholarship, blended with his praiseworthy concern for linking theory with practice, is most commendable.

Several individuals read and provided many useful comments on earlier drafts of this book. In particular, Elizabeth Whitt and Allan Cohen offered the kind of scholarly criticism that could not help but improve our work. Jean Kartje and Sandria Rodriguez produced thoughtful reviews of portions of our work. And three anonymous reviewers offered several discerning observations and probing insights that strengthened the book in numerous ways.

Finally, each of us would like to thank those who have, in both small and large ways, influenced our lives and work:

I, Jennifer Grant Haworth, express my deepest gratitude to Steve Haworth for his enduring and cheerful support. As a life partner, intellectual colleague, and cherished friend, I thank him for the humor, joy, and perspective he brings to my life. I dedicate this book to him. I also wish to thank Dorothy Lewis Sanville, Lee Sanville, and Captain Timothy S. Grant for their good patience and untiring emotional support. In addition, I am grateful to the many individuals who have invested in my continuing development as a teacher and learner, including Max Bailey, John Braxton, David Buckholdt, Sara Fagan, Janis Fine, Rebecca Ropers-Huilman, Michael Kane, Jean Kartje, Frank Lazarus, Maureen McLaughlin, Susan B. Millar, Anna Neumann, Maureen Noonan, L. Allen Phelps, Sandria Rodriguez, Patricia Scott, Elizabeth Whitt, and Terry E. Williams.

I, Clif Conrad—whose friends so graciously continue to share their wit and warmth and generosity of spirit with me—express my deep appreciation to the following people for their support: Pam and Erin and Abbi Conrad, Bob Barmish, Allan Cohen, Jay Griffin, Cryss Brunner, Paul Bredeson, Al Phelps, Noel Radomski, and Larry Leslie. In addition, I would like to dedicate this book in part to my four siblings—Lynn, David, Gail, and Tracey— who, in their inimitable ways, have enriched my life immeasurably.

# 1

## Perspectives on Academic Program Quality

*Quality ... you know what it is, yet you don't know what it is ... [I]f you can't say what Quality is, how do you know what it is, or how do you know that it even exists? If no one knows what it is, then for all practical purposes it doesn't exist at all. But for all practical purposes it does exist. . . . What the hell is Quality? What is it?—(Pirsig 1974, 184)*

What is a high-quality program? In higher education, the idea of program quality remains elusive. For more than a century, scholars have worked to conceptualize, improve, and evaluate program quality. Their efforts have generated an abundant and diverse literature.

In terms of general writings on academic quality, many scholars have published papers, books, and reports that address program, departmental, and institutional quality (Brown 1992; Mayhew, Ford, and Hubbard 1990; Millard 1991; Snyder 1993); identify alternative views of program quality (Astin 1980, 1982, 1985; Conrad and Blackburn 1986; Fairweather and Brown 1991); and review the literature on quality (Blackburn and Lingenfelter 1973; Conrad and Blackburn 1985b; Kuh 1981; Lawrence and Green 1980; Tan 1986).

In terms of research, many scholars have conducted empirical studies of program quality. The most popular of these, commonly referred to as studies of the quantitative attributes of quality (Conrad and Blackburn 1986), have been aimed at identifying "objective," quantifiable characteristics of programs and departments that are associated with (i.e., correlate with) programs assumed to be of high-quality.[1] For the most part, scholars have identified attributes of programs that have been judged to be of high quality as reflected in reputational rankings of graduate departments in the nation's leading doctoral-granting universities (Cartter 1966; Jones, Lindzey, and Coggeshall 1982; Roose and Anderson 1970).

There have also been various quality rankings of academic programs in colleges and universities, including both reputational rankings and objective indicator rankings (Webster 1986a). Scholars conducting reputational rankings, for example, have asked "experts"—usually faculty but occasionally department chairs or deans—to rate programs based largely on their judgments of the quality of program faculty. These rankings have been conducted primarily at the doctoral level in liberal arts and sciences disciplines, but there have also been rankings of professional fields at the undergraduate, master's, and doctoral levels.[2] The best-known include the first major reputational rankings of doctoral programs by Raymond Hughes (1925, 1934); Hayward Keniston's (1959) national rankings of graduate programs and institutions; two reputational rankings sponsored by the American Council on Education (Cartter 1966; Roose and Anderson 1970) that ranked doctoral programs nationally on the basis of faculty quality and program effectiveness; and a national ranking sponsored by the Conference Board of Associated Research Councils that ranked doctoral program quality in thirty-two disciplines (Jones, Lindzey, and Coggeshall 1982).

Widespread concerns about the subjectivity of reputational rankings have led some scholars to conduct "objective" indicator rankings of graduate programs that employ a quantifiable approach to evaluating graduate programs (Webster 1986a). Individuals conducting these rankings have selected, *a priori*, indicators identified with programs taken to be of high quality, such as faculty research productivity, faculty training, student achievement, and program resources. In turn, they have used these indicators as a basis to rank programs and entire institutions. Since the 1960s, most objective indicator rankings have emphasized faculty accomplishment, especially scholarly productivity (Webster and Conrad 1986). To wit, scholars have used faculty research productivity (as measured by publication records and citation counts) to rank programs in fields from anthropology and engineering to psychology and sociology (Beilock, Polopolus, and Correal 1986; Blair, Cottle, and Wallace 1986; Clemente and Sturgis 1974; Cox and Catt 1977; Glenn and Villimez 1970; House and Yeager 1978; Howard, Cole, and Maxwell 1987; Jones, Lindzey, and Coggeshall 1982; Knudson and Vaughan 1969; Lewis 1968; Liu 1978; Moore and Taylor 1980; Somit and Tanenhaus 1964; Webster and Conrad 1986; Webster, Conrad, and Jensen 1988; Wispe 1969). Other researchers have rated programs on faculty attributes, such as scholarly awards and peer recognition (Bowker 1965; Kaufman 1984).

With a knowledge of these writings and approaches to studying program quality firmly in mind, the remainder of this chapter is devoted to a discussion of five views of program quality that we derived from our analysis of the literature.[3] These views advance alternative conceptions of program quality and combine related attributes that are considered key features of high-quality programs. The five views are: Faculty, Resources, Student Quality-and-Effort, Curriculum Requirements, and Multidimensional/Multi-level. After exploring each of these views, we discuss their shortcomings and indicate how these limitations influenced our research.

## Views of Program Quality

We begin by describing these five views and identifying the major attributes that we associate with each of them. Then we examine support for the view in the literature, including relevant writings, empirical research on the quantitative attributes of high-quality programs, and literature on quality rankings (reputational and objective indicator rankings). Throughout, we draw on the literature that addresses program quality at the undergraduate, master's, and doctoral levels. The five views of program quality and the major attributes of each are as follows:

### Five Views of Program Quality

*Faculty View*
   Educational Training and Qualifications
   Scholarly and Research Productivity
   Research Funding
   Awards, Honors, and Prizes

*Resources View*
   Critical Mass of Faculty and Students
   Financial Resources
   Physical Facilities

*Student Quality-and-Effort View*
   Educational Qualifications and Academic Achievements
   Student Involvement
   Quality of Student Effort

*Curriculum Requirements View*
   Core and Specialized Course Work
   Residency Requirement
   Culminating Experience

*Multidimensional/Multilevel View*

Faculty Quality
Student Quality
Resources
Curriculum Requirements

## *Faculty View*

The most prominent view in the literature maintains that faculty—particularly those who are actively involved in creating and disseminating knowledge—are fundamental to high-quality programs (Blackburn and Lingenfelter 1973; Conrad and Blackburn 1986; Fairweather and Brown 1991; King and Wolfe 1987). Those advancing this view emphasize four faculty-related attributes of a high-quality program: educational training and qualifications; scholarly and research productivity; research funding; and awards, honors, and prizes. In so doing, they suggest that a high-quality program is one in which faculty have completed their doctoral training under the guidance of recognized scholars at highly-regarded research universities, are actively engaged in scholarship and research leading to publication, are successful in securing external research funding, and are recognized nationally by their peers for their scholarly contributions.

The faculty view enjoys direct empirical support from studies of the quantitative attributes of "high-quality" programs insofar as researchers have found strong positive relationships between all four of these faculty-related attributes and program quality. For example, several scholars have discovered strong relationships between measures of faculty educational training and qualifications and program quality (Clemente and Sturgis 1974; Conrad and Blackburn 1985a; Crane 1970), while others have found moderate to large associations between various measures of faculty scholarly productivity (such as mean number of research articles and books) and program quality (Abbott and Barlow 1972; Drew 1975; Drew and Karpf 1981; Glenn and Villemez 1970; Hagstrom 1971; Lewis 1968).[4]

Reputational rankings have also reinforced the faculty view of program quality by placing primary emphasis on faculty accomplishment (especially as reflected in scholarship and research) as judged by faculty peers. To a considerable extent, then, both quantitative attribute studies and reputational rankings—with their heavy emphasis on attributes related to faculty accomplishment—have contributed to the widespread view in American higher education that the quality of any academic program is closely related to the quality of its faculty.

## Resources View

One of the most conventional views of program quality maintains that adequate resources—human, financial, physical—are the *sine qua non* of high-quality programs. This view accentuates three attributes of a high-quality program: a critical mass of faculty and students, solid financial resources, and excellent physical facilities (including laboratories, computers, classroom facilities, and library facilities and resources).

The resources view is supported both directly through research on the quantitative attributes of program quality and indirectly through objective indicator rankings. As to the former, scholars conducting these studies have examined various resource-related attributes of high-quality programs. Some (Abbott 1972; Conrad and Blackburn 1986; Fairweather 1988; Fairweather and Brown 1991; Oromaner 1970) have found positive relationships between program size (as measured by the number of faculty and/or students)—a proxy for critical mass—and the quality of graduate programs. Others have discovered positive relationships between institutional and programmatic financial resources (such as endowments, expenditures per student, faculty salaries, research funds, and student-faculty ratios) and program quality (Abbott and Barlow 1972; Astin and Solmon 1981; Beyer and Snipper 1974; Janes 1969; Lavendar, Mathers, and Pease 1971; Morgan, Kearney, and Regens 1976). Still other researchers have uncovered positive associations between physical facilities and program quality. Several scholars, for example, have found that library strength (as measured by the number of library volumes and library expenditures) is an important attribute of high-quality programs and institutions (Cartter 1966; Jordan 1963; Perkins and Snell 1962).

Several objective indicator rankings, as reflected in the work of scholars who have ranked institutions on the basis of resources-related attributes, have also indirectly reinforced the resources view of program quality. For example, Charles Kelso (1975) ranked law schools according to a "resources" index; Donald Glower (1980) ranked engineering schools on the basis of the total amount of research spending; and Lyle Jones, Gardner Lindzey, and Porter Coggeshall (1982) ranked doctoral programs in terms of such resources-related attributes as number of faculty and students, number of program graduates, and library size.

## Student Quality-and-Effort View

Those advancing a student quality-and-effort view suggest that well-qualified, involved, and motivated students are the centerpiece of a high-quality program. They tend to emphasize three student-related attributes: the educational qualifications and academic achievements of entering students, student involvement, and the quality of student effort. In other words, a high-quality program is one that attracts students with outstanding educational backgrounds and achievements who, upon matriculation, are actively engaged in co-curricular as well as classroom activities and are committed to devoting significant and sustained effort to their studies.

Considerable support for the student quality-and-effort view is found both in quantitative attributes studies and in objective indicator rankings. Regarding the former, studies conducted at both the graduate and undergraduate levels have found positive relationships between various measures of student selectivity and program quality (Astin and Solmon 1981; Conrad and Blackburn 1985a; Hagstrom 1971). As to the latter, various individuals have ranked institutions largely on the basis of student-related attributes of academic achievement and, in so doing, have further reinforced the view that program quality is closely linked to the qualifications of entering students. Alexander Astin and Lewis Solmon (1979), for example, used first-year undergraduate and entering graduate student scores on standardized tests to develop quality rankings of institutions. Recently, magazines such as *U.S. News & World Report* and *Money* have similarly produced rankings of colleges in which the qualifications and academic achievements of entering students—as measured by entering students' high school class ranks or performances on the ACT (American College Test) or SAT (Scholastic Aptitude Test)—were used as key indicators of institutional quality.

Although most proponents of this view emphasize the educational qualifications and academic achievements of entering students, a growing number of scholars have stressed student involvement and the quality of student effort (Pascarella and Terenzini 1991) as important attributes of high-quality programs and institutions. For example, in two national studies he conducted on the impact of college on students, Alexander Astin (1977, 1993) found that the benefits of college are directly proportionate to students' involvement in educational experiences both in and outside of class. Moreover, George Kuh and his colleagues (Kuh 1981; Kuh, Schuh, and Whitt 1991) have documented that student learning and development is enhanced when students become actively involved in out-of-class activities with peers, faculty, and student affairs professionals. Finally, C. Robert Pace (1980, 1986) has found that the quality of student effort—that is, the student effort or initiative aimed at maximizing available resources--is fundamental to enhancing students' learning experiences.[5]

## Curriculum Requirements View

Perhaps the oldest view of program quality is one which suggests that coherent and rigorous curriculum requirements are at the core of high-quality programs. Those advancing this view tend to emphasize three quality-related attributes: core and specialized course work, residency requirements that encourage on-campus study, and a culminating experience—such as a thesis, research project, or comprehensive examination.

In addition to the extensive writings on accreditation (Young et al. 1983) and program review (Conrad and Wilson 1985), the curriculum requirements view enjoys considerable support in the undergraduate (Conrad and Pratt 1985; Schaefer 1990; Toombs and Tierney 1992) and master's education literature.[6] In particular, two major publications on master's programs illustrate broad-based support for this view. First, in its most recent policy statement on the master's degree, the Council of Graduate Schools (CGS)(1981, 3) states: "The Master's program should consist of a coherent pattern of courses frequently capped by comprehensive examinations and a thesis or its equivalent in a creative project." More specifically, the CGS policy statement recommends that "quality" master's degree programs consist of "a pre-planned and coherent sequence of lectures, seminars, discussions, and independent studies" (7); "a period of study on campus as a student in full-time residence" (8); "a component demonstrating creativity... [such as] a report of an internship, a case study, the organization and conduction of an advanced seminar, a music recital, a gallery showing of the student's works of art, the presentation of a play, and the reading of original poetry" (9); and "a comprehensive examination, which covers the field to be mastered" (9).

Second, in her comprehensive review of the literature on master's degrees, Judith Glazer (1986) found wide agreement that master's programs should include:

1. A common core of introductory courses appropriate to the discipline or field of study, such as foundations, theory, or research methods
2. A concentration or specialization in a subfield of study; for example, financial accounting, rehabilitation counseling, medical–surgical nursing, or creative writing
3. Cognate courses, often outside the department, to broaden the curriculum or to provide needed skills, such as statistics, computer programming, foreign languages, or behavioral science
4. An integrative experience to synthesize the program's content and translate theory into practice, such as seminars, on-campus practica, internships, and other field work
5. A summative experience to measure the student's achievement and cognitive growth by means of a thesis, research project, and/or comprehensive examination (17)

## *Multidimensional/Multilevel View*

Each of the above views of program quality has been questioned by those who believe that program quality is best viewed as a multidimensional/multilevel phenomenon (Blackburn and Lingenfelter 1973; Clark 1976;

Conrad and Blackburn 1985b; Fairweather and Brown 1991; Jones, Lindzey, and Coggeshall 1982; Kuh 1981; Solmon and Astin 1981). According to this view, program quality has multiple dimensions that span both the program and institutional levels. While there is considerable variation among its proponents regarding the relative importance of major dimensions of program quality, most seem to agree that faculty, resources, student quality and effort, and curriculum requirements are all dimensions of high-quality programs.

This eclectic view of quality finds support in two pockets in the literature: studies of the quantitative attributes of high-quality graduate programs and writings on quality assessment that have focused on identifying attributes of high-quality graduate programs. In particular, two studies of the quantitative attributes of high-quality programs provide empirical support for this view.

In the first, James Fairweather and Dennis Brown (1991) collected national data from three doctoral fields and then examined different dimensions of program quality—including size, resources, and student quality— at the institutional as well as the program level to develop and validate a framework for assessing academic programs. They found that "single-dimension" conceptions of quality were wholly inadequate and concluded that program quality should be viewed as a "multilevel/multidimensional" phenomenon.

In the second study, Clifton Conrad and Robert Blackburn (1985a, 1986) identified 32 attributes of high-quality master's programs. The attributes correlating the highest with program quality included individual and combined measures of faculty scholarly productivity, faculty grantspersonship, critical mass of students, student ability, and facilities. Conrad and Blackburn concluded that "factors associated with departmental quality are more multidimensional in regional colleges and universities than in departments at leading research universities" (1985a, 293).[7]

The Council of Graduate Schools (CGS) has been at the forefront of efforts to develop and refine methods of evaluating and strengthening graduate programs—efforts that lend support to a multidimensional/multilevel view of quality. In response to concerns about the shortcomings of peer ratings, CGS contracted with the Educational Testing Service (ETS) to develop more inclusive and reliable approaches for assessing quality in doctoral education. Three ETS researchers—Mary Jo Clark, Rodney Hartnett, and Leonard Baird—reviewed the literature and surveyed a national sample of graduate deans to identify attributes of high-quality doctoral programs. Among the attributes they identified were faculty training and scholarly productivity, student academic ability and satisfaction with program, physical and financial resources, and departmental operations (such as admissions policies, depth and breadth of course offerings, and degree requirements) (Clark, Hartnett, and Baird 1976).[8]

In the late 1970s, CGS appointed a task force of graduate deans to establish quality assessment criteria for master's programs. The task force identified six assessment criteria that had been underscored in the Clark, Hartnett, and Baird study of doctoral programs: faculty, students, resources, learning environment, curriculum, and alumni placement. After identifying various attributes for each criterion, the task force conducted a nationwide survey of approximately 200 graduate deans in which each dean was asked to evaluate and rank–order the relative importance of each criterion to the overall quality of master's education in their institution (Downey 1979, 90–91). Survey results indicated that graduate deans believed the following criteria (and related attributes) were most instrumental to program quality:

1. Quality of faculty, including instructional, scholarly, and artistic contributions, commitment to program, training, and experience
2. Quality of incoming students, including academic ability, commitment, and motivation
3. Resources, including faculty, facilities, services, and administrative support
4. Learning environment, including the competitiveness and rigor of the intellectual environment
5. Curricula, including academic offerings and degree requirements
6. Characteristics of recent alumni, including satisfaction with education (Ames 1979, 40)

Many writers on quality and quality assessment at the undergraduate and master's level have echoed the multidimensional assessment approach developed by the task force (Andrews 1979; Fisher 1979; McCarty 1979; Minkel and Richards 1981). For the most part, they have emphasized assessment criteria that traditionally have been used to evaluate program quality at the doctoral level—including faculty and student research productivity, faculty and student research awards and honors, and the availability of research equipment and suitable facilities (Conrad and Eagan 1990, 139).[9]

## Limitations of the Literature

In this chapter we have examined the literature on program quality, mostly in relation to five major views of program quality. This has provided a foundation for understanding contemporary conceptions of program quality in American higher education. Without minimizing the contributions of those who have preceded us, we conclude by highlighting seven key shortcomings of these views and of the program quality literature writ large. We then indicate how these limitations influenced our approach to research.

First, all five views of program quality focus primarily on program "inputs"—such as faculty scholarly productivity—rather than on attributes of programs themselves. As such, we have little understanding of what goes on inside the "black box" of programs that contributes to student learning (Kuh 1992, 354). With this limitation in mind, we decided to focus our research on identifying and examining how various program attributes enriched the overall quality of students' learning experiences. We chose this focus on the commonsense grounds that any robust conception of program quality must surely examine a wide range of potential attributes in order to find out what attributes contribute, and in what ways, to students' learning experiences.

Second, each of the five contemporary views of quality ignores critical relationships between program attributes and student outcomes. Research is needed both to identify program attributes that contribute to enriching learning experiences and to systematically identify the ways in which various program attributes affect student growth and development. Our awareness of this limitation led us to focus our inquiry around the search for such program attributes.

Third, the validity of the empirical research supporting current views of program quality is very much in doubt for several reasons. For one, in testing various quantitative attributes of quality, most researchers have used reputational rankings as the measure of program quality. Truth be told, these rankings have severe limitations as valid measures of program quality.[10] For another, many researchers have more or less assumed that attributes identified at the doctoral level are equally applicable to master's programs and undergraduate programs. Finally, most researchers have identified attributes (i.e., objective indicators) on an *a priori* basis and tested them without reference to clearly defined constructs or underlying theory. As Clifton Conrad and Robert Blackburn (1985b, 302) have noted, most scholars have used an "atheoretical" approach to identify attributes of high-quality programs: They have either selected attributes that are of personal interest to them or "rummaged through their data in search of any factors [attributes] that might conceivably be linked empirically to program quality" rather than identifying and testing potential attributes on the basis of a theory of quality. Put simply, researchers have had no theory to guide their selection of attributes, nor have they had a theoretical frame from which to interpret their findings. Accordingly, we chose to develop a theory "from the ground up" rather than risk being constrained by the views and attributes that have thus far been advanced in the literature.

Fourth, most of these views find support in studies of the "quantitative" attributes of high-quality programs. Program attributes that might help to explain variation in program quality that are not easily quantified—such as program leadership or faculty–student interaction—are rarely discussed, much less empirically studied. This limitation influenced our decision to use an open-ended, qualitative approach to inquiry that would allow us to identify attributes of high-quality programs that are not necessarily quantifiable.

Fifth, despite the volume of literature on program quality across degree levels, relatively little empirical research has been conducted on the topic. Aside from a few studies of the quantitative attributes of high-quality programs, few scholars have systematically investigated the various views and attributes that have been advanced in the literature. Reputational rankings, objective indicator rankings, conjecture, and opinion have added to the dialogue about program quality, but they are not adequate substitutes for systematic inquiry.

Sixth, all of the aforementioned views have been developed largely on the basis of investigations of doctoral and baccalaureate program quality. As such, little attention has been given to program quality at the master's level. Apart from a handful of empirical studies and some recommendations for evaluating master's programs, few people have looked at program quality in master's education on its own terms. For the most part, the literature treats program quality at the master's level as coextensive with the doctoral level, and master's education as unworthy of study as a separate and legitimate degree activity. The limited amount of scholarship at the master's level influenced our decision to use an open-ended approach to inquiry.

Seventh, the five views of program quality represented in the literature—as well as most writings on program quality generally—present the perspectives of a limited number of stakeholders, where "stakeholders" are defined as those people who have a vital interest in programs. Our understandings of program quality have been shaped almost entirely by a relatively small group of scholars, senior administrators, and faculty who work in highly-visible research universities. For the most part, the voices of administrators and faculty at less prestigious universities, and of students, alumni, and employers across all types of institutions, have not been represented. In order to present a more comprehensive treatment of program quality, we chose to ground our study in the perspectives of students, alumni, and employers—as well as faculty and administrators—who are actively involved in master's education at a broad range of institutions.

In summary, the limitations we identified in the research on program quality were critical to the design and analysis of our study. In light of the need for research (1) that identifies program attributes that contribute to enriching learning experiences that foster students' growth and development; (2) that is not limited to traditional "objective" attributes of quality;

(3) that focuses on the quality of master's programs on their own terms; and (4) the limitations of extant research, most notably the lack of any extant theory of program quality, we decided to use an open-ended, inductive approach to inquiry that was anchored in the development of a grounded theory of program quality. Finally, having learned that many "voices" were missing from the discourse, we chose to include a wide range of stakeholders' voices in our study.

## Endnotes

1. For detailed analyses of studies of the quantitative attributes or "correlates" of high-quality programs, see Conrad and Blackburn (1985b) and Tan (1986).

2. Some scholars have conducted cross-disciplinary reputational rankings of professional programs at the doctoral level. For example, Peter Blau and Rebecca Margulies (1974–75) ranked the top doctoral programs in eighteen professional fields of study based on the ratings of deans, and Allan Cartter and Lewis Solmon (1977) used faculty and deans to rank leading programs in law, education, and business. Other scholars have conducted reputational rankings of master's and doctoral programs in single professional fields, such as library science (Bookstein and Biggs 1987; Carpenter and Carpenter 1970; White 1987) and speech communication (Roach and Barker 1984a, 1984b; Trott, Barker, and Barker 1988). For further references on reputational rankings, see Lynn Hattendorf's (1989) annotated bibliography and David Webster's (1986b) historical overview of rankings of undergraduate institutions.

3. While we believe that these five views explicate the major conceptions of program quality represented in the literature, we do not suggest that these views are all inclusive. A number of attributes of high-quality programs advanced in the literature—including "attractiveness" and "distinctiveness" as suggested by William Bergquist and Jack Armstrong (1986)—are not included here on the grounds that they have enjoyed relatively little support in the literature.

4. Although some researchers—such as David Drew and Ronald Karpf (1981)—have found large correlations between faculty scholarly productivity and programs taken to be of high-quality, a word of caution is appropriate here. Most of these studies have examined quality at the graduate level in leading research universities in which faculty scholarly productivity was in all probability the criterion used to identify high-quality programs in the first place. As noted by Clifton Conrad and Robert Blackburn (1985b, 251–252): "The potentially self-fulfilling characteristic of this research raises the question of whether or not faculty-related characteristics in general and scholarly productivity in particular really are such central components of quality, especially in graduate and undergraduate departments located in institutions outside of the highly reputed institutions."

5. Pace's (1980, 1984) "quality-of-effort" scales have been used widely throughout higher education, and his work has influenced other scholars of program quality (Ory and Braskamp 1988; Young, Blackburn, Conrad, and Cameron 1989).

6.  C. W. Minkel and Mary P. Richards (1986) identified ten attributes of high-quality master's degree programs, including a core of planned course work and a culminating experience. Albeit in varying degrees, all ten attributes more or less represent curriculum requirements.

7.  Working with Denise Young, Robert Blackburn and Clifton Conrad subsequently replicated and extended their earlier work in a follow-up study. For the most part, they identified the same attributes as the best predictors of program quality, although they did not find correlations of the same magnitude as in the earlier study (Young, Blackburn, and Conrad 1987).

8.  Based on their preliminary information, the researchers conducted a follow-up questionnaire study and found that twenty-five to thirty attributes were useful in assessing the quality of doctoral programs. They grouped these attributes into two clusters: research-oriented and educational experience attributes. The former cluster included attributes related to doctoral program size, program reputation, physical and financial resources, student academic ability, and faculty research productivity. The latter cluster included attributes related to "student satisfactions, ratings of the teaching and the environment for learning, faculty interpersonal relations, and alumni ratings of their dissertation experiences" (Clark, Hartnett, and Baird 1976, 4).

9.  To be sure, a few scholars have suggested that these conventional criteria, taken by themselves, largely ignore important process and outcome considerations in undergraduate and master's education, such as the quality of student experiences and student outcomes (Clark 1979; Conrad, Haworth, and Millar 1993; Epstein 1979; Kirkwood 1985; Millard 1984).

10.  We share the widespread view that reputational rankings have substantial limitations (Astin and Solmon 1981: Clark 1976; Conrad and Blackburn 1985b; Conrad and Pratt 1985; Dolan 1976; Elton and Rose 1972; Fairweather 1988; Hartnett, Clark, and Baird 1978; Lawrence and Green 1980; Tan 1986; Webster 1981, 1986a, 1986b). From our perspective, the most important limitations of reputational rankings are: 1) They measure reputation and prestige rather than quality and, in so doing, conflate reputation and quality (thereby providing information more on "attributes of prestige" than on "attributes of quality"). 2) They rate mostly programs and departments in highly-visible national universities with strong research reputations at the expense of programs located in non-elite institutions. 3) They place primary emphasis on unidimensional evaluation criteria, especially faculty scholarly productivity and reputation. 4) They tend to reinforce the status quo in higher education, not least because of their primary emphasis on faculty quality. 5) They suffer from rater bias, such as overrepresenting scholars from national research universities who are likely to be influenced by the "halo effect" of prestigious institutions and are likely to give high marks to their alma maters ("alumni effects"). 6) Finally, they focus mostly on the doctoral level at the expense of the master's and undergraduate levels.

# 2

## Constructing a Theory of Program Quality

This chapter, which discusses how we developed a theory of program quality, is divided into two parts. In the first part, we introduce the definition of program quality that guided our theory development and sketch our overall approach to research and theory development. In the second part, we discuss our "positioned subject" approach to research, multicase study design, interview process, and data analysis procedures.[1]

### Overview

In broad strokes, we centered our inquiry around the construction of a theory of high-quality programs. As a beginning point, we broadly defined high-quality programs as those which, from the perspectives of diverse stakeholders, contribute to enriching learning experiences for students that positively affect their growth and development.

In advancing this definition, we fully recognize that others may choose to define program quality in other ways, such as on the basis of a program's "attractiveness" or "distinctiveness" (Bergquist and Armstrong, 1986) or the value of its credential in the workplace. This notwithstanding, we chose to define high-quality programs in terms of students' learning for two reasons. First and foremost, we did so on the grounds that bringing about student growth and development is arguably the driving purpose that cuts across all programs regardless of degree level. Hence, teaching and learning surely should be placed at the center of any definition of program quality. Second, our definition builds upon a growing consensus within higher

15

education that the development of student talents and abilities is at the core of the higher learning. This definition, which has been advanced and eloquently defended by Alexander Astin through his concept of "talent development" (1985, 17), has recently found strong support in the work of several scholars, policymakers, and external stakeholders (Association of American Colleges 1992; Bergquist and Armstrong 1986; Bowen 1977; Bruffee 1993; Chickering and Gamson 1987; Guskin 1994; Kuh, Schuh, and Whitt 1991; Study Group on the Conditions of Excellence in American Higher Education 1984; Sanford 1968; Southern Association of Schools and Colleges 1982).[2]

In keeping with this definition, we organized our research and theory development around a single overarching question: What program attributes contribute to enriching learning experiences that positively affect student growth and development? We grounded our research in the perspectives of 781 people, representing forty-seven master's programs in eleven fields of study, whom we had interviewed. These people were selected from six stakeholder groups: institutional administrators, program administrators, faculty, students, program alumni, and employers of program graduates.

Drawing on what we learned from these individuals about high-quality learning experiences, we systematically identified and intertwined attributes—and clusters of attributes—into a unified theory of program quality. Using the constant comparative method to analyze our interview material both within and across the forty-seven programs, we constructed an "engagement theory" of program quality. In effect, the engagement theory paints a picture of an "ideal" high-quality master's program. In reality, not one of the programs in our sample had all seventeen of the attributes included in the theory.

## Research and Theory Development

In conducting our research and constructing a theory of program quality, we used a "positioned subject" approach that grounded our research in the perspectives of diverse stakeholders with a vital interest in master's education.[3] This approach provided us with a strategy for research and analysis: we would focus on stakeholders' interpretations of the quality of students' learning experiences within individual programs—including how people described and made sense of them and what they believed contributed most to enriching their quality—always from their standpoints or perspectives.[4] In turn, through making comparisons and discerning patterns across these programs, we would develop a theory.

Consonant with our positioned subject approach, we used an open-ended, multicase study design that placed the perspectives of six groups of stakeholders at the center of our research. Next, we discuss our multicase study design, interview process, and data analysis procedures.

## Multicase Study Design

Our multicase study design was organized around a sampling strategy in which we selected cases (programs) from across the nation, and interviewees within each case, that were representative of program and interviewee characteristics that we believed relevant to the study. Hence, at the program level, we chose forty-seven programs from across the country that differed according to characteristics such as field of study, institutional type, type of control, and geographic location. Within each program, we selected individuals representing six different stakeholder groups and various other characteristics.

To provide for variation across the forty-seven programs in terms of field of study, we selected eleven different fields in the professions and liberal arts and sciences. From emerging professional fields we chose applied anthropology, computer science, environmental studies, and microbiology. We viewed these fields as representative of traditional liberal arts and sciences in which a non-university job market demand has developed for master's-educated people in recent years. From the traditional liberal arts and sciences, we selected English and sociology as core disciplines representing the humanities and social sciences.

To represent the range of institutions offering master's programs, we selected programs that differed in terms of institutional type (national, regional, liberal arts, or specialty) and type of control (public or private). Moreover, since master's programs in this country vary in other ways that might be relevant, we also chose programs that differed on the following characteristics: geographic location (East, West, South, or Midwest), levels of degree offerings within departments (master's-only; bachelor's and master's; or bachelor's, master's, and doctorate), student attendance patterns (full-time, part-time, or mix), type of delivery system (traditional day/evening, nontraditional weekend/summer, or nontraditional satellite), percentage of students who are minorities (high or low), and program prestige ("prestigious" or "non-prestigious").[5] Table 2.1 shows the distribution of the forty-seven programs across these six characteristics as well as by field of study, institutional type, and type of control.

Within each of the forty-seven programs in the sample, we interviewed individuals who held one of six stakeholder positions: institutional administrators, program administrators, faculty, students, alumni, and employers. We selected these particular groups because each had a vital stake in master's education.[6] To diversify our sample further, we interviewed people who differed in terms of personal characteristics such as race, ethnicity, and sex. Table 2.2 shows the distribution of interviewees by stakeholder group, minority status, sex, institutional type, and field of study.[7]

**TABLE 2.1  Characteristics of Case Study Sample**

| Pseudonym Institution | Field of Study | Type 1=National 2=Regional 3=Lib. Arts 4=Specialty | Control 1=Public 2=Private | Location 1=East 2=West 3=South 4=Midwest | Degree Levels[a] 1=M only 2=B+M 3=B+M+D | Student Attendance 1=FT 2=PT 3=Mix | Delivery System 1 = Trad. (day/eve) 2=Non-trad. (wknd/sum) 3=Non-trad. (satellite) | Percent Minority Student 1=High 2=Low | Program Prestige 1=Prestigious 2=Non-prestigious |
|---|---|---|---|---|---|---|---|---|---|
| Pierpont University | Business | 1 | 2 | 1 | 1 | 1 | 1 | 2 | 1 |
| Major State University | | 1 | 1 | 4 | 3 | 1 | 1 | 2 | 2 |
| Parks-Beecher University[b] | | 2 | 2 | 3 | 2 | 1 | 1 | 1 | 2 |
| Peterson University | | 2 | 2 | 1 | 2 | 2 | 2 | 2 | 2 |
| St. Joan's College | | 3 | 2 | 2 | 2 | 2 | 2 | 2 | 2 |
| Major State University | Education | 1 | 1 | 4 | 3 | 3 | 1 | 2 | 1 |
| Laramie University | | 2 | 2 | 2 | 2 | 2 | 2 | 2 | 2 |
| Chester College | | 2 | 2 | 1 | 2 | 2 | 1 | 2 | 2 |
| Southwest State University | | 2 | 1 | 2 | 3 | 2 | 2 | 2 | 2 |
| Lake College | | 3 | 2 | 4 | 2 | 2 | 2 | 2 | 2 |
| Major State University | Engineering | 1 | 1 | 4 | 3 | 3 | 1 | 2 | 2 |
| Prestige State University | | 1 | 1 | 2 | 3 | 1 | 1 | 2 | 1 |
| Middle State University | | 2 | 1 | 3 | 3 | 3 | 1 & 3 | 2 | 2 |
| Moore A & T University[b] | | 2 | 1 | 3 | 2 | 1 | | 1 | 2 |
| United Technological Univ. | | 4 | 2 | 2 | 1 | 2 | 3 | 2 | 2 |
| Major State University | Nursing | 1 | 1 | 4 | 3 | 2 | 1 | 2 | 2 |
| Barrett State Medical Center | | 1 | 1 | 2 | 3 | 2 | 1 | 2 | 1 |
| Peterson University | | 2 | 2 | 1 | 2 | 2 | 1 | 2 | 2 |
| Southern State University | | 2 | 1 | 3 | 3 | 2 | 1 | 2 | 2 |
| Western State Medical Center | | 4 | 1 | 2 | 3 | 2 | 1 | 2 | 1 |
| Major State University | Theater | 1 | 1 | 4 | 2 | 1 | 1 | 2 | 2 |
| Phelps University | | 1 | 2 | 1 | 1 | 1 | 1 | 2 | 1 |
| Helena State University[c] | | 2 | 1 | 3 | 2 | 1 | 1 | 2 | 2 |
| Trafalgar College | | 2 | 2 | 1 | 2 | 3 | 1 | 2 | 2 |
| National Conservatory College | | 4 | 2 | 2 | 1 | 1 | 1 | 2 | 1 |

| Institution | Field | | | | | | | | |
|---|---|---|---|---|---|---|---|---|---|
| Land-Grant University | Applied Anthropology | 1 | 1 | 2 | 2 | 2 | 1 | 2 | 2 |
| Atlantic State University | | 1 | 1 | 1 | 2 | 1 | 1 | 2 | 2 |
| City-State University | | 2 | 1 | 3 | 2 | 2 | 1 | 2 | 2 |
| Southwest State University | | 2 | 1 | 2 | 2 | 1 | 1 | 2 | 2 |
| Southeast State University | | 2 | 1 | 3 | 3 | 2 | 1 | 2 | 1 |
| Major State University | English | 1 | 1 | 4 | 3 | 1 | 1 | 2 | 2 |
| Phelps University | | 1 | 2 | 1 | 3 | 1 | 1 | 2 | 1 |
| Urban State University[b] | | 2 | 1 | 4 | 2 | 2 | 1 | 1 | 2 |
| Southwest State University | | 2 | 1 | 2 | 2 | 1 | 1 | 2 | 2 |
| Longmont College | | 3 | 2 | 1 | 1 | 2 | 2 | 2 | 2 |
| Phelps University | Environmental Studies | 1 | 2 | 1 | 1 | 1 | 1 | 2 | 1 |
| Major State University | | 1 | 1 | 4 | 1 | 1 | 1 | 2 | 2 |
| Carver A & M University[b] | | 2 | 1 | 3 | 2 | 1 | 1 | 1 | 2 |
| Vernon College | | 3 | 2 | 1 | 1 | 2 | 2 | 2 | 2 |
| Walton State College | | 3 | 1 | 2 | 2 | 3 | 1 | 2 | 2 |
| Major State University | Microbiology | 1 | 1 | 4 | 3 | 1 | 1 | 2 | 1 |
| Southwest State University | | 2 | 1 | 2 | 3 | 1 | 1 | 2 | 2 |
| Mountain State University | | 2 | 1 | 2 | 3 | 1 | 1 | 2 | 2 |
| Middle State University | | 2 | 1 | 3 | 2 | 1 | 1 | 1 | 2 |
| Appleby State University | | 2 | 1 | 4 | 2 | 1 | 1 | 2 | 2 |
| Major State University | Sociology | 1 | 1 | 4 | 3 | 1 | 1 | 2 | 1 |
| Major State University | Comp. Sci. | 1 | 1 | 4 | 3 | 1 | 1 | 2 | 1 |

[a] M = master's degree
B = bachelor's degree
D = doctoral degree
[b] Predominantly black institution
[c] Predominantly women's institution

*Source:* From Clifton F. Conrad, Jennifer Grant, and Susan Bolyard Millar, *A Silent Success: Master's Education in the United States,* 1993, pp. 34–35. Reprinted by permission of the Johns Hopkins University Press.

**TABLE 2.2   Distribution of Interviewees**

| *By Stakeholder Group* | *Number of Interviewees* |
|---|---|
| Institutional Administrators | 85 |
| Program Administrators | 95 |
| Faculty | 167 |
| Students | 184 |
| Alumni | 147 |
| Employers | 103 |
| Total | 781 |

| *By Minority Status* | |
|---|---|
| African-American | 60 |
| Asian-American | 12 |
| International | 19 |
| Hispanic | 11 |
| Native American | 3 |
| White Nonminority | 676 |
| Total | 781 |

| *By Sex* | |
|---|---|
| Men | 430 |
| Women | 351 |
| Total | 781 |

| *By Institutional Type* | |
|---|---|
| National Universities | 303 |
| Regional Colleges and Universities | 333 |
| Liberal Arts Colleges | 84 |
| Specialized Institutions | 61 |
| Total | 781 |

| *By Field of Study* | |
|---|---|
| Established Professional | |
| Business | 78 |
| Education | 76 |
| Engineering | 90 |
| Nursing | 90 |
| Theater | 76 |
| Total | 410 |
| Emerging Professional | |
| Applied Anthropology | 100 |
| Computer Science | 15 |
| Environmental Studies | 71 |
| Microbiology | 89 |
| Total | 275 |

| Traditional Arts and Sciences | |
| --- | --- |
| English | 82 |
| Sociology | 14 |
| Total | 96 |
| | |
| Grand Total | 781 |

*Source:* From Clifton F. Conrad, Jennifer Grant, and Susan Bolyard Millar, *A Silent Success: Master's Education in the United States,* 1993, p. 36. Reprinted by permission of the Johns Hopkins University Press.

## Interview Process

In keeping with our positioned subject approach, we conducted our interviews as dialogues: While interviewees did most of the talking, we presented ourselves as participants in a conversation. With the exception of students (whom we interviewed in focus groups), we sought to encourage sustained dialogue through face-to-face individual interviews. A small number of interviews were conducted over the telephone with employers and alumni who were not available at our research sites.

We developed a broad set of topics to guide the interview process. These topics explored students' learning experiences in master's programs, including their "character" and "quality" as well as those program characteristics that interviewees believed contributed most to students' enrichment. Rather than using these topics as a formal interview protocol, we encouraged each interviewee to establish the direction of the dialogue. Once they felt that we genuinely wanted to understand their views and grew accustomed to the open-endedness of our interviews, most interviewees seemed to enjoy establishing the general direction of the exchange.[8]

To be sure, some interviewees needed prompting.[9] When this occurred, we often asked questions such as: "What do you think are the most important characteristics of the program?" "What have you and others learned?" "What activities or events have been most instrumental in helping you learn advanced knowledge in your field? In developing your skills?" "Where does the 'real learning' take place for students here?" Still, we self-consciously sought to limit the amount of prompting we did and, in most instances, the people we interviewed were very forthcoming.[10]

## Data Analysis: Constant Comparative Method

We organized our data analysis around the construction of a theory of high-quality programs—a theory based on research we had conducted at the master's level, but one that we believed could be extended (albeit tentatively) to the undergraduate and doctoral levels as well.[11] On the basis of what we learned from interviewees across the forty-seven master's programs in the sample, our data analysis was informed throughout by our systematic endeavor to identify and weave together attributes and clusters of attributes of high-quality programs into an integrated theory.[12] To that end, we used the constant comparative method to analyze our interview material first within and then across the forty-seven programs. Over an extended period of time, we gradually constructed a theory of program quality made up of seventeen attributes divided into five clusters.

In keeping with our definition of a high-quality program, a single overarching question guided our data analysis: What program attributes contribute to enriching learning experiences for students that positively affect their growth and development? To flesh out specific program attributes, we concurrently addressed three sub-questions. First, what actions do stakeholders take to implement or enact the attribute? Second, what consequences do these actions have for enhancing students' learning experiences? Third, what positive effects do these learning experiences have on students' growth and development?

Prior to beginning data analysis, we developed two decision-rules to guide our identification of attributes of high-quality programs. First, each attribute had to be considered important by interviewees in at least three of the six stakeholder groups represented in our sample. Second, each attribute had to be considered important by stakeholders in at least two-fifths of the programs in the forty-seven-case sample.[13]

Our data analysis followed the four stages of the constant comparative method. In the first stage, we reviewed the interview transcripts for all 781 people interviewed in the study.[14] In so doing, we used our guiding questions and decision-rules to record in a codebook—on a program-by-program basis—data incidents that interviewees in three or more stakeholder groups in each program considered important. In addition, we recorded incidents in which interviewees identified attributes of high-quality master's programs that they felt were missing in their program. Through this "open sampling" technique, we coded data into the following categories: attribute, reasons why the attribute was considered important by stakeholders, actions taken by stakeholders to enact the attribute, conditions constraining the realization of the attribute, ways in which the attribute enhanced students' learning experiences, and effects of the attribute on students' growth and development. Once this open-ended coding process had been completed, we tentatively identified thirty-nine attributes of high-quality programs through a cross-case analysis.[15]

In the second stage of data analysis, we focused on systematically refining and testing the attributes identified in the first stage in order to construct a theory of program quality. Guided by our initial list of program attributes, we revisited our codebook as well as original interview material and then—on a program-by-program basis—systematically developed, refined, and tested the emerging theory. As we proceeded through the programs, we continued to remain open to attributes that we might have missed in the first stage. For the most part, this cross-program analysis was informed by two considerations: the fleshing out and refining of program attributes—including actions, consequences, and effects—through constant comparison across the forty-seven programs and, equally important, the systematic search across programs for evidence that supported, refuted, or modified the program attributes identified through this process.

This analytic procedure led to the gradual construction of a preliminary theory of program quality during the second stage. While many of the attributes of high-quality programs we had identified in the first stage were modified and refined (sometimes by integrating two or more into a single attribute), others were refuted by negative evidence or insufficiently supported by the data. The remaining attributes were confirmed by the data with little modification. These cross-program comparisons, by drawing attention to differences and variation across programs as well as to similarities, also contributed to our depth of understanding and, in turn, to the overall development of the theory. For each attribute, these comparisons helped us understand better the actions taken by stakeholders to enact the attribute, the ways in which the attribute enhanced students' learning experiences, and the positive effects of these learning experiences on students. Using the decision-rules that an attribute had to be voiced by at least three stakeholder groups and in at least two-fifths of the programs, we identified twenty-three program attributes in our emerging theory of program quality by the completion of this second stage.

In the third stage of data analysis, we further delimited and tested the theory. Guided by our inventory of program attributes and using discriminate sampling on a program-by-program basis, we took two more sojourns through our revised codebook. We first reexamined each program with the intent of developing, insofar as possible, a more parsimonious and inclusive set of program attributes. We then revisited each program to test the theory further, especially in light of our decision-rules. In particular, we systematically looked for negative evidence to refute each of the attributes included in the emerging theory. After completing this second journey and agreeing between ourselves that the guidelines of "theoretical saturation" had been met, we prepared a revised outline of the theory that included seventeen attributes that we grouped into five clusters.[16] For each attribute, the outline included the actions taken by stakeholders to enact the attribute, ways in which the attribute enhanced students' learning experiences, and the effects that these learning experiences had on students' growth and development. This outline provided the foundation for the fourth and final stage in the constant comparative method: writing a theory of program quality.[17] (Readers interested in an expanded treatment of our method may wish to consult the technical appendix.) In the following chapter we present our engagement theory of program quality.

## *Endnotes*

1. The discussion of our multicase study design and interviews draws upon material previously published in *A Silent Success: Master's Education in the United States* (see pp. 28–41).

2. From our perspective, the most compelling support for our definition is found in the work of Alexander Astin (1985, 60–78), especially his concept of "talent development." We also note that the growing emphasis throughout higher education on student learning outcomes finds support in many objective indicator rankings that have reinforced the notion that program quality is closely linked to the achievements of students and program alumni. Robert Knapp and Hubert Goodrich (1952) ranked institutions in terms of the proportion of alumni who earned doctoral degrees; Robert Knapp and Joseph Greenbaum (1953) ranked institutions according to the proportion of students who earned graduate fellowships; Ervin Krause and Loretta Krause (1970) ranked undergraduate colleges on the basis of the number of bachelor's graduates who contributed articles to *Scientific American*; William F. Dube (1974) ranked undergraduate colleges according to the number of alumni who entered medical school; Donald Glower (1980) used the number of alumni listed in *Who's Who in Engineering* as one of two criteria for ranking engineering schools; and Carol Fuller (1986) ranked undergraduate institutions on the basis of their success in producing graduates who went on to complete a Ph.D. degree.

3. This approach assumes that people, as "positioned subjects" (where "subjects" refers to people with particular needs, perceptions, and capabilities for action, and "position" refers to the setting in which they are situated), actively interpret their everyday worlds. The basic idea implied in our use of the term "positioned subject" has long been used by anthropologists to describe a particular interpretive approach to research (Geertz 1974, 1983; Rosaldo 1989). In recent years, scholars in many disciplines have articulated similar approaches. See, for example, the work on "standpoint epistemologies" by Sandra Harding (1986, 1991) and Dorothy Smith (1990). In our study, we used Jon Barwise and John Perry's (1983) relation theory of meaning as the philosophical underpinning of our positioned subject approach. For a discussion of this theory, see the technical appendix in *A Silent Success: Master's Education in the United States*.

4. We also viewed each program as located, or positioned, within a particular setting.

5. We also included four programs at three predominantly black institutions and one program at a predominantly women's institution.

6. Depending on a researcher's approach, stakeholders might be defined in different ways. For example, critical theorists (Giroux 1988; McLaren 1989; Tierney 1989a, 1989b; Weis 1985) are particularly attuned to "oppressed" and "privileged" stakeholders. Most scholars using traditional approaches have relied heavily upon the perspectives of administrators and faculty at national universities and in national professional organizations, but a growing number have included a broader range of stakeholder perspectives (Chaffee and Tierney 1988; Clark 1987; Conrad 1989, Kuh, Schuh, and Whitt 1991). In our case, if a person—whether "powerful" in the cultural, political, and economic mainstream or not—had a vital stake in master's education, we considered him or her a stakeholder.

7. We spoke with an average of sixteen stakeholders in each case, with a low of twelve interviewees and a high of twenty-four.

8. With the permission of interviewees, we taped nearly all of our interviews and took extensive notes. Interviews typically were sixty to ninety minutes in length.

9. We inevitably provided interviewees with various cues. For example, our note-taking sometimes seemed to provide such a cue. By pausing to take notes, we sometimes communicated to interviewees that what they had said was particularly important. They often responded to such cues by commenting on our notes, either explaining that what we had written was not that important or, more often, elaborating on the point.

10. We attribute their candor to several factors. For one, many interviewees told us that they were pleased with our promise to keep their responses confidential. For another, most interviewees seemed to accept our explanation that our aim was to listen carefully to their perspectives as the basis for understanding the nature and quality of students' learning experiences, not to evaluate their programs, per se. And not least important, most interviewees clearly seemed to appreciate our interest in their views.

11. In developing our theory of program quality, we drew heavily on Jennifer Grant Haworth's (1993) Ph.D. dissertation entitled "A Grounded Theory of Program Quality in Master's Education."

12. We could have chosen to limit our analysis to interviewees from a subset of programs which—on the basis of reputational rankings or our analysis—we identified as high-quality programs. Instead, we chose to include interviewees from across all forty-seven programs in our sample. We did so for two reasons. First, and most important, nearly every one of the 781 interviewees in our study expressed definite views on those aspects of their master's experiences that did and did not contribute to a high-quality learning experience for students. To study only a subset of programs or, alternatively, to have rank-ordered programs in terms of their overall quality as the foundation for analysis, would have silenced the voices of many interviewees in our study. Second, while we did find that there was considerable variation in overall quality across the forty-seven programs in our sample, we learned that there were attributes of master's programs that did and did not contribute to students' master's experiences regardless of their overall program quality.

13. As positioned subjects, we each brought our own "position" to data analysis and theory construction. For example, we each brought understandings of pro-

gram quality based on our awareness of the literature on program quality. At the beginning of our analysis, we used these understandings as "a conceptual entree— a beginning logic, however simple or obvious, for linking datum to datum, for making initial sense out of what would otherwise be disparate bits of information" (Neumann and Bensimon 1990, 681). These understandings were points of departure—not referent points—in our analysis. We continuously sought to anchor our analysis in the voices of interviewees: stakeholders' perspectives were the primary foundation for generating attributes and clusters of attributes and, in the end, our theory of program quality. By maintaining fidelity to stakeholders' voices, we sought to remain open to new understandings and interpretations throughout the entire data analysis process.

14. We also reviewed the program summaries which, as discussed in the technical appendix, we had prepared earlier for each of the forty-seven programs included in the study.

15. As the first step in this analysis, we identified all of those attributes of high-quality master's programs that had been emphasized by at least three stakeholder groups in at least two-fifths of the programs. In the second step in this analysis, we engaged in spirited exchanges in which we questioned one another about the evidentiary foundation and coding of data incidents in the first stage of analysis. Based on these conversations, we modified our initial coding scheme. In the third step of this cross-program analysis, we prepared an outline that listed thirty-nine attributes of high-quality programs and included other pertinent information as well, such as the ways that each attribute enhanced students' learning experiences.

16. None of the attributes of high-quality master's programs that we identified had strong associations with characteristics built into our sample, such as field of study, institutional type, type of control, and full-time or part-time student population.

17. To ensure that interviewees did not uncritically conflate "quality" and "satisfaction," we invited many to distinguish between the two. In doing so, some interviewees told us that satisfaction and quality were linked in that "satisfaction" was a prerequisite to a quality program. They did so on the grounds that being satisfied with their program encouraged them to invest in their studies. For the most part, however, interviewees told us that student satisfaction often was not enough to ensure that students had a "high-quality" learning experience.

# 3

An Engagement Theory
of Academic Program
Quality

In this chapter, we introduce our theory and, in so doing, advance a new perspective on program quality. This theory is anchored in our definition of high-quality programs—namely, those which provide enriching learning experiences that positively affect students' growth and development—and is based on the weight of the evidence of the 781 people we interviewed. In broad strokes, the theory emphasizes one major idea: that student, faculty, and administrator engagement in teaching and learning is central to a high-quality program.

## Engagement Theory

According to our theory, high-quality programs are those in which students, faculty, and administrators engage in mutually supportive teaching and learning: students invest in teaching as well as learning, and faculty and administrators invest in learning as well as teaching. Moreover, faculty and administrators invite alumni and employers of graduates to participate in their programs. In short, the theory accentuates the dual roles that invested participants play in constructing and sustaining programs of high quality.

More specifically, the theory holds that participants in high-quality programs invest significant time and energy in five separate clusters of program attributes, each of which contributes to enriching learning experiences for students that positively affect their growth and development. The five clusters of program attributes are: diverse and engaged participants, participatory cultures, interactive teaching and learning, connected program requirements, and adequate resources. Figure 3.1 provides a visual representation of the theory.

In keeping with the engagement thesis, the most important of these clusters is diverse and engaged participants. In high-quality programs, faculty and administrators continually seek to attract and support faculty and students who infuse diverse perspectives into—and who are engaged in—their own and others' teaching and learning. Faculty, students, and leaders who invest time and effort in their programs strengthen students' learning experiences in ways that significantly enhance students' personal, intellectual, and professional development.

Stakeholders in high-quality programs also invest heavily in participatory cultures. Program administrators, faculty, and students—as well as institutional administrators, alumni, and employers—develop and sustain cultures that emphasize a shared program direction, a community of learners, and a risk-taking environment. Program cultures that share these attributes greatly contribute to the quality of students' learning.

Program administrators, faculty, and students in high-quality programs also make strong investments in interactive teaching and learning. Through critical dialogues about knowledge and professional practice, faculty-student mentoring, cooperative peer learning projects, out-of-class activities and integrative, hands on learning activities, stakeholders actively participate in and contribute to one anothers' learning.

Program administrators, faculty, and students in high-quality programs invest in a fourth program cluster: connected program requirements. To wit, faculty and program administrators design program requirements that challenge students to develop more mature and unified understandings of their profession and its practice as they engage in planned breadth and depth course work, apply and test their course-related knowledge and skills in a professional residency, and complete a tangible product (such as a thesis, project report, or performance).

Finally, faculty, program administrators, and institutional administrators in high-quality programs devote substantial time and effort to providing monetary as well as non-monetary support for students, faculty, and basic infrastructure needs. Investing in this program cluster helps to ensure that faculty and students have the resources they need to concentrate fully on teaching and learning.

Table 3.1 summarizes the engagement theory. For each of the theory's seventeen attributes, this figure identifies the actions that stakeholders take to implement the attribute, sketches the major consequences that these actions have for enriching students' learning experiences, and indicates the

**FIGURE 3.1  Engagement Theory of Program Quality**

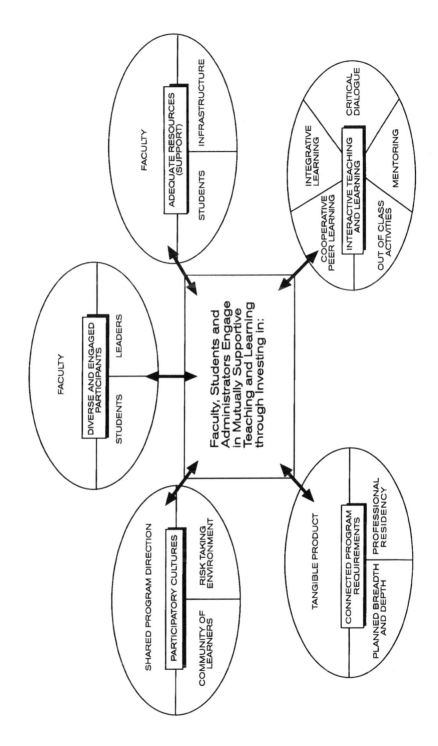

positive affects that these learning experiences have on students' growth and development.

In presenting the theory, we emphasize that the clusters of attributes that make up our engagement theory represent an "ideal" high-quality program. Further, while each of the attributes discussed in the following chapters was present in at least two-fifths of the programs in our sample, no single program encompassed all seventeen attributes. We encourage readers to use the theory as a "common analytical yardstick" (Turner 1978, 35) for reflecting on similarities and differences between their programs and this "ideal" program.

**TABLE 3.1  Overview of Engagement Theory**

*Cluster One: Diverse and Engaged Participants*

| | Actions | Consequences for Learning Experiences | Effects on Students |
|---|---|---|---|
| **Diverse and Engaged Faculty** | Faculty and administrators adopt multidimensional hiring policies to attract faculty who will bring diverse theoretical and applied perspectives and a commitment to teaching. | Faculty infuse diverse perspectives into their classroom lectures, discussions, and out-of-class interactions with students. | Students who study with faculty who accent multiple viewpoints develop richer, more creative understandings of knowledge and professional practice. |
| | Faculty and administrators establish reward structures that support faculty for engaging in diverse scholarly activities and for investing in students. | Faculty dedicate significant time and energy to teaching, including outside-of-class involvement with involvement with students. | Students who learn from committed scholar–teachers become more inspired professionals who are more committed to their profession and to their ongoing professional growth and development. |
| **Diverse and Engaged Students** | Faculty and administrators establish admissions policies to attract diverse students who will bring a multiplicity of disciplinary and experientially-based perspectives and who will invest in their experience. | Students contribute fresh perspectives to discussions they have with one another and with faculty. | Students who share diverse perspectives creatively expand and enrich one anothers' understandings of theory and professional practice. |
| | Faculty and administrators screen and admit students whose professional interests and goals match those of their curriculum and faculty. | Students invest time and energy in their own and others' learning through active participation in formal and informal learning activities. | Students who invest in learning inspire one another to commit more fully to their professions. |

*(Continued)*

31

**TABLE 3.1** *(Continued)*

*Cluster One: Diverse and Engaged Participants (Continued)*

| | Actions | Consequences for Learning Experiences | Effects on Students |
|---|---|---|---|
| **Engaged Leaders** | Faculty and administrators recruit department or program chairs who will "champion" their program. | Leaders effectively promote their program to internal and external audiences and are adept at securing resources to sustain it. | Leaders who provide students with program leadership opportunities help them become more highly-skilled, self-confident leaders. |
| | Institutional administrators and faculty engage in activities aimed at supporting program leaders. | Leaders attract and support diverse and engaged faculty and students. | Engaged leaders provide the kinds of support that empowers faculty and students to invest in teaching and learning experiences which, in turn, help students become more competent, committed, and creative leaders. |
| | | Leaders encourage participants to assume informal program leadership roles. | |

*Cluster Two: Participatory Cultures*

| | Actions | Consequences for Learning Experiences | Effects on Students |
|---|---|---|---|
| **Shared Program Direction** | Faculty and administrative leaders invite stakeholders to join them in developing a shared program direction. | Stakeholders share an overall program direction that both informs and animates their actions and provides a common thread which knits together students' learning experiences. | Students develop more distinct professional identities in programs in which participants share a common focus. |
| | Leaders sustain shared understandings of program direction by encouraging faculty, students, alumni, and employers to participate in ongoing evaluation efforts in which they examine | | "Connected" learning experiences help students to develop a keener sense of professional direction and a greater awareness of where and how they wish to invest their professional energies upon graduation. |

| | | |
|---|---|---|
| | the fit between their program's teaching and learning activities and its overall direction. | |
| | Leaders sustain shared understandings of program direction by communicating it to internal and external audiences. | |
| **Community of Learners** | A leader—or group of leaders—takes responsibility for helping to build a learning community. | Participants experience their program as a "learning community" in which faculty and students teach and learn from one another more or less as colleagues. |
| | Faculty develop more collegial and less hierarchical relations with students. | Participants experience camaraderie among and between faculty and students that supports and complements the overall sense of community. |
| | Administrators, faculty, and students construct in- and out-of-class teaching and learning experiences to facilitate and sustain co-learning among program participants. | The collegial interactions students have with one another and with faculty improve their communication and teamwork skills.<br><br>Students develop a greater appreciation and respect for the value of collaborative approaches to inquiry, problem-solving, and leadership. |
| **Risk-Taking Environment** | Faculty and administrators develop a supportive learning environment in which students are encouraged to explore new ideas and test developing skills. | Supported and challenged to take risks, students regularly question orthodoxies, advance alternative perspectives and approaches, and engage in learning activities that press the boundaries of their potential. |
| | Faculty and administrators take risks themselves, encourage students to follow their lead and to stretch and grow in new ways. | Students who engage in—and learn from—risk-taking activities become more competent, self-assured professionals.<br><br>Since risk-taking ventures require students to wrestle with their profession in new and creative ways, they become more imaginative and resourceful professionals. |

(Continued)

33

**TABLE 3.1** *(Continued)*

*Cluster Three: Interactive Teaching and Learning*

| | Actions | Consequences for Learning Experiences | Effects on Students |
|---|---|---|---|
| **Critical Dialogue** | Faculty and administrators emphasize a two-way, interactive approach to teaching and learning that nurtures ongoing dialogue among program participants. | Faculty and students engage in disciplined and mutually-enriching dialogue in which they constantly question one another, examine assumptions and differing points-of-view, and generate critically informed understandings of knowledge and professional practice. | Students who engage in critical dialogues with faculty and other students learn to think in a more holistic, questioning, and discriminating manner. |
| | Faculty and administrators infuse a critical sensibility into these interactions by encouraging students to take an inquisitive stance on knowledge and professional practice. | | The critical and holistic thinking skills students refine through critical dialogue helps them to become more creative and self-confident problem-solvers. |
| **Integrative Learning: Theory with Practice, Self with Subject** | Faculty and administrators invest in teaching and learning activities—such as "real-world" lectures and hands-on learning—that invite connections between theory and practice. | Students participate in learning activities in which they connect theoretical and applied knowledge to complex problems, issues, and situations in the real world. | Students who participate in integrative learning activities approach problem-solving from a more holistic standpoint. |
| | Faculty and administrators model for students how they integrate knowledge and practice as they work with students in class, on-stage, in the laboratory, or in the field. | | Because they are challenged to connect theoretical and applied knowledge to real-world issues, students become more adept at translating and communicating theoretical and technical knowledge to others. |

| | | | |
|---|---|---|---|
| Mentoring | Faculty take an interest in students' career goals and tailor courses of study to their educational objectives.<br><br>Faculty periodically instruct students on a one-on-one basis in order to sharpen their understandings of knowledge and professional practice.<br><br>Faculty regularly provide students with feedback on their professional skills development. | Students receive individualized advice, guidance, and feedback from faculty in various ways: working together in the lab, field, or studio; in formal meetings; and through informal interactions. | Students become more aware of their strengths and weaknesses, thereby strengthening their professional competence and enhancing their confidence.<br><br>The mentoring students receive from faculty helps to advance their careers in the university and non-university workplace. |
| Cooperative Peer Learning | Faculty use in- and out-of-class group activities to promote cooperative learning among students.<br><br>Faculty themselves engage in collaborative research and team-teaching activities; in so doing, they model peer learning for students and emphasize the importance they place on it in their program and profession. | Students participate in group activities in which they contribute to, and support, one anothers' learning in ways that enrich their understandings of knowledge and professional practice. | Cooperative learning experiences improve students' interpersonal and teamwork skills.<br><br>As students teach and learn from one another in study groups, research teams, or theater companies, they become more self-confident in their professional abilities. |

(Continued)

**TABLE 3.1** *(Continued)*

*Cluster Three: Interactive Teaching and Learning (Continued)*

| | Actions | Consequences for Learning Experiences | Effects on Students |
|---|---|---|---|
| **Out-of-Class Activities** | Faculty, administrators, and students develop and sponsor formal and informal out-of-class program activities. | Students—and occasionally faculty—participate in a variety of informal, out-of-class activities in which they explore topics of mutual interest and enrich one anothers' learning. | The interactions students have with one another in out-of-class activities improves their oral communication and interpersonal skills. |
| | Faculty and administrators support—financially and otherwise—out-of-class activities as an integral part of their program. | | As students interact with and learn from one another and from faculty in out-of-class activities, they develop a greater appreciation for collaborative approaches to inquiry, problem-solving, and leadership in their fields. |

*Cluster Four: Connected Program Requirements*

| | Actions | Consequences for Learning Experiences | Effects on Students |
|---|---|---|---|
| **Planned Breadth and Depth Course Work** | Faculty and administrators meet periodically to determine the knowledge, skills, and practices they expect students to learn. | Students complete a combination of core and specialized course work in which they learn both generalized and specialized knowledge. | The advanced knowledge, skills, and practices students learn in core and specialized courses enhances their professional competence. |
| | Faculty and administrators develop core and specialized course work requirements in line with these expectations. | | Since core and specialized course work challenges students to think about their fields in both "broad" |

|  | | | |
|---|---|---|---|
| **Professional Residency** | Faculty and administrators design professional residency experiences with students' career interests and goals in mind. | Residential learning experiences challenge students to build bridges between what they learn in classes and what they encounter in "real-world" settings, thereby helping them to develop more robust and connected understandings of their professions. | and "deep" ways, they develop more holistic understandings of knowledge and practice that improves their workplace effectiveness. |
|  | Faculty and administrators maintain ties with employers, alumni, and community members that, in turn, help them identify and secure residency sites and supervisors for students. |  | The successful application of knowledge and skills in their professional residencies helps students to develop into more confident and competent professionals. |
|  | Once students are involved in their residencies, faculty members and site supervisors regularly provide them with regular guidance and feedback. |  | A professional residency strengthens students' professional identities. |
|  |  |  | The confidence, knowledge, and professional networks students develop in their residencies enhances their job prospects upon graduation. |
| **Tangible Product** | Faculty and administrators design tangible product requirements in light of their program's overall direction and goals. | In developing a tangible product, students are challenged to draw upon and knit together relevant principles, practices, and skills that they have learned in their programs to create a product that is of value to the field as well as to them personally. | The research and writing associated with thesis and project work improves students' analytical and written communication skills. |
|  | Faculty and administrators support students throughout this culminating activity, providing them with guidance and feedback as needed. |  | By assuming major responsibility for their projects from start to finish, students develop into more confident and independent professionals. |

*(Continued)*

**TABLE 3.1** (*Continued*)

## Cluster Four: Connected Program Requirements (*Continued*)

| | Actions | Consequences for Learning Experiences | Effects on Students |
|---|---|---|---|
| **Tangible Product** (*Continued*) | | | As a culminating—and often an integrative—activity, this learning experience helps students to develop a "big picture" perspective on their professions. |

## Cluster Five: Adequate Resources

| | Actions | Consequences for Learning Experiences | Effects on Students |
|---|---|---|---|
| **Support for Students** | Institutional and program administrators, as well as faculty, secure monetary resources for student assistantships, fellowships, and travel to professional conferences. | Students who receive financial aid for full-time study, or who complete their studies part-time in programs with nontraditional delivery formats, are in a better position to concentrate on their learning. | Students who utilize career planning and placement services are more likely to secure employment in their field upon graduation. |
| | Faculty and administrators design nontraditional course delivery formats to support the educational needs of working professionals. | Students who take advantage of career counseling and job-search strategies and develop professional networks that better prepare them for locating employment upon graduation. | Since financial aid and nontraditional course delivery formats provide students with the support needed to invest more fully in their learning experiences, they indirectly help students to become more committed, lifelong learners. |
| | Faculty and administrators provide career planning and placement assistance to help students prepare for and locate employment upon graduation. | | Since support facilitates student investment in many other attributes, it further intensifies many of the effects that these attributes have on students. |

| | | | |
|---|---|---|---|
| **Support for Faculty** | Campus and departmental administrators allocate monetary resources for faculty salaries, sabbaticals, and travel to professional conferences. | When faculty are adequately supported, they invest significant time and effort in teaching and mentoring students. | Students who study with faculty who take an active interest in them became more self-confident professionals. |
| | Campus and departmental administrators establish reward structures that support faculty for their involvement in teaching and learning. | | Since support facilitates faculty investments in other attributes, it further intensifies many of the effects these attributes have on students. |
| **Support for Basic Infrastructure** | Campus and departmental administrators, as well as faculty, secure monetary resources to purchase requisite equipment and supplies; to ensure suitable laboratory, performance, and classroom facilities; and to support institutional library and computer needs. | When basic infrastructure needs are met, students are in a better position to learn advanced knowledge and techniques. | Students who study in programs with up-to-date equipment and facilities become more technically-competent professionals. |
| | | | Since this kind of support in-directly complements student investments in other attributes, it further intensifies many of the effects these attributes have on students. |

# 4

# Diverse and Engaged Participants

Based on evidence from hundreds of interviewees, we identified "diverse and engaged participants" as the first cluster of attributes in our engagement theory of quality. As the people who took responsibility for teaching and learning, these participants played a pivotal role in constructing and defining the quality of learning experiences that students had in their programs.

In this chapter, we describe the first three attributes in the theory: diverse and engaged faculty, diverse and engaged students, and engaged leaders. For each, we discuss the actions that faculty and program administrators took to enact the attribute, describe the consequences of their actions for students' learning experiences, and examine the effects of these learning experiences on students' growth and development.

## Diverse and Engaged Faculty

Throughout our study, we became increasingly aware that diverse and engaged faculty were fundamental to high-quality programs. In many programs we visited, faculty not only infused a variety of scholarly and experiential perspectives into their teaching, they also invested significant time and energy in teaching students. In so doing, these faculty consistently elevated the quality of students' learning experiences in ways that enhanced their growth and development.

## Actions

Faculty and administrators invested in two activities to ensure that they had diverse and engaged faculty teaching in their programs. First, they developed hiring policies that valued faculty who had varied theoretical and applied perspectives and a dedication to teaching. Second, they established reward structures that supported faculty for engaging in a broad range of scholarly activities and for investing in teaching.

Across our sample, faculty and administrators told us that they intentionally sought to attract diverse and committed scholar–teachers to their programs. To this end, they established hiring policies that emphasized a variety of criteria, including educational background, research productivity, scholarly diversity, professional experience in the non-university workplace, teaching and advising competence, and dedication to student learning.

In Southwest State's microbiology program, for instance, several faculty and administrators pointed out that they had crafted hiring policies with diverse and engaged faculty in mind. As we came to understand it, the program's hiring policy strongly valued individuals who, in the words of the department chair, were "academics [and] not just researchers. . . ." We want [new faculty] to grow as teachers as well as researchers," he told us emphatically. "We don't want [people who will] just come here with a set of notes and use those [notes] for the next fifteen years. . . . The people we're hiring now are here because they know that what counts is adding quality work to the literature and doing well as teachers."

Faculty and administrators in Moore A&T's engineering program offered a similar view. As one professor told us, he and his colleagues had recently developed a set of "multidimensional" hiring criteria to attract faculty who were "not only good research and grants types," but who also had "great teaching ability and cared about students." These criteria, the department chair emphasized, sent a clear message to prospective hires that their department was not "for everyone":

> [In this program], you have to really be interested in advising students. Faculty are on campus from 9 to 5 and they are here for informal as well as formal contact. When we hire faculty we stress this informal contact—that getting grants and publishing papers isn't enough. Like members of a small company, faculty have to be willing to be involved in many aspects of the master's program—not just their own specialty.

Alongside "multidimensional" hiring policies, faculty and administrators established reward structures that supported diverse and engaged faculty. These included promotion, tenure, and merit review policies that recognized and rewarded faculty for their participation in a range of scholarly endeavors as well as for their involvement in various teaching-related activities.

The theater program at Helena State is a representative program in which faculty and departmental administrators influenced the development of a more supportive institutional reward structure. As we learned from many stakeholders, in recent years the chair of the fine arts department had held many conversations with key campus administrators, including the university's graduate dean and the academic vice-president, concerning the need to incorporate a broader "definition of scholarship" into the institution's promotion and tenure guidelines. These discussions, according to one high-ranking campus administrator, helped him to develop "an understanding of the varied nature of scholarship . . . particularly in a milieu where the scientific model of research has dominated. . . . You have to understand what a show . . . mean[s] to an artist. You have to understand what kinds of things master's students in theater do." Animated by this new perspective on scholarship, this administrator worked with others to revise Helena State's promotion and tenure policies so that they supported theater faculty both for their involvement in professional artistic performances and for their investments in various teaching-related activities, including classroom instruction and university-sponsored theatrical productions.

In a much larger number of programs we studied, faculty and program administrators crafted merit review policies at the departmental level that rewarded faculty for participating in a broad range of scholarly activities—including teaching. A Walton State administrator, for instance, told us that "committed teaching" was a high priority in his department. As he put it: "In many institutions graduate study is a vehicle for freeing the teacher from classroom commitments, but here, at the graduate level, the commitment that the instructor has to teaching [is supported]. My job in the program is not to carry out my own research program. If I can do both, good . . . but the first thing I have to do is carry out my commitment to teaching." With a slightly different twist, the chair of City-State's applied anthropology program stressed that the expanded definition of scholarship he and his colleagues had woven into the department's reward structure ensured that faculty were recognized not only for refereed publications and good teaching, but also for externally-funded applied research projects, technical reports, and local consulting assignments that broadened and deepened their perspectives on professional knowledge and practice.

## Consequences for Learning Experiences

The efforts faculty and administrators put into attracting and supporting diverse and engaged faculty consistently enriched the overall quality of students' learning experiences. As we learned, these faculty infused diverse perspectives into their classroom lectures, discussions, and out-of-class interactions with students. Equally important was their dedication of time and energy to teaching and learning that benefitted students in myriad ways.

During our study, we found that many faculty shared diverse theoretical and applied perspectives with students. The chair of Major State's education program, for example, elaborated on the range of perspectives that he and his colleagues infused into their interactions with students:

> We have a long history of putting ourselves out on a limb. We sort of take unpopular, not widely held positions at the time and, very often in the process of doing that, [we] become a bellwether for things to come. . . . Students in our classes walk away with their heads spinning at the frequency with which they've encountered questions that never occurred to them. They are exposed to orthodox and rival perspectives: neo-Marxist, feminist, and international perspectives. They all exist here in our classes.

In a similar vein, a professor in St. Joan's business program told us that faculty intentionally incorporated theoretical and applied perspectives into their class discussions and lectures. "There's a place for theory in [our program]," he explained, "but that's just one piece of the puzzle. The other piece includes the practicalities of the workplace. Here we try to hit on both. . . . [Our faculty] take the theory, apply it to real-life practical experience, and then demonstrate how the theory can be translated into money for a corporation's pocket."

Many students and alumni emphasized the value they placed on learning from faculty who shared diverse points of view on knowledge and professional practice. A graduate of Major State's environmental studies program, for instance, told us how much he enjoyed taking classes from "faculty who had spent time working in other jobs and who brought some business or real-world working perspectives, not academic, back into the classroom and shared that [with students]." A Middle State engineering student made the same point through a negative example. As he put it, his master's experience would have been "greatly improved" if his professors would have "had a broader base of knowledge across the electrical engineering field": "Their knowledge is limited to what [two local industries] offer. They also lack a lot of practical knowledge about what's going on in engineering."

Along with students and alumni, many employers valued faculty who introduced students to multiple views on knowledge and practice. As an employer of Appleby State's microbiology alumni said of the wide-ranging perspectives faculty shared with students: "To do that, [to] foster [those] perspectives, is all people stuff. It's not equipment stuff and it's not textbook stuff. It's hiring the right professors." An employer of Phelps' theater graduates reiterated this theme in his interview, underscoring the important role that faculty played in developing "multidimensional actors" for his theater company. As he told us:

> *I think that students really need to develop their own style with the help of a lot of different teachers [who represent different viewpoints]. [And Phelps' program accomplishes this because it] uses a lot of team teaching in the best sense of the word. Different viewpoints from all of the different faculty are tolerated and, in fact, encouraged [by faculty] in terms of not forcing the acting students to choose between different viewpoints but, rather, to have them understand that there are sixteen different ways of looking at the same thing.*

In addition to sharing differing perspectives with students, many faculty in our study committed significant time and energy to their teaching. We came to appreciate that this commitment was grounded in a broadly-shared belief among faculty that promoting student growth and development was an essential—if not the fundamental—purpose of higher education. A faculty member in Middle State's microbiology program touched upon this when he remarked, "You know, I don't care about making myself look good. I mean, that's not a big deal [to me] at all. But what I want to see is students learn and really do well. That's where I get my kicks." In much the same spirit, a microbiology professor at Appleby State candidly told us: "If I felt like I wasn't helping students, I'd get out of the field. I'd go wash dishes or something. But I do feel like I'm making a difference. I hope so anyway. I hear the feedback and I think we are doing the right thing [with our master's students]—helping these people to reach their own potential, develop themselves, and helping to facilitate them to a better life."

Inspired by a commitment to student learning and development, these and other like-minded faculty were committed to their own classroom teaching as well as various out-of-class instructional activities—including supervising tutorials, internships, and independent studies; directing student theses and practicum reports; and working with students on research and service-related projects. For example, in Southwest State's applied anthropology program, one professor told us that he and his colleagues "put a tremendous amount of energy into nurturing interactions between faculty and graduate students": "This is a very labor-intensive program of advising and supervising education outside the classroom in terms of tutorials, individually-directed readings, taking students out for lunch, and simply being open to drop-by chats." Reflecting upon the time and effort that faculty devoted to teaching in its M.B.A. program, a professor at Peterson University commented: "We have very dedicated, committed teachers walking down these corridors. They may not be the most published, but they are very dedicated to teaching the discipline. They really care. They really give a damn."

The time and effort that faculty committed to teaching and learning was not lost on students and alumni in our study. Indeed, many spoke effusively about their professors, describing them as student-centered teachers who genuinely cared about their growth and development. As an Appleby State microbiology alumnus said to us: "The professors they have here, as I remember them, are not ones who were just there to show off. And I really mean 'show off' how much they know and impress you. They were interested in a genuine attempt to get you to learn the information." In a similar vein, a Middle State microbiology student offered these words of praise for the program's faculty: "[They] really care about students. They really want students to succeed. Most are willing to go out of their way to see [that] this is done. They work with you . . . they care that students learn."

Not to be overlooked, students and alumni in some programs told us that they would have had far richer learning experiences if faculty had been more interested in their teaching. An alumnus of Middle State's engineering program, for instance, offered this biting appraisal of his professors: "They didn't care about teaching, just their research. I felt the faculty used me to do their research. I paid good money to go there, but not to go and bust my ass [sic] so that they could publish. I needed to get a good education and I spent a lot of time teaching myself. They didn't give enough." A Mountain State alumna was similarly disappointed with her professors, describing them as "self-centered, publish-or-perish type[s]" who could "care less about students": "The [prototypical] new faculty member is a high-tech, Wall Street businessman sort-of scientist. They are getting to be self-centered little capitalists. . . . The new faculty [in the program] are pushed to get grant money and they are always complaining about teaching under-graduates or master's students."

Whether they expressed positive or negative accounts, interviewees across our sample made it clear that diverse and engaged faculty are an essential feature of high-quality programs. Perhaps a faculty member-turned-corporate executive best captured the critical role that diverse—and, especially, committed—faculty play in creating and sustaining high-quality programs when he stated:

*When you look at education in general, whether you're talking bachelor's, master's, or Ph.D., you're really talking about a function where you're taking people at a very valuable time of their lives, and trying to help them make decisions and function within society in particular ways. I think that anything we do in that area depends very strongly on the leadership capabilities of the people. Within every university that I've been associated with, it's the compassion of the faculty and the leadership—it's the faculty that care about the students and, to some degree maybe, have the kind of personality that students can relate to and interact with, that makes all the difference.* . . . *It doesn't matter how you design the program on paper. If it's not executed by faculty advisors, by faculty willing to take students into the lab and provide the research training experience, by faculty who teach the courses [then an essential quality link is missing in the program].*

Indeed, across the forty-seven programs in our study, we found that the major difference between students who had high-quality learning experiences and those who had mediocre ones often boiled down to this all-important attribute.

## Effects on Students

Students derived two major benefits from their interactions with diverse and engaged faculty. First, students who studied with diverse faculty graduated with richer and more creative understandings of knowledge and professional practice. Second, students who learned from engaged scholar–teachers became more inspired professionals who, in turn, committed themselves more fully to their own growth and development.

Many students and alumni in our study credited the diverse perspectives that faculty shared in their classes with enriching and expanding their thinking on various field-related topics and issues. An alumna of Longmont's English program, for instance, told us that by studying with faculty who were "on the cutting edge—not only of teaching strategies, but also of canon development"—she had "stretched" herself "intellectually in all kinds of new directions": "They're teaching Native American literature and black poets here. [In my Ph.D. program at another university] we never get that in regular classes. I get so excited about [Longmont] because it's so exciting for me." In much the same spirit, three Southern State nursing students described how faculty had broadened their thinking:

*[Student 1]: A major strength of this program is the intellectual diversity among faculty—different theoretical perspectives like feminism and critical theory.*

*[Student 2]: It's the perspectives they include when they're doing their lectures. For example, we had a lecture last week and it was specifically about how the profession of nursing has been held back because it is essentially a women's profession.*

*[Student 3]: I think the new perspectives are widening the whole perspective of being human, and specifically, of being female. I must be pretty naive, but I wasn't aware of all of that. . . . It's making me think [in new ways].*

*[Student 1]: I've heard feminist perspectives in the issues classes . . . a little bit in the education and administration courses. . . . I think since I've been in this program I have become more politically aware of some issues that I never thought of before. If anything, this program has encouraged me to look into these things [from a variety of new perspectives] and to become more knowledgeable about them.*

Besides expanding their understanding of knowledge and practice, students and alumni told us that learning from committed scholar–teachers affirmed and inspired their own sense of professionalism. An alumna of Longmont's English program expressed this outcome:

*I suppose many people tell you that not only are the professors tremendously erudite, but they're tremendous teachers so they're great models as teachers. I got so many new insights into works that I [had] taught for many years and thought I knew a lot about. [But] then dealing with these teachers—some of them made such tremendous connections—things I never thought of. That certainly affected the way I looked at a lot of works I taught. I've tried to be like them. I think they've been such an inspiration.*

Similarly, a Middle State microbiology student said that the "caring support" she received from faculty had led her to invest more fully in her own learning. As she put it: "The faculty really care about you in this program. And you'd be surprised—they have their own families and their own problems, but somebody takes time out for you. . . . When you have an instructor, and you have a question and you can talk about it, then you're willing to go and find out even more about it on your own."

While many other students and alumni expressed countless variations on this theme, their accounts emphasized a common, unifying idea: When scholar-teachers genuinely cared about students' growth and development, they inspired students to delve more deeply into their studies, to produce higher-quality work, and to become more inquisitive, inspired professionals.

## *Diverse and Engaged Students*

In working through the nearly 800 interviews in our study, we became increasingly aware that diverse and engaged students are also vital to high-quality programs. Time and again, interviewees stressed that committed students who shared different points of view—perspectives variously grounded in their racial, ethnic, gender, and socioeconomic backgrounds as well as their workplace, educational, and life experiences—markedly enhanced the quality of students' learning.

## Actions

Faculty and program administrators used a two-part recruitment strategy to attract diverse and engaged students to their programs. First, they established admissions policies that placed a high value on students who would bring to their studies varied disciplinary and experientially-based perspectives as well as a passion for learning. Second, they screened and admitted only those students whose professional interests and goals meshed well with those of their program's curriculum and faculty.

Across our sample, faculty and administrators crafted admissions policies and criteria with diverse and committed students in mind. Along with using traditional indicators of student quality (such as standardized test scores and undergraduate grade-point averages), they sought out culturally diverse students (in terms of race, ethnicity, gender, age, and socioeconomic status) with varied educational, life, and non-university workplace experiences who were clearly committed to their own and others' learning.

At Phelps University, for example, faculty pointed out that they emphasized two criteria—diversity and commitment—when admitting students to their environmental studies program. Two professors elaborated on the importance of these criteria:

> [Faculty 1]: We want to bring in good people—people who are bright and energetic and have the energy to pursue their ideas. That's the number one criterion: We are looking for people who are going to go out and make a difference [in the environmental studies field]. But that isn't enough. . . . There's a big need to bring in people with other perspectives so more approaches can be attempted and identified—people from civil engineering, biology, the social sciences, [and] the liberal arts.

> [Faculty 2]: We want ethical, smart, gung-ho, creative people. We look for exactly those kind of people. . . . If someone has had interesting experiences with the Forest Service or the Nature Conservancy or the Peace Corps, we're very impressed with that.

Faculty and administrators in other institutions emphasized similar criteria in their admissions policies and practices. An administrator at Laramie University, for example, said that while "the university need[ed]" and was "concerned about" students' GRE (graduate record examination) scores, faculty in its global education program paid far more attention to other criteria in the selection process—including just how invested students would be in their ongoing learning and development as professional educators. As he put it: "I tell students that we're interested in what you've done in the classroom, with what your professional goals are, and how you're going to take the skills you're going to learn in this program and go back into the classroom and be a more competent, polished, professional educator." On a different note, a Trafalgar administrator amplified on the reasons behind his colleagues' decision to admit students with diverse educational and life experiences into their master's program in theater:

> Some people might argue that these are the people we need to eliminate [from our program]—the ones who are untrained. But what we get are these incredibly lively minds who come from excellent schools, with excellent undergraduate work, and have a career's worth of work. We have, for example, a successful software designer with a degree in aeronautical engineering from M.I.T. who also happens to be a playwright. In one sense, he knows nothing about theater. . . . But he brings a whole new perspective [to the study of theater and playwriting] because of that. I think graduate programs need to make room for people like that.

Faculty and program administrators used a second strategy when recruiting diverse and engaged students: they screened and admitted only those individuals whose goals and interests meshed well with those of their programs. Faculty accomplished this in many ways, such as sponsoring program information sessions for prospective students and requiring individual interviews as part of the admissions process.

A Laramie administrator, for instance, said that he held three or four information sessions a year in which he introduced prospective students to the purposes and orientation of the school's global education program. As he explained, these sessions played an important role in attracting students who were, first and foremost, committed to becoming "global educators":

> When I do these sessions, I say to people, "I want you to go into this program with your eyes wide open. There are lots of wonderful options out there for you at our institution . . . and the other institutions with whom we compete." But then I say to them, "You should look at all of those programs, but if you really want to do global education which is a far narrower focus, then this is the place for you to be."

At Middle State University, faculty required on-campus interviews of all potential microbiology master's students to ensure, as one professor put it, "a good fit between the student's interests and what our faculty can provide to the student." And, at Phelps University, an administrator highlighted the important role that the admissions review process played in its master's program in theater. As he explained, faculty carefully reviewed each of the more than 800 applications for admission received each year and selected only those four or five dozen students whom they believed had the requisite "talent," "desire," and "commitment" to succeed in the program.

## *Consequences for Learning Experiences*

Faculty and administrative efforts to recruit diverse and engaged students had important consequences for students' learning. As we were told by many interviewees, these students not only infused a variety of perspectives into their discussions with others in and outside of class, they also invested in teaching and learning activities that considerably enriched the quality of their own and others' learning.

Throughout our study, interviewees emphasized the medley of perspectives that diverse and engaged students contributed to their programs. A Longmont administrator made this point unambiguously in referring to the novel insights students (the vast majority of whom were experienced elementary and secondary school teachers) shared in class discussions:

> *The thing that's most special about this place is the students themselves. You could look at the brochure and say that it's the faculty members that make this place what it is, but they come here because [interviewee emphasis] of the students. Quite a few of them have told me that—that they would not come here if they knew they would find, say, [Ivy League] students here. . . . They're looking for the types of people we have here--people from all over the country who don't necessarily have an academic background. . . . The faculty have come to expect that these students who are nontraditional are the ones who contribute the most valuable insights— who think of things that the professor never has. The professors say it is very refreshing to come to [Longmont] because of that other view, to see how the rest of the world is reacting to literature.*

In much the same spirit, two environmental studies students at Phelps University highlighted the varied professional and educational backgrounds of their peers, stressing that this diversity produced an abundance of perspectives on knowledge and practice in the program. As one of them remarked: "The capabilities of the student body are tremendous here. We [the students] take lots of opportunities to learn about what other people have done and to teach others about our own professional experiences. Most of us have been in very responsible positions for two or four years, and we really do have a lot to learn from each other." The other student echoed this view: "There's an attitude among students here that we all bring a really good depth and breadth of knowledge and professional experience to this program. We're fascinated by our classmates here."

Students and alumni frequently told us how much they enjoyed—and valued—peers who shared multiple points of view. A Major State business student illustrated the appreciation he had for his diverse classmates:

*It's really intriguing to see how many different perspectives [that] health
professionals, engineers, communications, public relations, and folks who
have worked in banking [bring to the classroom]. I think they add a lot. . . .
When you get into classes which lend themselves to discussion, people
have very different perspectives on things and I think that's a real strength
of the program. . . . When I've been in classes that have had [students with]
work experience and there's been class discussion, I've learned a lot more. . . .
I'm not so grade conscious—[instead] I'm looking and listening based on
the experiences others have had and I'm comparing them to my own experiences with a particular subject or situation.*

In much the same vein, an alumna of Peterson's nursing program fondly
recalled the workplace-related knowledge and experiences that her peers contributed to class discussions. "I remember the first graduate course I took here,"
she said, "because it was full of practicing nurses who brought such a wealth of
experience with them. And [there was a lot of sharing] but it was never boast-
ful—it was always in a very helping kind of vein like 'this is how I do it where
I work.' So this really helped me in my work—just sitting here and getting
ideas from my peers in these classes." An M.B.A. student at St. Joan's College
claimed that one of the "biggest pluses" of the program was "being with students who are in the real world": "I like hearing about their experiences. I like
that real-world edge. I learn so much from them."

Besides sharing varied perspectives with their peers and with faculty,
many students in our sample devoted considerable time and energy to their
studies. Students demonstrated this commitment in a variety of ways: by
actively participating in class discussions, being involved in research projects
or artistic productions, and engaging in cooperative peer learning activities
both in- and out-of-class.

On numerous occasions, interviewees provided us with rich insights
into the energy and enthusiasm that animated students' involvement in classroom activities. A Pierpont administrator, for example, metaphorically described students in the school's M.B.A. program as "vacuum cleaners" who
"sucked up new ideas and information in their classes." A professor at
Longmont College conveyed this same idea with a memorable phrase she
had coined. "I call it the 'piranha fish factor,'" she said, "which means that
you say something in class, and they [the students] are just into it, because
they are all just so anxious to sort things out. It's something to do with their
motivation and their sense that they have a very small amount of time to get
something very special."

Students' commitments to learning also extended beyond their participation in the classroom. As we learned from many interviewees, these students also invested heavily in out-of-class activities. A Mountain State faculty
member illustrated this when he described the commitment that one of his
students had to his research:

*He brought an idea to me and a chemical engineer . . . about a new kind of bio-reactor. When we first looked at it, we said it would never work, but as we looked at it more and more we decided it probably would work. We've written a proposal to NSF [the National Science Foundation] to try to get the thing funded. We've filed a patent application running through the [state's] research foundation. This was an idea he brought to us, and convinced us that it would work. . . . He's the type of student who teaches me a lot.*

Not surprisingly, faculty and students valued the commitments that students brought to their studies. A professor in Major State's environmental studies program, for instance, extolled the dedication of his students, emphasizing how "rewarding" it was for faculty to work with individuals who were passionate about their graduate work:

*The students [here] are an extraordinarily exciting bunch of people. That's what really attracts the faculty, from my point of view. The students who come in [to this program] are so good, so interesting, so exciting. In fact, faculty have repeatedly told me that the students in [this program] are better than the students in their home disciplines. That may mean many things—not necessarily that they're brighter, but that they are more animated, committed, engaged.*

In a similar spirit, a Phelps theater student underscored how much he valued learning from classmates who he considered "the most motivated, the best in their fields."

Across our forty-seven-program sample, diverse and engaged students emerged as an important attribute of high-quality programs. As many interviewees helped us to understand, students who shared diverse perspectives and engaged in their own and others' learning infused a vitality and richness into the learning process that greatly enhanced the overall quality of students' experiences.

## Effects on Students

Diverse and engaged students contributed to one anothers' growth and development in two major ways. First, students who shared diverse perspectives with one another creatively expanded and enriched their understandings of theory and professional practice. Second, students who were committed to their own and others' learning inspired one another to invest more fully in their professions.

Students and alumni frequently told us that the diverse points of view they shared with one another helped them to develop more creative understandings of knowledge in their fields. A Longmont alumna, for instance, credited the "diversity of [Longmont's] student body" with "challenging" her "to enter into a dialogue [with others] that create[d] new perspectives and new ideas and points of view": "When you have a student body that comes from traditional East Coast schools, and Indian reservations, and rural school districts, and the odd guy from an urban school [gesturing to a fellow student] who says, 'I don't want to have anything to do with this stuff,' it is a tremendously provocative place." A Peterson business student offered a similar appraisal. As she related, the practice-based and multicultural views her peers contributed to class discussions led her to develop a broader perspective on her field:

> *You get people from all walks of life in this program. You get a real cross section of [this metropolitan area] here. The students are not only from one social or economic class . . . you get people from different industries, older seasoned people, younger people out of undergraduate [school], and a very integrated racial/ethnic student population. It's interesting to get people from different countries, too. They really add a perspective that you just don't think about.*

Interviewees also emphasized that committed students generated an enthusiasm for learning that nurtured—and, in some cases, renewed—one anothers' professional commitments. During our visit to Lake's education program, for instance, a secondary school teacher told us that while he had originally pursued his master's "to earn a credential," his classmates had inspired him "to commit myself to teaching again." At Longmont College— a nontraditional, summer's-only English master's program for elementary and secondary school teachers—a student similarly discussed how her class- mates had revitalized her commitment to teaching and learning:

> *Change can happen and a place like this makes you believe that. You're with teachers who work their butts off ten months of the year. They come here, sacrificing their vacation, to study all summer. The whole attitude is that "I'm learning these strategies, and I have these people to connect with, and I can take these ideas back with me and can return next year." And instead of feeling zapped, you feel energized.*

## Engaged Leaders

In analyzing our interview material, we identified engaged leaders as an- other important characteristic of high-quality programs. Time and again, we found that the investments that engaged department and program chairs made in their programs markedly enhanced the quality of students' learning.

## *Actions*

Faculty and administrators used two strategies to attract and retain engaged leaders. First, they recruited department or program chairs who would invest time and energy in championing their programs. Second, institutional administrators and faculty engaged in various activities that were aimed at supporting leaders.

In several programs we studied, faculty and administrators told us that they hired leaders who would be visible and articulate "champions" for their programs. More specifically, they recruited leaders who would advance their program's mission, secure needed resources for it, and involve faculty, students, and staff in program governance.

At Southwest State University, for example, a professor in the applied anthropology program described the leadership qualities that he and his colleagues had looked for in a new department chair. "We wanted someone," he recounted, "who was committed to applied anthropology [and] someone who had a good track record getting grants, who had good administrative experience, who was energetic. We wanted someone who could implement our vision." Similarly, a number of faculty and administrators associated with Major State's environmental studies program mentioned that during their last search for a chairperson, they had intentionally sought to recruit a leader who would not only champion the service-oriented mission of the program to institutional administrators, but who would also aggressively secure additional funding from internal and external sources.

Once they had recruited "champions" for their programs, institutional administrators and faculty supported leaders in direct and indirect ways. In some instances, institutional administrators provided direct support in the form of new faculty lines, graduate assistantships, or increased budgetary allocations. In others, faculty and institutional administrators supported leaders indirectly through voluntary participation in new program initiatives and service on committees.

The applied anthropology master's program at City-State University is a representative case in which program leaders received both direct and indirect support from institutional administrators. As a senior campus administrator told us, he actively supported the chair's recent efforts to expand and strengthen the program's applied orientation for both financial and service-related reasons:

> *Personally, I think the possibilities of master's education at urban universities haven't as yet been explored. I'm particularly interested in master's in certain areas—applied emphases in anthropology, sociology, psychology, geography, criminology. . . . We [administrators in the College of Arts and Sciences] sit around and try to figure out how to give money to these*

*applied programs because it's like putting money in the bank—we know they will give us a return on our money. You give anthropology $5,000 and suddenly their enrollments go up by ten percent—they know how to handle [the financial support] so well. . . . I'm currently working on a committee to find ways to market and advertise these programs. Most people in the community have no idea what these applied programs can do.*

In other programs, faculty engaged in sundry activities that indirectly supported leaders. An applied anthropology professor at Southwest State, for instance, mentioned that several "old guard" faculty members had participated in a series of "retooling" workshops initiated by the program chair, thereby lending support to his efforts. At Southern State, a nursing professor explained that she and a few of her colleagues backed the chair's recent curricular revision efforts:

*One of the things that's happened around here in the past year is that faculty have begun to share articles with each other. They're talking with each other in the halls about some of the things that we've [the chair and the curriculum committee] been talking about, rather than . . . that kind of "na-na" stuff that goes around. There are still some people who are in that mode, but for the most part, the whole energy of the faculty has really shifted so there's more enthusiasm about what's going on [with the curriculum] here.*

Finally, many faculty told us that they supported their leaders in "little ways" such as by voluntarily chairing committees, working on new projects, and expressing appreciation to leaders for their efforts.

## Consequences for Learning Experiences

The commitments that institutional administrators and faculty made to attracting and supporting engaged leaders enhanced students' learning in three, largely indirect, ways. One, these leaders effectively championed their programs to internal and external audiences and adeptly secured resources to sustain them. Two, leaders put considerable effort into recruiting diverse and engaged participants to their programs. And, three, leaders invited faculty and students to assume informal leadership roles in their programs, thereby enhancing their ownership in them.

Many interviewees in our study described their leaders as "champions" who enthusiastically promoted their master's programs to campus administrators and employers. At Major State University, for instance, several environmental studies faculty described their chair as a strong advocate who effectively educated institutional administrators on the value of this interdisciplinary, service-oriented master's program. In our interview with him, the chair elaborated on his advocacy:

> [*I'm constantly imploring campus administrators*] *to decide on the front end that you're going to commit to this kind of educational realm, not as the only thing that a great university does, but as a* legitimate [*interviewee emphasis*] *thing that a university does. You don't go around apologizing for it. . . . If you look at our* [*graduates*] *some years out, they still have that synoptic point of view and set of interests; we're training people with great capability, with a critical level of thought.  The plea I make [to campus administrators] is that we're not lesser or better, we're different. It's a legitimate and important kind of academic activity.*

In much the same way, a number of faculty in Southwest State's applied anthropology department told us that their chair was constantly promoting the master's program to university administrators. The chair himself amplified this point, stressing that he spent "a good part" of his time trying to "educate the administration": "I constantly get into committees and I talk about the innovations we are doing and the changes we are making in the program." We learned that his efforts had yielded considerable fruit: over the past few years, institutional administrators had allocated five new faculty lines to the program and increased its budgetary support.

Such efforts were not lost on students. Indeed, many told us how much they appreciated leaders who promoted the mission of their programs and secured adequate resources for them. A Southwest State alumna, for instance, commended the department chair for winning "a lot of institutional and community support" for the master's program in applied anthropology. A Phelps theater graduate offered these words of praise for his program chair: "He coordinates everything. In a week when you can see seven shows going on, you see that someone is administering this. He's amazing."

We learned that leaders also invested in their programs in a second way: they devoted significant time and energy to recruiting faculty and students who were strongly committed to teaching and learning. Many interviewees in Southwest State's applied anthropology programs, for example, indicated that their chair had attracted several well-known scholar-teachers by strategically taking advantage of campus incentives to hire women and people of color. Several also mentioned that his "national student recruitment strategy" had brought many enthusiastic learners to the program. Stakeholders in other institutions conveyed similar accounts, from those who highlighted the efforts that Moore A&T's chair put into hiring "multidimensional" engineering faculty, to those who applauded the investments that Laramie's director made in attracting committed students to the school's global education program.

Many interviewees stressed how much they valued leaders who took the recruitment process seriously, noting that their efforts greatly improved the quality of students' learning experiences. During our site visit to Longmont College, for instance, several students, alumni, and employers complimented program leaders for "choosing great faculty" who were strongly committed to "making a difference" in students' lives. A professor at City-State, offering a similar appraisal, told us that the master's program in applied anthropology owed much to its former chair for "attracting self-initiating faculty who really wanted to pursue research interests in the local region" and who were "committed to teaching students."

Finally, many leaders in our study invited faculty and students to assume active roles in the governance of their programs. Many did this by developing program cultures in which participants were welcome to express their views, to advance new ideas, and to exercise informal leadership in both small and large ways. In so doing, leaders not only listened to faculty and students, but they also invited them to share responsibility for building and sustaining enriching learning environments for all program participants.

Such was the case in Southeast State's applied anthropology program. According to a professor we interviewed there, when the idea of a master's program arose in the department, the chair played an instrumental role in getting "faculty to come together as a group" and to "talk over their options . . . [to decide] what kind of master's degree would make sense." This collaborative approach, she indicated, cultivated a sense of shared ownership among faculty for the master's program and led many to make a major commitment to it. In much the same vein, an environmental studies professor at Phelps University said that leaders regularly invited students' input on matters germane to the program and its curriculum. He used the following anecdote to illustrate how students often served as "great sources of change" in the program:

> *Our tropical resources program is a good example. It was probably one of the first ones created, although lots of places are now developing one. You know, I'd like to say it was the vision of the faculty that created it. But it was much more a vision—a demand, actually—of the students who saw the global-scale problem as critical and they demanded that the school do something about it. And what that has done is [that] it hasn't just created a program. Practically every professor has some element of what they do now that was different from what it was in the past—[because of] the addition of [this] international and tropical dimension. That's an example of how the program is student-driven.*

Again and again, interviewees told us that they strongly valued collaborative leaders who listened to and "empowered" them. A Peterson nursing professor, for example, praised program leaders for being "very accepting people" who were "always interested in what faculty and students had to say." Similarly, a Phelps' environmental studies administrator said appreciatively of her dean's leadership:

> *He's the one who really gives the atmosphere here. He's stepping down this summer which, to me, is a great loss. The top man, you know, always fosters the atmosphere in any institution, and he fosters this. He will always talk at our staff meetings, telling everyone that things are going well because of them. And he makes everyone feel 10-feet tall—"it's not because of me but because of you people." He knows how to run a place, and he's an excellent administrator. He's not somebody standing over you and nitpicking. When he gives you a job, he gives you the authority that you need to do it, and that's the end of it.*

In light of these and other comparable accounts, we came to appreciate the important role that engaged leaders played in fostering high-quality programs. Throughout our study, stakeholders emphasized that leaders who championed their programs—by promoting their missions, securing adequate resources, recruiting diverse and engaged participants, and creating program cultures in which faculty and students were invited to participate actively in leadership and governance—contributed in myriad ways to enhancing the quality of students' learning experiences.

## Effects on Students

We learned that engaged leaders favorably affected students in two ways. First, the leadership opportunities that program chairs and others provided to students indirectly helped students to develop into more confident leaders. Second, since engaged leaders provided the kinds of support that empowered faculty and students to invest in other attributes in our theory, they indirectly intensified many of the effects that these attributes had on students.

Many students and alumni told us that the leadership roles they assumed in their programs—whether small or large—had improved their self-confidence as leaders. Two graduates of Lake's education program, for instance, said that in taking responsibility for various discussions and projects in their courses, they had become more confident in their abilities to lead and persuade others. As one alumna told us: "I'm on a Task Force—the parochial schools in the town are studying if they should consolidate and all that. I volunteered for the task force because I really feel I have a lot to contribute. . . . I don't think I would have had the confidence [to have joined before my master's]. At the meetings I speak quite a bit." The other said that she also actively participated in governance processes at her school: "At our faculty meetings, well, you know it takes guts to get up there and speak. And I do that now." The principal who employed both of these graduates confirmed that these teachers had "begun to exercise leadership [in the school]": "[They're much] more involved in decision-making processes in matters of curriculum and course scheduling."

With a slightly different twist, a Phelps theater alumna said that the leadership positions she assumed in the program's professional theater challenged her to become a more confident, skilled administrator. As she put it:

> *I walked into [my new job] and I started to hire people. I knew how to do this because I had extensive experience dealing with high stakes agents [in my master's program]. The only difference here was that there was more money involved. But, yes, it [working in various leadership positions in the theater] helped me a lot. I could walk in the door and do lots of things, including casting, publicity, and budget forecasts. I felt very confident that I could do these things and do them well.*

Engaged leaders indirectly affected students' growth and development in a second, no less important, way: Leaders who successfully championed their programs, acquired needed resources, and attracted and supported diverse and engaged participants provided the kinds of support that empowered faculty and students to invest more fully in other clusters in our theory. In particular, their efforts were central to developing participatory cultures and in securing adequate resources. As such, engaged leaders amplified the effects that the attributes in these two clusters had on students.

# 5

## Participatory Cultures

Having learned through our research that high-quality programs are anchored in collegial and supportive cultures that invite widespread stakeholder involvement, we identified "participatory cultures" as the second cluster of attributes in the engagement theory. In this chapter, we explore three attributes of participatory cultures: a shared program direction, a community of learners, and a risk-taking environment. As in the previous chapter, our discussion of individual attributes is divided into three parts. We first examine the actions that program administrators and faculty—and, to a lesser extent, students, alumni, and employers—took to develop and sustain the attribute within their programs. We then describe how these actions enhanced students' learning experiences. Finally, we discuss the positive effects that these experiences had on students.

### Shared Program Direction

After several excursions through our interview material, we came to understand that a shared program direction is an important feature of high-quality programs. In many programs, administrators, faculty, students, alumni, and employers worked together to build shared understandings of and support for an overall program direction. This shared direction provided a common thread that helped to knit together students' learning experiences in ways that greatly enhanced their growth and development.

### Actions

Administrative, faculty, and student leaders used three strategies to develop and sustain a shared direction in their programs. First, they invited program stakeholders to join them in constructing a shared direction. Second, leaders encouraged faculty, students, alumni, and employers to participate in evaluation efforts in which they examined the fit between their program's teaching and learning activities and its overall direction. Third, leaders nurtured and sustained shared understandings of their program's direction by frequently communicating it to internal and external audiences, both on and off campus.

Time and again, faculty and administrative leaders told us that they worked closely with other stakeholders to develop a shared direction for their programs. To this end, many invited faculty, students, alumni, and employers to serve on formal committees, advisory boards, or self-study teams in which they could share ideas, negotiate differences, and cultivate common understanding.

The applied anthropology program at Southwest State illustrates the participatory approach that some leaders used to develop and sustain a shared program direction. We learned during our site visit that several years earlier an unfavorable university-wide review had placed the department on shaky ground with institutional administrators. The review team wrote in its report that, among other weaknesses, the master's curriculum was "outdated" and that the unit lacked the direction and resources to make it "a top university department." Shortly after the report was released, the department chair resigned. The new chair promptly initiated a self-study and invited faculty to work with him in carving out a clear direction for the department in general, and the master's program in particular. As he told us:

> The first thing I did was take the mission statement, which had never been looked at since I first came, and say "Here's the mission statement." I gave it to everybody and said, "If you're happy with it the way it is, fine; if you'd like to see it revised in some fashion, please do so. Send them back to me and I will collate them, summarize them, and give them back to everyone without anyone's name on them." That's the process [I used], you're [faculty] the focal point. I redistributed this [the mission statement and faculty comments], and they saw what everyone else was thinking, and I did that for several iterations. There was some talk about applied [anthropology] and that came out in there. And I finally drafted a composite mission statement and sent it back [to faculty]. And then we got agreement on that.

The department chair described how he had worked closely with faculty to craft a set of clearly expressed and mutually supported goals for the master's program:

> Now I said, "What are our goals? What goals can be derived from this mission statement?" So we did that [same] process again . . . [which] had a tendency to build consensus, so people began to agree. So we got our

*goals [and] we decided to concentrate our energies on designing [an ap-*
*plied anthropology master's] program . . . [to prepare students] for practi-*
*tioner-oriented careers.*

We interviewed other leaders who likewise indicated that they actively
involved stakeholders in developing a shared direction for their master's
programs. The chair of Southwest State's microbiology department, for example, noted that he nudged faculty and employers to "decide what kind of
master's graduate" they wanted and then worked with them to develop
program purposes that addressed their expectations. In much the same vein,
an administrator in Moore A&T's engineering program said that he involved
faculty and students in decisions about program direction in order to "get
them all onboard with a shared mission."

Besides inviting stakeholders to play an active role in crafting a shared
direction, leaders often asked faculty, students, alumni, and employers to
take part in ongoing program evaluation efforts. To this end, some leaders
built a network of advisory boards, alumni councils, and employer committees. Other administrators and faculty sponsored faculty retreats and open
forums with students in which they examined the congruence between their
program's teaching and learning experiences and its overall direction. Regardless of their approach, leaders encouraged stakeholder participation in
these evaluation activities not only to sustain a clear program focus, but
also to nurture shared understanding and a sense of ownership among diverse constituents.

Illustrating the point, the chair of Southwest State's applied anthropology program told us that he had organized a practitioner advisory council
to ensure that "real-world feedback" became a "central feature" of program
evaluations. Consisting of "some of the nation's most prominent anthropologists employed outside of academe," he noted that the advisory council provided feedback on curriculum materials, participated in formal program reviews, and assessed students' knowledge and skill development (as
interns or staff in their employment). At Pierpont University, an administrator in the M.B.A. program said that faculty met annually to assess the relationship between "what we say and what we actually do [in the program]."
This annual review, he emphasized, helped faculty and administrators to
clarify and reinforce the overall direction and goals of the program and to
"pay more attention" to its curriculum. On a similar note, a Southwest State
faculty leader told us that he and his applied anthropology colleagues periodically held open forums to elicit student feedback on their program.

Administrative, faculty, and student leaders engaged in one other activity to develop and sustain a shared program direction: they frequently
communicated their program's direction and purposes to stakeholders at
various activities and events. Administrators and faculty at City-State and
Laramie, for instance, reinforced the practitioner-orientation of their applied

anthropology and global education programs during orientation sessions for new students. In the theater programs at Phelps and NCC, administrators published alumni and employer newsletters to keep constituents attuned to program goals and informed of new developments. And in many programs we studied, administrative, faculty, and alumni leaders put considerable effort into building a shared understanding of their program's direction—including its purposes and goals—with constituents at social gatherings both on and off campus.

## Consequences for Learning Experiences

Leaders' efforts to develop and sustain a shared program direction consistently enhanced the quality of students' learning experiences. When leaders took such initiatives, stakeholders shared a common focus that not only informed and animated their actions, but also provided a unifying thread that helped to knit together students' learning experiences in meaningful ways.

At many sites, interviewees articulated similar descriptions of the direction, or focus, of their programs. The applied anthropology program at City State University serves as an instructive case-in-point. During our visit there, each person interviewed emphasized the program's community-centered, practitioner-oriented direction. In speaking with the department chair, for instance, we were told that the program prepared master's-educated practitioners who not only had "an understanding of their region," but also the knowledge and tools to "come up with solutions for the region." An alumna provided a similar take on the program when she described it as "tied to real things and needs in the city." And an employer told us that there was "no equivocation" by faculty on the program's focus: "They have a good idea of what kinds of graduates they're turning out. They are really trying to prepare practitioners for the workplace."

City-State's stakeholders were not alone in articulating shared understandings of their program's overall direction. An administrator in Laramie's global education program, for example, told us that while there was "diversity, politically, within [its] faculty," all "agree[d] on what the goals of this organization are and who we are": "I think there is a feeling here about what our mission or goal is. The students definitely share this mission." A Major State environmental studies professor also stressed that administrators, faculty, students, alumni, and employers were united on their program's interdisciplinary and applied orientation: "We share the conviction that this is really the way that this [solving environmental problems] has to be done," he commented. "It is not just an engineering problem or just a political problem—it is all of it together."

We learned that when participants shared a common understanding of their program's direction, this shared focus provided them with an integrative thread to knit together students' learning experiences. Such was the case in Major State's environmental studies program, where interviewees told us that the interdisciplinary emphasis on "training people to go into applied settings . . . [and] manage water resources" permeated every aspect of the curriculum. Besides completing forty-five credits of interdisciplinary course work in the natural, social, and biological sciences, students were taught applied skills relevant to the management of water resources, such as technical writing, policy-oriented statistical and budgeting methods, and remote sensing techniques. In addition, students completed an out-of-class team project in which they tackled, in the words of a former program administrator, "a question in the real world that has to do with managing a water resource—that involves people, institutional structures, resorts, government, citizen groups, politicians, [and] lawyers." Whether in class or in the field, this concentration on preparing students for the interdisciplinary challenges of water resources management helped to connect students' learning experiences throughout their time in the program.

Turning to a different example, interviewees at Parks-Beecher University told us that the preparation of African Americans for corporate leadership positions provided the integrating strand in their master's program. Both in and out of class, students participated in various activities that sharpened their interpersonal, leadership, and technical skills as well as provided them with information on real-world business practices. In terms of formal course work, faculty required students to complete a core sequence of business courses, assigned a variety of "real-world" case studies, and invited business executives to give guest lectures. Outside of class, faculty and students organized numerous activities that facilitated students' preparation for careers in business, including a mentor/mentee program, job interviewing and dress-for-success workshops, and colloquia on "key topics" in corporate America.

Many students and alumni stressed how much they valued the "connected" learning experiences they had in their programs. Two Laramie alumni, for example, were enthusiastic in describing how their entire master's experience had been organized around the theory and practice of curriculum development. As one of them said: "In the summer [of our first semester], we made lessons out of the world politics class. . . . Then we had four quarters of a curriculum lab that guided us toward this end result [a final curriculum product]. . . . Our focus [throughout the program] really was [on] how to write curriculum." "Yes," the other alumna added, "We wrote curriculum. . . . [It] was great because we walked out with the actual curriculum in our hand." A Major State environmental studies alumnus told a similar story, noting how a single idea had cut across all of his experiences and connected them in a way that proved invaluable to his understanding of the field:

*The concept of river basin management pervades this entire program—it's the notion that economists could study water resources management and never understand it, wastewater and flood control engineers could study it and never understand it, fisheries experts could study it and never understand it. [In this program] you learn that you have to integrate all of these fields in order to understand the system.*

To be sure, our sample included some programs in which a shared program direction was noticeably absent. Often hindered by ineffective leadership or faculty infighting, these programs typically had multiple or diffuse missions and unclear priorities that severely diminished their overall quality. This appeared to be the case at Trafalgar College, where a professor panned the theater program for being "all things to all people." As he put it: "We [the faculty] can't resolve what we should be offering or what we should be focusing on. As a result, our students often don't get the specialized training they need." A faculty member at Major State painted a similar picture of the theater program:

*This is a department that has not decided what it wants to be when it grows up. We have not decided if we want to educate generalists, specialists—we don't know. This department could be anything they wanted to [be] if it said this year, "This is what we're going to make a priority and this is what we're going to go for." But no one is willing to do that because if they do that they'll have to give something up from their program if their program is not the one that is the priority. It's been a problem since I've been here, and it will continue to be.*

Students and alumni were even less sanguine about the quality of such programs, often complaining that they had fragmented and disconnected learning experiences. A Major State theater alumnus said of his master's program:

*In some ways the program needs to be reevaluated very, very seriously in order for them [faculty] to understand what their intention is. They [faculty and administrators] are very ambiguous. They are trying to do two things simultaneously. They are trying to give you an intellectual background and an historical perspective on the whole world of literature and the cultural basis of theater, while they are simultaneously trying to do the acting process in studio form. So what is required is that you spend incredible hours working on your body and voice and then you go home and the intellectual side, the left brain side, is requiring you to do all this incredible stuff, too. The body can't do it. Just literally, the body can't do it. You cannot process the kind of information corporeally that you are being demanded to do and still keep the rational focus. And you shouldn't.*

Other students echoed this interviewee's remarks. At Trafalgar College, a theater student nearing completion of his studies criticized faculty for failing to "zone in on what was important": "They didn't provide the courses or the individual attention that I needed. . . . If I had to do it all over again I wouldn't come here. This program did not meet my needs." An applied anthropology student at Atlantic State likewise said that the program suffered from a nagging "lack of focus": "There is little agreement among the faculty in this program about the skills they believe every practicing, applied anthropologist should have. I'm not even sure the faculty can articulate what those skills are—in fact, I think that the faculty emphasize different skills." Frustrated and disillusioned, this student reluctantly went on to tell us that several of her peers were "thinking about dropping out" of the program. "[We're] disappointed with the courses and [we're] hearing that a lot of graduates from last year didn't find jobs."

Across the forty-seven programs in our study, interviewees offered both affirmative and negative accounts that underscored the importance of a shared direction to high-quality programs. A Western State professor summarized the importance of this attribute when she noted that while there was great diversity among nursing administrators and faculty, a common focus on "nursing as caring" permeated their entire program. Such a unifying theme, she remarked, encouraged faculty to "discuss diverse ideas and issues and be very constructive. We're all working toward the same goals and I just love being a part of it."

## Effects on Students

We came to understand that a shared program direction contributed to students' growth and development in two ways. First, in programs in which participants shared a common focus, students developed more distinct professional identities. Second, and closely related, students who had "connected" learning experiences became more keenly aware of where and how they wanted to invest their energies after graduation.

Many students and alumni in our study said that the focused character of their master's experiences had sharpened their professional identities. Two microbiology students at Appleby State, for instance, credited the program's ubiquitous emphasis on "thinking like a scientist" with slowly but deliberately changing the way they defined themselves. As they explained:

> [Student 1]: *This is a really hard thing to pin down, but I feel like a scientist now. In the past, I felt like a good old boy or something . . . now I feel something different. Being a scientist, I think, doesn't just entail what you know but it also involves a fascination with the way things work and the*

*way you look at life. I think the science has become a part of myself. It's not just something that I do. It's something that you live almost, I guess.*

*[Student 2]: I feel that same way. I feel like a scientist who just happens to be a microbiologist. . . . I think there is a lot to being a scientist.*

Many faculty also stressed that students forged richer and more distinctive understandings of themselves as professionals in programs in which a shared program direction was present. A professor at Phelps University, for instance, told us that while many of her dramaturgy students initially felt "confused" about their professional role at the beginning of their studies, by the end of "three years of collaborative work with others in numerous productions, these students felt confident about who they are and where they come from and where they are going. They know what a dramaturge is and what their role is [in the professional theater]." Similarly, a Peterson nursing administrator remarked that, during her many years at the university, she had "seen students leave the program" with a much-improved "sense of their own professionalism": "I've seen that transformation occur over and over again."

The connected teaching and learning experiences students had in these programs also helped them to clarify where and how they wanted to invest their professional energies upon graduation. An alumna of City-State's applied anthropology program illustrated this outcome nicely, noting how her community-centered master's experience had served to focus and define her professional niche:

*The way I want to use anthropology is to take the concepts of anthropology and the information that anthropology produces and then utilize that to find avenues of empowerment. And one avenue might be to get the resources of the university more into the community. And that's the goal with the leadership training thing that I've been working on now. . . . I think that there are a number of things that the university can do for the community that will empower and train and provide information to people who might not ever come through the door.*

A Middle State microbiology student made the same point in a slightly different way. She told us that the pervasive emphasis placed on basic laboratory science in the program had opened up a new trail for her to explore in medical school:

*Immunology is so fascinating that I may do research in immunology when I'm in medical school. . . . Microbiology was a closed field to me [as an undergraduate]. I just thought they were these little microbes—I wanted a heart or some lungs that I can look at and work on. Taking microbiology, I now understand what microbiology is all about. It's broadened my horizons. I'm interested in this—I never thought I would be.*

Finally, a Southern State nursing alumna said simply that her master's experience had refocused her professional interests and, in doing so, provided her with a "path for a journey for a lifetime."

## Community of Learners

As we worked through the nearly 800 interviews in our study, we discovered that a "community of learners" is another fundamental attribute of high-quality programs. Interviewees across our sample told us that an ethic of collegial teaching and learning imbued the culture of their programs such that faculty, students, and administrators interacted with one another more or less as partners within a community of learners. Membership in such a community greatly enriched students' learning experiences and positively affected their growth and development.

## Actions

Faculty, administrators, and students engaged in three activities aimed at developing and sustaining a community of learners in their programs. First, a leader—or group of leaders—took responsibility for helping to build a learning community. Second, faculty developed more collegial and less hierarchical relations with students. Third, administrators, faculty, and students constructed in- and out-of-class teaching and learning experiences to facilitate and sustain co-learning among program participants.

In many programs we studied, faculty, administrative, and student leaders deliberately went about building learning environments that nurtured a sense of community among participants. Some did this through encouraging faculty and student involvement in collaborative teaching, research, and service projects. Others sponsored out-of-class social activities that brought together faculty and students in informal settings.

A faculty member in Walton State's environmental studies program, for instance, worked closely with colleagues to "create an environment that enhanced a kind of collectivist learning—we are intentionally trying to build an environment that builds contact with students." At Laramie University, a program administrator mentioned that a "conscious goal" of his was "to provide an environment which encouraged" a sense of community: "I provide the vehicles for doing this, for bonding the group together. I see that as a very important part of our master's experience." Similarly, a Southwest State applied anthropology professor noted that his department chair sponsored social gatherings to foster a sense of community among program participants. "He puts a lot of effort into social things—about every six weeks he has a party at his house. He tries very hard to develop a sense of collegiality and a quest for quality in this department."

To nurture and sustain a community of learners, faculty and administrators developed collegial relationships with master's students—relationships, many interviewees told us, which de-emphasized traditional faculty–student hierarchies. Many faculty said that they did this not only because they believed students had useful insights and worthy ideas to contribute, but also because they often learned a great deal from interacting with students as co-learners.

During our visit to Southwest State's applied anthropology program, we observed many collegial interactions among faculty and students. When asked about this, the chair of the department responded, "We have a shared philosophy that students are very important and they need to be treated as developing professionals, as current and future colleagues. We're more focused on colleague-building rather than [on] a faculty-over-student kind of relationship." Several Middle State faculty likewise indicated that collegiality was the norm in their microbiology program. One professor, for instance, pointed out that faculty "treated students as our partners," while another candidly remarked: "We work together like colleagues every day and we respect each other. . . . There is a healthy respect for talent and ability both ways."

Not surprisingly, faculty and administrators in these "communities of learners" were often critical of traditional, hierarchical views of the faculty–student relationship. Many emphasized that they openly discouraged students from viewing them as "authoritative experts" and, instead, invited students to interact with them as co-learners. As a Southwest State applied anthropology professor put it: "I don't enjoy those students who want to maintain that [Dr. Smith] kind of thing. They want me to . . . tell them what to do. . . . I want them to tell me what they want to do and then we can work out a collegial compromise. I'm not the authority—I'll guide, but don't ask me to prescribe." An administrator in Appleby State's microbiology program expressed his views on this issue in this way: "I believe that the essence of a quality program is that the faculty get behind the graduate students and make them feel as colleagues, not as serfs. They feel as though they are really participating in the intellectual discovery of knowledge, rather than just being the passive recipients of knowledge."

Along with building communal learning environments and cultivating collegial relationships, faculty and administrators worked closely with students to create in- and out-of-class learning experiences that facilitated and sustained co-learning among program participants. Many faculty and administrators, for example, required students to complete immersion experiences (such as extended work in the field with faculty members) and a set of core courses (which insured that students not only had contact with several faculty members, but also had a common base of knowledge and experiences from which to draw during the program). Moreover, faculty and students often developed colloquia, symposia, journal clubs, and brown bag seminars in which program participants were encouraged to learn from one another outside of class. No less important, many faculty and students invited students to engage in collaborative research, performance, and service-related projects in which their teaching and learning extended far beyond traditional classroom boundaries.

## Consequences for Learning Experiences

Administrative, faculty, and student efforts to develop and sustain a community of learners enriched participants' mutual learning experiences in two important respects. First, participants encountered their programs as "learning communities" in which faculty and students taught and learned from one another more or less as colleagues. Second, a camaraderie animated participants' interactions that advanced and complemented this sense of community.

Interviewees in numerous programs in our sample stressed that a "community of learners" provided the cornerstone of their teaching and learning experiences. An environmental studies professor at Phelps University, for example, considered a "sense of community" as one of the program's "trademarks": "I think it's one of the things that we hold most dear about the place." A Longmont English student related that the "biggest selling point" of his master's was the enduring support he experienced as a member of the "[Longmont] community," while, at Moore A&T, a professor said of the communal feeling that enveloped faculty in students in its engineering program: "There's a sense of family you get around here. It's like a nurturing process. And I'm not going to say that it's all due to professors. It's due to the students as well. . . . We support one another here."

When we asked interviewees to elaborate on what contributed to a "sense of community," they consistently highlighted the collegial, oftentimes collaborative, relationships that bonded faculty and students together in their programs. Many emphasized that both faculty and students viewed one another as important sources of knowledge and understanding, and that they routinely sought to learn from one another through classroom interactions, joint research projects, and collaborative theatrical productions.

Illustrating this point, a Southwest State applied anthropology professor told us that she and her colleagues regularly invited students to work on research projects and to co-author papers. As she explained, such collaborations were "a very applied kind of thing":

> *Sure, I'm teaching them, but I'm working with them as colleagues. . . . I think that's one of the major differences between us and a typical academic department where the senior faculty members do all of this stuff and the message that comes through is, "This is too difficult for poor little you to do. Just trust me and I'll give you a job." I don't think that's good. . . . We really do believe in nurturing professionalism here. Collaboration and colleagueship are part of that.*

A Helena State professor also stated that faculty–student collaboration was a central feature of the theater program. "When we're working on productions," he emphasized, "there are no division lines of faculty [and] student. . . . [In this program] people are expected to produce as equals regardless of whether they're faculty or students."

Many students and alumni spoke with enthusiasm about the collaborative teaching and learning that occurred in their programs. The following anecdote from an Appleby State alumnus says much, for example, about the co-learning that took place among faculty and students in the microbiology program:

> *The instructors that I had were really interested in what they were doing, and it almost seemed like . . . everybody was getting together and doing this learning. I still remember the day when we made DNA, when we actually wound this material out on a glass rod—and how many years ago that was! It was something we all worked together on. We were like colleagues, and it kind of gave you a good feeling, and you learn so much from it.*

Drawing on another example, a Peterson nursing alumna described the co-learner roles that professors and students enacted in one of her courses:

> *Once a week we would assemble for a [clinical] seminar—where everyone would gather together and discuss patients and different styles of handling things. But, you know, we really didn't even need a faculty member there. Everyone looked forward to it. Students would get up and make a presentation on this or that—we pretty much ran the seminar ourselves. Sure, the faculty member would ask a question here and there, but you never felt like you were on the spot and you were up there and people were going to try and humiliate you. It wasn't like that at all. It was very collegial.*

Not surprisingly, many students and alumni stressed that they valued being treated as "contributing members" of their learning communities.

Reflecting on her master's experience, a Helena State alumna openly relished how she and her peers had worked together to ensure the success of the program's theatrical productions: "You might have the lead in the production," she remarked, "and then mop the floors after the rehearsal. I mean, there was no star system here. Everyone [faculty and students] worked together. The main goal was a successful production." A Major State student was equally positive about his team-based research experiences, observing that they made him feel like "I was part of something important, that I wasn't just another grain of sand on a whole beach. I was really doing things other than just doing my homework. I was made to feel like I was part of something that mattered."

We came to understand that "learning communities" consisted of more than collegial and collaborative interactions between faculty and students. Many people told us that a camaraderie also existed within faculty and student subcultures that supported the overall sense of community in their programs. A Moore A&T administrator, for example, summarized the view of many of his colleagues by describing the engineering faculty as "one big family": "We show lots of respect and collegiality toward one another." At Southwest State, a professor underscored the "sense of collegiality and cooperation" that held the applied anthropology faculty together, while at Middle State, a microbiology professor emphasized that he and his colleagues functioned as a collaborative team: "We [the microbiologists] work as a group and there's lots of interaction here. We go to meetings together and we're very supportive of one another. There aren't any prima donnas here."

Many students and alumni in our sample also spoke of experiencing a "sense of student community" in their programs. This sense was based largely on the supportive camaraderie students generated among themselves as they taught and learned from one another both in and out of class. A Longmont English student touched upon this:

*With the students [here], I find a great deal of community. . . . Let's put it this way, at the university I attended as an undergraduate there were people who hid books because all they wanted was to get the top spots in the top law schools, and there are only so many spots. But here I don't see that. Everybody is trying to help one another. I don't think I've ever seen anyone not give me a helping hand when I asked for it, and a lot of times they help me when I didn't ask for it, which is good. I know I've grown a lot because of that.*

Two Vernon College students portrayed the "sense of community" they experienced in their environmental studies program this way:

*[Student 1]: The program is hard, it's rigorous, but there is a sense of community that holds us together so we can get through it. There is more*

*camaraderie . . . and this is important. It's not like regular programs where graduate students don't know what the others are doing.*

*[Student 2]: The support that you get from the other students helps keep you going. If someone really bogs down and falls behind [we help take care of them]. . . . The five or six of us who continued into the second year really worked together.*

To be sure, many students in our study told us that their learning experiences would have been richer if their peers and professors had interacted with them on a more collegial and less hierarchical—and sometimes adversarial—basis. A Phelps English student, for instance, said that his professors "never treated" him like a "colleague": "I felt like I was expected to act like a graduate student [because] I didn't have any expertise." On a slightly different note, a recent graduate of Major State's English program objected strongly to the highly competitive relationships faculty cultivated among students. This adversarial practice, she explained, had made her master's "a grueling experience" in which "students were consumed [wholly] by their grades": "[F]ar from supporting one another as fellow sufferers, [we] actually avoided interacting with each other. We were placed into strong competitive relationships. I was terrified the whole time I was in the program."

In summary, interviewees provided a substantial body of evidence that led us to identify a "community of learners" as an important feature of high-quality programs. A Longmont alumnus provided the most compelling testimony to the salience of this attribute:

*What makes [Longmont] happen isn't just the professors, or the quality of the students, or what happens in the classrooms. It's this sense of us as a community, bonded together and tied into this thing that [Longmont] epitomizes for us. . . . It's a psychological landscape, it's a sense of identity, of belonging to this project. . . . What I'm suggesting is that not only is it a nice perk when that happens, but that it may well be integral to creating the dynamic. It's like a synergy that happens. It's because of this notion that we learn together: I'm not just learning in my class—there is an intensive interaction because of that. It happens at meals, it's just always happening. . . . Intense interactions are typical, never stop around here. That's part of what makes this place work. And it would suggest to me that that's what would energize a graduate community at any university. But it means you have to pay a lot of attention to things outside of the curriculum, and the quality of the professors, and the academic demands that you make on your students. You have to look at the students as a whole, and at their life together. That's what helps create an academic community.*

## *Effects on Students*

Participating in a community of learners enriched students' growth and development in two major ways. First, the collegial interactions that students had with one another and with faculty strengthened their communication and teamwork skills. Second, owing in large part to the contributions that others made to their learning within these "communities," students developed a greater appreciation of and respect for the value of collaborative approaches to inquiry, problem solving, and leadership.

Many students and alumni credited their collaborative learning experiences with improving their communication and teamwork skills. In Middle State's microbiology program, for example, one student told us that her involvement in group-oriented research projects had enhanced her awareness of how her "performance impacted others": "I began to understand that I was not a solo operator. I had to be concerned with how I presented information and how I guided people's understanding of it." A Carver A&M environmental studies student similarly observed that, in his master's program, he was learning how to get others "to pull their shoulders together and share": "I'm seeing that [solving environmental problems] is not a one-man game. If you look in the lab [I'm in], you'll see that everyone works in pairs so that they can compare and contrast and exchange ideas. . . . We really try to help each other out."

Learning communities positively affected students' growth and development in another way: The diverse contributions that faculty and students made to one anothers' knowledge and understanding helped them to develop a greater appreciation for the value of collaborative activity. A Helena State alumna expressed this outcome:

> *One thing that I feel [Helena State] taught me above all else was that you can be confident in your own abilities and yet gain so much from the people around you. . . . When you get ten minds together it can make an incredibly exciting production. And the production teams here—being able to work on them and being a student observing them—just gave you incredible insight. . . . The atmosphere was electric.*

An Appleby State microbiology alumnus likewise indicated that he had come to value "team approaches" to science when, in referring to the "bouncing back and forth" of ideas that occurred in his research team, he remarked: "There was a lot of group interaction and we experienced successes and failures together. We learned a lot from one another. . . . I really think that group approach [to solving scientific problems] was beneficial."

## Risk-Taking Environment

In culling through our interview material, we identified a risk-taking environment as yet another important attribute of high-quality programs. On repeated occasions, stakeholders told us that their programs had supportive and challenging learning environments in which students felt "safe" to take risks in their learning. These risk-taking ventures significantly improved the quality of students' learning.

### Actions

Faculty and administrators laid a foundation for risk-taking in their programs in two interrelated ways. First, they developed a supportive learning environment in which students were encouraged to explore new ideas and test developing skills. Second, faculty and administrators took risks themselves, encouraging students to follow their lead and challenge themselves to stretch and grow in new ways.

Many faculty and administrators in our study encouraged and supported risk-taking by providing students with numerous opportunities to discuss ideas, explore alternative viewpoints, and experiment with new approaches in "safe" learning contexts that were free from excessive competition, ridicule, or penalty. Through these risk-taking activities, faculty challenged students to develop their potential and to learn from their mistakes as well as their successes.

The theater program at the National Conservatory College (NCC) is a model case where faculty and administrators worked together to develop a challenging and supportive learning environment. In paging through the program's brochure, we observed that it was described as a "safe harbor" in which students were "encouraged to participate wholeheartedly in experimental work—to risk and even to fail—while maintaining and developing their critical faculties as professional actors." In exploring this point with interviewees, we learned that faculty and administrators created this "safe harbor" by eliminating all formal auditions, providing students with multiple opportunities to play unconventional character roles, and stressing a "yes attitude" that supported students' risk-taking. As one faculty member told us: "We believe that a simple 'no' is a non-repeatable act of power. 'Yes' creates a supportive environment and opens up creativity. It creates a positive atmosphere [that is] safe and nonjudgmental. It keeps people open [to trying new things]." An administrator took this perspective a step further, explaining that faculty encouraged students to say "yes to everything because this leads them [students] into the unknown":

*[We tell our students that] you may not like it [this role or dialect or characterization], you may hate it, but you have to try it and then you can decide. . . . Our program's philosophy is to treat everyone as an individual and to push them to find their strengths as an actor. Other programs mold students to fit their vision of "this is what an actor should be." We try to have students create their own mold instead of having them fit into our mold.*

Faculty and administrators in other programs also emphasized that they tried to create program environments in which students felt at once challenged and supported to take risks in their learning. A Moore A&T administrator, for example, said that while faculty "expected students to work hard" and "challenged them to develop their potential," they did not "excuse students quickly" when their grades faltered or their experiments failed. Instead, he explained, faculty gave students a "little bit of extra help" to guide them through rough spots. An applied anthropology professor at City-State expressed a similar view, noting that faculty buttressed their high expectations for students with strong support. "Sometimes I give the students too much rope and they flounder," he remarked. "But I tell them that professional people feel that way a lot . . . that if they feel comfortable all the time they aren't being challenged—to feel uncomfortable means you're plowing new ground. But I tell them that if they fall flat on their faces, we're here to pick them up."

Time and again, faculty emphasized that such opportunities were vital to helping students appreciate the valuable role that risk-taking—and its byproducts, success and failure—played in the learning process. As a faculty member in Phelps' theater program told us: "The most valuable thing we can offer students is that there is benefit in failure. They have a right, in a school of drama, to fail. I believe we give them this right with the little productions we have every weekend. When these fail or succeed, we sit down with the students and talk about why [they failed or succeeded]." A Middle State microbiology professor provided a similar rationale when he said of the laboratory research opportunities he provided to students:

*I give students lots of research problems to work on. And I tell my students right up front: "It's not my problem, it's your problem, but my door is always open and I'm here to bounce ideas off of. And when you're stuck, come in and talk to me." See, I expect students to tell me how to do things. You have to push them a little bit; it builds up their confidence. I believe you have to do this—and you have to permit them to make mistakes. I tell my students that's how you learn how to do research—by learning from your mistakes.*

Besides establishing supportive climates, we learned that faculty and administrators cultivated a risk-taking environment in a second way: they took risks themselves and encouraged students to do likewise. Many faculty told us that they modeled risk-taking behavior to students in their classes, on stage, or in the laboratory. Moreover, many said that they openly discussed their professional experiences with students, often elaborating on the lessons they learned from their mistakes.

In Phelps' theater program, for instance, every faculty member we interviewed stressed that their involvement in the professional, non-university theater sent a clear message to students that their "teachers" were constantly challenging themselves. At Southwest State, a microbiology professor said that by modeling risk-taking for students in the laboratory, he helped "students to know that it [scientific research] can be done": "[It] makes them feel that they can make advances, and that induces them to go into science—to have someone doing it [in front of them] who is their teacher." And in City-State's applied anthropology program, a faculty member told us that he discussed his failures—as well as his successes—with students because "telling them about my mistakes makes them feel better; it helps them to know that the people who are teaching them are human, too."

## Consequences for Learning Experiences

The investments that faculty and administrators made in developing and sustaining a risk-taking environment greatly enhanced the quality of students' learning experiences. In our study, interviewee after interviewee told us that when students felt supported and challenged to take risks, they were much more likely to question orthodoxies, advance alternative perspectives, and engage in learning activities that pressed the boundaries of their potential.

Students and alumni across our sample highlighted the trusting and supportive character of their learning environments. Many told us that even as faculty challenged them to take risks that would unleash more of their talents, they also supported them when they needed a discerning ear, a critical eye, or a helping hand. An Helena State theater alumna said of her program's "nonthreatening environment":

> Faculty allowed students to be vulnerable but, at the same time, safe within that vulnerability so that they felt trusted. They built a trusting environment, a trust among students and their advisor. Taking those risks was important. . . . [This is] a very open and supportive environment. I never felt threatened by anything here. I had experienced jealousy among departments elsewhere . . . but I did not experience that here.

A Moore A&T engineering student described the supportive—and demanding—nature of his program's learning environment in this way: "You're pushed to get the work done [and] you have a lot of pressure. But I like being here. I like the more one-on-one setup with the instructor. You can walk into an office and talk to your advisor and talk about the problems you're having. . . . The faculty are really motivated to educate you."

Within the context of these supportive and trusting learning environments, students felt "safe" to engage in risky learning experiences that stretched them in new and unanticipated ways. A student at NCC, for example, told us that she was constantly experimenting with new roles, dialects, and acting styles because "NCC's motto is 'Try it, maybe it will work for you.' " To illustrate her point, she discussed a "scary" project she had recently completed that involved writing and performing a one-act play with two other students in the program. From her perspective, this was "a good way to start out the program—it threw me into unmapped territory. I learned how to let go, how to get out of my own head . . . how to go over the top."

Along these same lines, we interviewed two Appleby State microbiology students who openly discussed some of the risks they were taking in their studies. One of them told us how he had started to "move away from the textbook" and "to question everything in the lab": "I've been constantly analyzing, reflecting, [and] reapproaching how I do things." "And the faculty really encourage that, too," the other student interjected. "They try to move you away from what they call 'cookbook' approaches and into thinking for yourself." Both of these students agreed that making the transition from "dependent" to "independent" scientist was "scary" at first, but that in taking the risk they had begun to "think like microbiologists."

Students and alumni told us repeatedly how much they valued being challenged to take risks in their learning. A Longmont student observed that the intensely intellectual, yet noncompetitive, character of the master's program in English "pushed" him to do his "best possible work":

> *You respect your teachers very highly, and you want them to respect you. You're invested, and I accomplish things here—I know others do [too]—that you don't think are physically possible and that are at a very high level of language, of communication, thinking, ideas. You'd think that people would be competitive. But there's no such thing as a bell curve here. . . . You're not really competing with other people, you're competing for quality.*

In much the same spirit, a Helena State theater alumna said that the program's simultaneously supportive and demanding environment had challenged her "to take risks and to trust [her]self."

On a different note, some students and alumni indicated that the quality of their learning experiences had been severely undermined by the competitive and sometimes intimidating environments faculty promoted in their programs. A Major State English alumna, for instance, told us that since faculty relied heavily upon students' grades when assessing their applications for doctoral study, this practice "bred a fair amount of paranoia among students about their professors": "Whether their professors approved of them, whether they would pass them on exams, and whether they were going to get through this place." Unwilling to jeopardize their admission chances, many students in this master's program—far from taking risks in their own learning—conformed to faculty expectations and demands. One alumnus explained:

> *As a student, there's a kind of decorum or posture that you should be careful to assume, I think, in class because you're afraid of alienating someone who you need desperately professionally at the time. . . . You don't want to piss anyone off. I felt like I was walking on eggshells with people. There were very significant messages which were being imparted by faculty as to whether the department was going to employ you or not [as a teaching assistant] and whether the professors were taking you seriously [enough to consider admitting you into the Ph.D. program].*

We learned that the situation in Major State's theater department was similar. There, several graduates and students reported that the program's intimidating learning environment had literally required them to "toe the line" to faculty demands. "It's clearly [an] abuse of the system," one alumnus said. "People have finished three years of M.F.A. [master's of fine arts] work and [they have] still not been given their degree because [a certain faculty member] decides they aren't worthy to be a director. . . . Very few people get out of the directing program here. They all put the hours in, they all put the years in, and they walk out without their degree." Not surprisingly, these stakeholders—as well as several others we interviewed—felt that the "probational" and idiosyncratic nature of faculty evaluation in their programs produced counter-productive environments in which students seldom felt supported, let alone encouraged, to take risks.

Whether they used affirmative or negative examples to convey its importance, we learned from interviewees across our sample that a risk-taking environment is a vital component of high-quality programs. On countless occasions, stakeholders told us that students learned much when they engaged in "safe" risk-taking learning experiences that challenged them to become more than they thought possible.

## Effects on Students

Students who took risks within the context of a supportive learning environment enhanced their growth and development in two important ways. First, students who engaged in—and learned from—risk-taking activities graduated as more competent and self-assured professionals. Second, and closely related, since many risk-taking ventures required students to wrestle with their crafts in new and creative ways, they helped them develop into more imaginative and resourceful professionals.

Many interviewees told us that they witnessed a shift in students' self-confidence as they successfully completed challenging assignments and projects in their master's programs. An administrator in Middle State's microbiology program said that he saw this "change occur over and over again" as students tackled increasingly difficult problems in the laboratory. "Once these kids learn that they can do it," he remarked, "they move beyond. It's like a snowball effect. As the confidence level increases [with each new successfully-managed challenge], they're not willing to accept the old levels of performance anymore. They think they can do better than that. They rise to new levels of challenge." In much the same way, an employer of Major State's engineering program indicated that the research challenges that students "stared down" and successfully completed in the program gave them "a leg up" on others in the workplace. As he put it: "My master's-trained employees [from Major State] are real go-getters. . . . They're just a lot more confident that they can start and finish the task."

Students and alumni often corroborated these faculty and employer accounts. In describing the risks faculty challenged her to take in her writing, a Southwest State student said that she had "discovered"—and become much more self-confident in—her authorial "voice": "Now I'm not afraid to say, 'I don't buy that at all. I think this is where the text is at.' And I may be the only one who thinks so, but I'm going to write my paper on that because that's what I believe. So, discovering a voice and gaining confidence—all of those things go together." Similarly, a Phelps theater alumnus credited the risks he took in his master's with "stretching" his skills and confidence as an actor "in incredible ways." "I may have possibly done the best work of my life there," he observed. "I did things there that I may never have the opportunity to do again. . . . I feel a lot more powerful and self-assured as an actor now than I did before I entered the program."

We also discovered that students benefited from risk-taking in a second way: as they questioned orthodoxies, explored alternative perspectives, tested their skills, and advanced new interpretations, students developed into more creative and resourceful professionals. One student in Appleby State's microbiology program articulated this:

*After having survived some problems in the lab that, at the time, appeared impossible, you learn "possibility thinking." For example, as an undergraduate, I tackled a research project that I gave up on, basically. The problem never was resolved. But now, I have not given up on the ultimate goal of my thesis research, although I still haven't achieved success there yet. Sure, it's frustrating, but I think there is a way around it now. I'm much more persistent. I see more possibilities.*

With a slightly different twist, an NCC theater student elaborated on how her risk-taking ventures had helped her to find and strengthen her own creative voice and style:

*One of the school's philosophies that we hear around here all the time is "only by attempting the absurd can we achieve the impossible." And students are encouraged to do a lot of that around here—to take risks and try out new things. That's been really valuable for me. I've tried risky things and I've failed, but it was in failing that I discovered my own voice and the impact I can have on an audience. I actually found my edge by going beyond it. I believe that an actress must dare herself to fail, otherwise she will just fit into someone else's mold instead of creating her own mold.*

Finally, a student in Middle State's microbiology program described the positive impact that risk-taking had on her professional development in this way: "I think differently about things now. I approach things differently—I realize there's not always a right answer. I now question more. I see how things relate. I realize that everything isn't just black and white. . . . I'm doing things that I never thought I would be doing. There's a real sense of accomplishment in that."

# 6

Interactive Teaching
and Learning

We identified interactive teaching and learning as the third cluster of
attributes in our engagement theory of program quality. As we came to understand, high-quality programs are constructed around an interactive model
of communication in which faculty, students, administrators, and staff actively contribute to one another's learning.

In this chapter, we discuss the five program attributes that we associate with interactive teaching and learning: critical dialogue, integrative learning, mentoring, cooperative peer learning, and out-of-class
learning activities. For each, we consider how administrators and faculty fostered the attribute in their programs, examine the consequences
of these actions for students' learning experiences, and discuss the positive effects that these learning experiences had on students' growth and
development.

## Critical Dialogue

Critical dialogue emerged as a distinctive feature of high-quality programs
in our study. We learned that when faculty and students jointly questioned
extant knowledge, challenged core assumptions in their fields, and generated critical understandings of knowledge and professional practice, students had far richer learning experiences that noticeably enhanced their
growth and development.

## *Actions*

Faculty and administrators paved the way for critical dialogue in their programs in two closely related ways. First, they emphasized a two-way, interactive approach to teaching and learning that encouraged dialogue among program participants. Second, faculty and administrators infused a critical sensibility into these interactions by encouraging students to take an inquisitive stance on knowledge and professional practice.

In numerous programs in our sample, faculty and administrators used an interactive approach to teaching and learning that encouraged students to share their ideas, opinions, and experiences. A Lake College program administrator helped us to understand this approach more fully when she remarked: "[We use] a democratic way of teaching. Our teachers and students dialogue with one another. We encourage student sharing. These teachers come together and are encouraged to discuss serious questions." The director of Longmont's English program said that the faculty there invited all the students "to be part of the discourse. We don't use a language that excludes people. . . . If we're going to have students in our classrooms, then all of them have to be invited into the discourse."

Many faculty and administrators told us that they used an interactive approach because they believed students had bona fide ideas to contribute and deserved to be treated as valued participants in the learning process. A Southern State nursing professor stated her views on students this way: "I believe students are valuable sources of knowledge. I'm always encouraging them to share their knowledge in class." A faculty member in Lake's education program said much the same, noting matter-of-factly that he saw "students as experts in their own right" and treated them as such in his classes.

In concert with an interactive approach to teaching and learning, faculty and administrators often infused a critical sensibility into their conversations with students that challenged them to scrutinize and question their own and others' understandings of knowledge and practice. Faculty used a variety of interactive teaching and learning activities to promote this "critical dialogue," including small and large group discussions, role-playing exercises, and student-led seminars.

The nursing program at Southern State University is a representative case in which faculty and administrators fostered critical dialogue with students. During our visit there, several faculty indicated that they had recently embraced a new approach to teaching that encouraged students to question and critically probe "orthodox" perspectives on nursing theory and practice. As one explained:

> *One of the things that we're trying to do is to raise the consciousness of students to things that people buy into without questioning. . . . If you*

*accept things without questioning them, then you're buying in. That's what we try to do at the master's level—to get people to question the systems that they are in and the way things are done. For example, why do women and children have poorer health care, why aren't they valued more, why doesn't everyone have access? We want to give a bigger picture of the way the world is.*

To nurture this critical perspective in students, faculty had begun to emphasize ongoing dialogue and reflection in their classes. An administrator provided us with a flavor of this "dialogical" approach:

*What we're doing now is sharing with each other and [discussing] how it's working. Like, for example, in the pathophysiology course, the instructor who teaches the course has stopped lecturing. There are certain articles that are assigned for the evening and she has told the students that this is your class, here are some things we might discuss, but we can do it in whatever way you choose to do it. Even some of the content has already changed—bringing in the critical thinking, the feminist perspectives, and questioning things that nurses often think are carved in stone. . . . And we're questioning that with the students. We're asking them if they think that's the way our knowledge really is.*

In other programs in our sample, faculty and administrators used various interactive teaching strategies to encourage students to embrace an inquisitive stance on knowledge. At Southwest State, for example, a professor explained that he and his colleagues engaged in "lots of discussion" with students to help them "understand that basically anthropological theory is the underlying assumptions that you carry into a situation. All we want to do is to get students to be more explicit and systematic about those assumptions. . . . This idea of grounding—of knowing what your assumptions are and why you believe them—is very important." A faculty member in Phelps' environmental studies program approached this task from a different angle, using role-playing to stimulate student discussions of how different assumptions influenced policy-making. Finally, a Peterson nursing professor told us that she conducted all of her classes "like seminars" in which she constantly challenged students to "examine critically . . . taken-for-granted issues" and to question the conventional wisdom of the profession.

## Consequences for Learning Experiences

For the most part, the efforts that faculty and administrators put into fostering critical dialogue greatly enhanced the quality of students' learning experiences. In many programs we visited, faculty and students engaged in disciplined and mutually-enriching interactions in which they constantly questioned one another, examined assumptions and alternative points of view, and generated critically-informed understandings of knowledge and professional practice.

Many students in our study highlighted the interactive nature of their learning experiences. A student in St. Joan's business program, for instance, described his master's experience as a "conversation" in which faculty encouraged him to "participate in the management" of his own education. At Longmont College, an English alumna described the invitational nature of faculty–student dialogue:

> *Overall, the teachers here are far more involved with the students than at other places [I've been]—[they're] willing to give up control and not feel threatened by it. In many other schools, the professor barges ahead because they don't want to be interrupted or questioned. They don't want to lose footing—because a student could run by, pass them by, at any moment. There's not a sense here that the faculty feel threatened by you—more that they are inviting you to join them. . . . Different pedagogy is stressed here: students are in groups. You're put in charge of your own learning more here, and [you're] respected here [more], than in any other school. And there is this sharing.*

Within the context of these two-way, interactive learning experiences, many students and alumni emphasized that faculty encouraged them to think in new and demanding ways. A microbiology student at Middle State University, for example, said that faculty "constantly asked [the kinds of] questions" that challenged students to "think, not regurgitate information": "They tell us that there are no right or wrong answers. Rather the questions they ask are, 'How would you approach this problem?' They want us to think and discuss things with them. . . . We ask lots of questions back and forth." In much the same vein, a Southern State nursing alumna stated that faculty there told students "to be free thinkers": "They encourage thinking as opposed to just following strict guidelines. [They want us] to think in a different light." From her perspective, this "free thinking" invited participants to probe issues in greater depth, to articulate diverse viewpoints in disciplined ways, and to explore underlying assumptions and perspectives that often were at the root of competing views.

Many students and alumni told us that critical dialogues were among the most demanding and rigorous learning experiences they had in their master's programs. Referring to the "constant questioning" he engaged in with his peers and professors, for example, an alumnus of Walton State's environmental studies program candidly remarked: "[Walton State] doesn't make it easy—[like] this is going to be the right answer. You're constantly asked 'What is your bottom line, what are your limits, what are your values, what are you making your choices on?' It was not an easy road." A Laramie education student made this point in a slightly different way: "We talk a lot about things that we normally do in our jobs, or that reflect our personal beliefs about the way the world works, and we examine them and test them out against other people. . . . We have a lot of arguments around here."

Students and alumni also told us how much they gained from their dialogical interactions with one another and faculty. Some, for instance, said that these exchanges had been invaluable in challenging them to think through and critically evaluate ideas with others. A Southwest State alumna said of the critical dialogues one of her anthropology professors had encouraged in class:

*He was great. He really was a critical thinker and he wanted us to be, too. He encouraged a lot of exchange in class—and that's what made the class so good. I mean, sure, you can learn a lot when a professor sits up in front of the class and lectures and talks about stuff we're reading. But when you sit back and you actually have to start formulating ideas [and] you have to talk back and carry on a conversation and use your brain, that's when you really begin to learn.*

A Helena State theater alumna was equally positive about the ongoing, critical exchanges faculty fostered with students. "We were constantly saying, 'what if, what if, what if?' " she recalled. "Faculty expectations were high. . . . They expected that you would be successful; they expected you to pull your own weight; and they expected you to question if you had concerns or problems. . . . They stressed thinking and individual growth." From her perspective, such conversations had "forced" her to move beyond "regurgitating information" to "doing a great deal of thinking and problem solving and research," thereby pushing her to "take risks and to trust" herself.

Other students and alumni emphasized that dialogical interactions helped them to develop critically-informed perspectives on knowledge and practice in their fields. A Southwest State English student—who clearly relished the open-ended interactions in his courses—touched upon this particular benefit of critical dialogue:

*Here the concept of discourse community tends to be very, very strong. People want to hear what other people have to say. As far as the books, you're going to get basically the same books no matter where you are. . . . [that's] fairly consistent. What isn't consistent is the people. And the whole concept of critical study of literature has to revolve around this concept of discourse. People talking about why a certain author is great. What is so good about this. Or why they feel someone is horrendous and shouldn't be in the canon. . . . And that has been my experience in all of my education here. I learned far more about these ideas in my classes than I learned from reading Shakespeare by myself.*

For their part, many faculty and administrators told us that they also benefited from their interactions with students. As a professor in Phelps' theater program put it, such conversations with students "kept her clean": "It is really good to have their [students] feedback and their challenges. They really do that for me. . . . I think the benefits are really mutual." Referring to her interactions with master's students, an administrator in Peterson's nursing program similarly remarked, "These students keep me humble. As much as I have to offer to them, they offer an incredible amount to me . . . a lot of these people are out in the real world on a daily basis. These students constantly remind me what's happening out there. . . . These students change me as much as I have helped them to change."

Conversely, students and alumni in some programs indicated that they would have had higher-quality learning experiences if faculty had fostered more "critical" dialogue—let alone dialogue—in their classes. From their standpoint, authentic dialogue seldom occurred because faculty either were indifferent to learning from students or were so preoccupied with communicating their own views that they rarely invited others to share their perspectives.

For example, a theater student at Trafalger College told us that some of his professors sent a clear message that they "had better things to do" than to talk with master's students—an attitude that had led some of his classmates to leave the program. Several students and alumni in Major State's English program articulated a different concern, noting that while faculty often invited them to raise questions in class, many had such "strong personalities" that free-flowing, open discussions were rare. As one recent alumnus explained:

*Certain identities are formed within a department and they are not of subtext; they are on the surface and they are carried around openly and self-consciously portrayed, and the identities are shifted around what are called "ways-of-knowing" and that, I think, describes a lot of the professors. Basically, in a spiritual sense, faculty live and die by those identities. I mean they spend their whole lives forming them. . . . And you have some people who are very inflexible about the kind of critical approaches you as a student can take to the pursuit of knowledge in your literary endeavors. And these are the kinds of things that you start to discover, either quickly, blatantly, easily, or painfully . . . in your courses.*

In light of both positive and negative evidence, then, we came to appreciate that critical dialogue has important consequences for the quality of students' learning experiences. In many programs we studied, interviewees told us that developing students' thinking abilities through critical dialogue was, in the words of a City-State program administrator, a signature feature of "what every [good] master's program should be."

## Effects on Students

Critical dialogue had two positive effects on students' growth and development. First, as a result of the ongoing, dialogical interactions they had with faculty and one another, students became more holistic, critical, and discriminating thinkers. Second, these interactions contributed strongly to helping students become more self-assured and creative problem-solvers.

Many interviewees indicated that dialogical learning experiences challenged students to think in ways that stressed holism, constant questioning, and critical analysis. An alumna of Southwest State's applied anthropology program, for instance, told us that her interactions with others helped her to develop a "different kind of thinking":

> *I learned how to step out of my own value system—and that's really hard. That takes time. I remember I started to get so mad at everyone around me because I kept seeing how locked in they were by their own assumptions. . . . You would think you'd get this thinking process in your bachelor's, but you don't. . . . It's a whole different experience at the master's level. You learn how to look at yourself and different cultures in a more critical way. You just don't go along with the flow; you just don't accept everything that everyone says and does anymore. You really get critical. You really begin to question.*

Along these same lines, an alumna of Southern State's nursing program credited the dialogical character of her master's with "transforming" the way she approached her professional practice. As she put it: "Before I was just a robot, I was a good staff nurse. But it wasn't like anything I can do now. Everything now has to be questioned. At that time [during my master's] I began looking through a different lens. It made things very difficult, but I enjoyed it. I found it very refreshing and very valuable."

Many faculty and employers corroborated these student and alumni accounts. An administrator in Peterson's nursing program pointed out that the dialogical conversations students engaged in made them "think on a theoretical basis": "They begin to see things in a bigger perspective. . . . And I think that's what students get in this program—a framework for seeing more and more of the world. They can conceptualize now, they begin to think theoretically and critically." In much the same vein, an employer of St. Joan's business graduates attributed the program's interactive, question and debate format with changing one of his employee's thinking:

> *Before [this employee] received his master's, every question could be answered by a tally sheet. Now, he can see shades of gray. It used to be you'd know what he'd say before you asked him. Then [during his master's] he started to hesitate, wrinkle his brow, and think a bit. Then he started to weigh the issues: "Maybe the guy can't pay his bill, but maybe we shouldn't shut him down. If we can help him along, maybe he'll be able to pay his debt and stay in business for us." He's really become a part of the decision-making team now.*

In addition to encouraging students to question and approach issues in more critical and holistic ways, many interviewees stressed that critical dialogues positively affected students in another way: many left their programs as more creative, self-confident, problem-solvers. An alumna of Southern State's nursing program informed us, for example, that the "constant questioning" she engaged in with her peers and professors helped her to become a more holistic and creative problem-solver. She relayed the following story to illustrate her point:

> *[During my master's, I began] to think, "O.K., if I look at this from the medical model perspective, I would say, 'What's the pathology? What's the treatment?' " And that's how I looked at things in my bachelor's program. Having a master's degree I now look and say, "How well is this person doing? What is this person's strengths? What is it that they need? What is their social support? How can I interface what I know into their lives to help improve their lives?" It's not just pathology [anymore]. . . . My focus is "How can I help this person? How can I educate them? Support them?" It's a much more holistic approach.*

Employers in many other programs in our sample likewise underscored the impact of critical dialogue on students. After mentioning that faculty encouraged students to become "more analytical—to look at things that they can do in their classrooms and to do it at a higher level," a Lake College employer told us that their education graduates were highly-adept at "look[ing] at different ways of learning [and] ways of managing their own classroom. They look at different ways of teaching and they manipulate these more than other teachers. . . . One of my [Lake] alums is now looking at changing his perspective and trying some new approaches in his teaching." Similarly, an employer we interviewed at Southern State praised the dialogical inquiry that occurred among nursing faculty and students and then, unprompted, offered this comment on the program's graduates:

*I think nurses [from Southern State's program] are much more inquisi-
tive. . . . Before they were trying to get their technical skills down and now
they begin to see that artistic side of nursing at the master's level. I think
at the bachelor's level all you learn is how to give an injection, whereas at
the master's level . . . they learn to do other things than [how to] just give
an injection—they learn to take the time to go into the patient's room and
to find out more about why this person is hurting. [They consider] alternative measures that could be used; they begin to see the total picture and
they begin to assess on a much higher level. . . . These graduates are more
open to ideas and are more aware of the gray areas in problem-solving. . . .
They're more independent, more autonomous, and more creative [than before they received their master's].*

## Integrative Learning: Theory with Practice, Self with Subject

Integrative learning is still another important attribute of high-quality programs. In our study, students had far richer learning experiences when they
were challenged to link what they were learning to tangible situations and
issues in the outside world, and to link theory with practice, self with subject, learning with living. We came to appreciate that such integrative learning substantially improved the quality of students' experiences in ways that
considerably enhanced their growth and development.

### Actions

Faculty and administrators fostered integrative learning in their programs
in two ways. First, they invested in teaching and learning activities that
invited connections between theory and practice. Second, faculty and administrators modeled how they integrated the two as they worked with
students in class, on stage, in the laboratory, or in the field.

In many programs, faculty and administrators planned teaching and
learning activities that brought together theoretical and applied knowledge.
Some faculty, for example, tied the concepts they were presenting in lectures to messy, "real-world" problems. Others used "hands-on" activities
that encouraged students to make clear connections between theory and
practice. Regardless of the approach, these faculty and administrators believed strongly that students needed to learn both the theoretical and the
real-world dimensions of their disciplines, and that students could learn a
great deal from participating in activities that blended the two.

Many faculty in our sample indicated that they actively and self-consciously drew on real-world problems and issues to present students with
more than "textbook" understandings of knowledge in their classes. A

faculty member in Land-Grant's applied anthropology program, for instance, said that he integrated cultural resource management law into his archaeological theory course to provide students with a richer and more authentic perspective on their field. As he put it: "I see too many courses that are taught by professors who don't do contract archaeology and all they do is read the laws. My courses are far more than that. I do talk about what's happening out there in the real world and I use my more recent experiences to illustrate points." In a similar vein, an education professor at Laramie University told us how he tied global education concepts to curriculum development and instructional practices in his lectures:

*I'm the one who talks with students initially about how we're going to take this concept of . . . nation states—which can be fairly "ivory tower" and esoteric—and translate that into something that third-graders [or ninth-graders] can do. . . . I give them the opportunity to talk about "how do you take this concept of conflict resolution and bring it down to make it work with the elementary children [in your school] when we talk about global education?" It's [conflict resolution] not just a concept of things that happen on the other side of the world, but children have to be able to learn to get along with who's sitting next to them and to be able to play together in the school yard. And that's also global education. They don't need to be talking about India to be a global educator.*

Other faculty told us that they used "hands-on" learning activities to help students connect the knowledge and skills they were learning in class to problems and situations outside the university. These hands-on activities included role-plays, case studies, simulations, field trips, artistic performances, field research, and laboratory experiments.

For example, during our trip to Walton State, an environmental studies professor described a specific role-play that he and one of his colleagues used to help students unite theory with practice. "We break the group into quarters," he began, "and we ask each group [to play a different role] like the Chamber of Commerce, the City Council, a national environmental group—those kinds of things. Then they have to testify before [the other instructor] and me—we're two senators who come as a subcommittee [to address the environmental policy issue]. It's great. I mean, students really get into it and present some fascinating information." At Helena State a theater professor told a similar story about requiring students to construct sets for university-related productions in her lighting and stagecraft class. She explained her rationale behind this requirement:

*What you learn from a book helps to make what you do on stage easier, but when you do stuff on stage, there are things that happen that aren't in the books. . . . So we have to give the grad students the opportunity to do what it is that they need to learn in real production contexts. What I try to teach in class always ends up going back to "see how this ends up in the production." . . . The more times I can say, "This is what it looks like on paper, and this is what it looks like in real life, and what makes this [on paper] look like this [on stage]," the better. If they just get it in class, they still don't have a clue [about the practical applications].*

Faculty and administrators used a second strategy to foster integrative learning in their programs: they actively "walked their talk," modeling for students how they blended theory with practice and self with subject in their own professional lives. This modeling often took place when faculty shared their professional experiences with students in class or worked alongside them on various hands-on projects in the laboratory, field, or studio. In addition, faculty invited full-time, non-university workplace professionals into their classes—as role models in their own right—to share their experiences with students.

A Major State music education professor, for instance, told us that he had recently "become very aware of the importance of the personality of the teacher, the performance of the teacher, [and] the modeling that goes on." This self-awareness, he explained, led him to incorporate what he "read and experienced" in his performances more intentionally into his classroom teaching. A business professor at Peterson University—who also owned several small businesses—provided a similar account. After telling us that modeling was "key" to good teaching, he shared the following anecdote to illustrate his point:

*This student came in to see me—he was laid off [from his job]. He said to me, "You really affected me." I asked him how. He said, "Well, I don't know if you remember, we were talking about a case that had to do with the relationship between two partners and you told a personal story about a problem you had with your partner. And I thought that anybody who opened themselves up like that—well, I ought to pay attention to what that man says." And it made me wonder about how I taught. And it got me thinking [that] what they [students] learn is modeling. Everyone who has gotten as far as me—all of us have a model, someone who has changed our lives. We need people like this to change our lives.*

Many faculty also invited non-university workplace professionals into their classes to model for students their integrated understandings of knowledge and practice. A professor in St. Joan's business program, for instance, said that she brought in representatives from the Canadian Trade Council, the Federal Reserve Bank, and the U.S. Departments of Commerce and Labor to provide her multinational business students with practical perspectives on monetary theory, principles of fair trade, and the trade imbalance. Along these same lines, a Southwest State faculty member told us that he invited applied anthropologists working in cultural resource management, economic development, and agricultural development to guest lecture in his classes. These practitioners, he explained, served as key "role models" to students and helped them to develop "a sense of how applied anthropology works [outside the university]."

## Consequences for Learning Experiences

The time and effort that faculty and administrators put into fostering integrative learning had important consequences for the quality of students' learning. In many programs we studied, students participated in learning activities in which they connected theoretical and applied knowledge to complex problems, issues, and situations in the real world. These integrative experiences challenged students to weave the principles and practices of their disciplines more fully into the fabric of their own lives.

Many students and alumni said that faculty set the tone for integrative learning when they moved beyond narrow, "textbook" presentations of knowledge and connected what they were teaching in their classes to tangible issues in the real world. A student in Middle State's microbiology program nicely illustrated this point, noting how, in her immunology class, the professor not only lectured on the immunological characteristics of AIDS (acquired immune deficiency syndrome), but also provided a context for understanding the real-world effects of the disease. She explained: "He brought in some of the AIDS patients he was working on in the clinic, and they talked to us. It wasn't just textbook and it wasn't just 'here, you have an assignment to do.' It was real. You could talk to these people and see what the disease did to them mentally and physically." A Peterson business alumna similarly recalled how professors wed theory and practice in her classes:

> In general, if they gave us the theory, they would say here is theory A, B, C, and D. Then they would tell us that they knew for a fact that Theory B worked because they were using it in their own business right at this moment. . . . In other words, they were telling me practical information rather than just plain theory and [they applied it to their own experiences and told me if it worked]. I learned that just because Theory A sounds logical, it doesn't mean that it works. Yes, it sounds very logical but when you get out there in the real world and you're dealing with clients it's a whole different ball game.

We learned from many interviewees that just as faculty members high-lighted connections between theory and practice in their lectures, they also stepped aside and provided students with hands-on learning opportunities to discover and test these connections for themselves. Students and alumni often spoke enthusiastically about such hands-on learning activities, which included laboratory experiments, games, simulations, fieldwork assign-ments, theater productions, and case studies.

By way of illustration, two global education students at Laramie Uni-versity discussed the hands-on games they played in their classes—games, they informed us, that helped them to discern how various theoretical con-cepts informed curriculum development. As one student stated, "We spent time in one class playing the kinds of games kids would play, and which have international learning consequences. We got so much from it that we forgot we were supposed to be learning from it." The other student elabo-rated on this point:

> *There were always some principles at work [in these games], like "dependencia"—the way Third World countries are economically depen-dent on industrial countries. One of these games [that faculty used] would easily illustrate this concept and help engage the students in substantive discussions of what "dependencia" is. Questions like: "Are countries prompted by necessity to be cooperative?" So, these things illustrate dif-ferent approaches to teaching and development of curriculum.*

Other interviewees across our sample shared similar stories, telling us that through various hands-on activities, theory and practice worked hand in glove in many of their courses.

Many students and alumni told us that integrative lectures and hands-on activities were among their most rewarding learning experiences, em-phasizing that they greatly appreciated these opportunities to connect theory with practice in meaningful, tangible ways. A Phelps environ-mental studies student put it this way: "Here I learn most when, either individually or in a group, I am asked to apply concepts that we're learn-ing and discussing in the classroom to a situation—to work the concepts through in real life." A Peterson business student offered a comparable perspective:

> *When I have to go out and actually collect financial indicators from my own work setting or for a case study, I really feel like I'm being bumped up to another level of education. It's no longer hypothetical; it's real-world stuff. In this program, somewhere along the line, after faculty make you learn the theory, they then make you deal with the realistic and that moves you up to a different level of thinking. That's what I enjoy.*

Employers valued these integrative learning experiences for the same reasons as students and alumni. Time and again, they noted that hands-on projects, in particular, helped students to weave the principles and practices of their disciplines more meaningfully and accurately into their own professional practice. An employer of Major State's computer science graduates said of the "realistic" class projects students completed in the program:

> *I appreciate that the faculty force reality unto students by making them do more realistic projects instead of just stuff on paper. The projects usually are a scaled-down version of something that actually happens in reality. For example, in the programming class . . . students actually build something like a compiler. Yeah, it's a bit like a toy, but there are some elements of reality to it and the framework that students use [to build it] gives them an understanding of the theory that [in turn] helps them really grasp in a pragmatic sense what a compiler really is like. . . . They have some fundamental understanding of the theory and definitely some experience from the practical [side].*

A Walton State employer also spoke appreciatively about the integrative learning experiences students had in the school's environmental studies program. In particular, she commended faculty for using a variety of hands-on learning activities that were "relevant to the kinds of issues and problems [we're] addressing [in the field]": "I think [that's valuable because] it makes [for] less of a break for the student. It's less of going off for two years and doing the thing and then coming out, emerging like a butterfly. It's more of an integrative experience of continual application and testing back and forth."

To be sure, integrative learning was conspicuously missing in some programs we visited. Many students, alumni, and employers in these programs told us that faculty emphasized theoretical knowledge to the exclusion of applied, practical knowledge. Moreover, faculty seldom connected the theoretical concepts they presented in their lectures to problems or issues in the real world, nor did they provide students with hands-on learning opportunities to bridge the theory–practice gap. Interviewees stressed that this lack of integration seriously diminished the quality of students' learning experiences.

Students and alumni within this subset of programs frequently criticized the "overly-theoretical" orientation of their programs. Many reproached faculty for teaching theories and concepts from an "ivory tower" perspective that largely ignored the realities of the non-university workplace. A Pierpont business alumnus brought this point to the surface when he tersely said of his professors: "They gave all this theory, but they never made reference to the *Wall Street Journal*. They stayed in theory so much that when you got out, you couldn't comment on what was really happening."

A Major State sociology alumnus voiced a similar criticism when he related this story about one of his professors:

> *I remember at one of these graduate cocktail parties, I was talking to a sociology professor, and he was talking about his work in a [South American country]. He was telling me about some of his findings. And I said, "Well, did you suggest to the [country's] government any policy changes?" And he looked at me stunned, just stunned. "You mean I should suggest policy changes based on my findings?" And I said, "Well, yeah. Because why else would you be doing this?" And he just laughed, [acting] like I was completely nuts.*

Students, alumni, and employers in these programs also reprimanded faculty for failing to provide students with hands-on learning opportunities that, in their view, would have helped students to make stronger and more vital connections between theory and practice. An applied anthropology student at Atlantic State, for example, criticized her professors for spending too much time "talking about anthropological theory" and not enough "doing anthropology": "I'm getting tired of just talking about what we could do." A student in Major State's business program said that faculty rarely assigned case studies, group projects, or class presentations that challenged him to link what he was learning in class to "complex, real-life situations": "That's the kind of experience you should get in an M.B.A. program," he said disappointedly, "but we really aren't getting that experience here." Similarly, an employer of Major State's nursing graduates told us that faculty needed to incorporate more hands-on clinical experiences into the program: "There seems to be less emphasis on clinical expertise there and more on [the] theoretical," she observed. "[The faculty have] a belief that if students have the framework they can apply it. It's a fairly weak program clinically."

Across the forty-seven programs in our study, interviewees provided many affirmative and negative accounts identifying integrative learning as a key attribute of high-quality programs. A Major State environmental studies administrator vividly captured the value of integrative learning when he described such educational experiences as being analogous to a "souffle": "[They] provide an opportunity for synthesis—you put these ingredients together, and it rises and becomes a new entity. Suddenly everything starts to fit in. You see how things interrelate. . . . For the people for whom it works, not only do you connect and link together focused pieces of information, but it all moves up to a different level of conception of how you look at it."

## Effects on Students

Integrative learning positively affected students' growth and development in two important ways. First, learning activities of this kind helped students to approach problems and issues in their fields from a more holistic stand-point. Second, because integrative learning experiences required students to blend theory and practice, they became more adept at communicating complex theoretical and technical knowledge to others in their work settings.

Many interviewees in our study told us that integrative learning activities challenged students to develop more holistic perspectives on problems and issues in their fields. In discussing the role plays, hands-on activities, and integrative lectures he had experienced at Walton State, a second-year environmental studies student remarked that he had been taught how to "synthesize everything": "From how much memory a computer uses, to how we look at how we write, and how we regulate what we put into the waters. I've been taught to think critically, to think broadly, and to draw connections that I have never seen before." An alumnus of Longmont's English program similarly credited an activity that one of his professors had required with forever changing the way he approached the teaching of writing. As he explained:

> *He [a Longmont professor] taught me how to teach each child's text as if it was a real text—not just an adolescent text. That was profound for me. I had to analyze a nine-year-old's story in terms of adult literature. And, ever since then, I try to look at my students' texts as important texts— whereas other teachers just look for problems in punctuation. . . . I want to take what I learned there and look at multiple voicing in texts, at how to treat all texts in a certain way—without necessarily putting them in a hierarchy. Think how that impacts the teaching of English.*

For their part, many employers corroborated these student and alumni accounts. An employer of several City-State applied anthropology alumni, for instance, said that the hands-on learning activities students completed in the program helped them to develop "a different way of looking at the world": "That's what they bring and that's why I hire them. . . . I think they will be able to think holistically—that they will be able to see systems, that they will be able to pull things together. . . . It has obviously been worth it to me to get that piece. . . . They bring a world view that's really helpful." A Walton State employer was equally delighted with the holistic problem-solving approach students learned in its environmental studies program. As he told us, "They have a broader perspective and understanding of the system and the world and the context for their technical work. And that's really valuable. . . . I think they have that understanding of the big picture and how the pieces fit together and how the system works."

In numerous programs we studied, interviewees emphasized that integrative learning also helped students to become more adept at communicating theoretical and technical knowledge to others. A microbiology student at Middle State University conveyed this outcome as follows:

*A lot of nurses have asked me to explain things to them and I can see in the doctor's eyes that they're impressed. I've come into the limelight a little bit more at work. I'm called upon to solve more problems and to train people. . . . I've taught a few nurses a few things. I've explained things to them and I haven't stuttered over it or had to use my notes. I can just tell them because I know it. I can explain it . . . and I can even tell them how to do an experiment on it.*

Along these same lines, a Southwest State student made it clear to us that her hands-on classroom and fieldwork experiences had taught her how to "convert academic jargon" into prose that "gave archaeology back to the public."

An environmental studies administrator at Major State further made this point when he told us that the hands-on projects students completed in the program enabled them to "explain to employers that 'I understand not only academically, but practically, what it means to work on a problem like this because I have dealt with the community, with a state agency, those crazy roles, and I understand what the media can and cannot do.' " In much the same way, an employer of Lake's education alumni said that the program's "practical, theory-into-practice" orientation produced graduates who had "an improved interpersonal, professional approach with parents": "They can sift through information and move it into a larger perspective and then use this information constructively in working with parents and students."

## Mentoring

Mentoring is another important characteristic of high-quality programs. In many of the programs we studied, faculty and administrators provided individualized advising, instruction, and direct feedback to students that strengthened their professional skills and advanced their understandings of knowledge and practice. This mentoring consistently improved students' learning experiences and enhanced their personal and professional development.

## Actions

Faculty and administrators engaged in three activities designed to promote mentoring in their programs. First, they took an interest in students' career goals and tailored courses of study accordingly. Second, faculty periodically instructed students on a one-on-one basis in order to sharpen their understandings of knowledge and professional practice. Third, faculty provided students with regular feedback on the development of their professional skills.

In our study, individual advising was the most common way that faculty and administrators mentored students. Many faculty and administrators used advising sessions to learn more about students' career interests and, then, worked with them to develop individualized courses of study consonant with their interests.

A professor in Major State's microbiology program described how he mentored students through the advising process in this way:

> *I think a very important aspect [of the master's program] is to look at a person's heart. And I mean this sincerely, [to help students] find what they want to do. . . . I try to tell students that you're getting a master's, but really your avenues are expanding. And they expand in many ways: You can go into industry. You can go into a clinical laboratory. You can even go on and get your Ph.D. But that this is a time for you to evaluate your life, also, and to make some decisions. . . . I think students are looking for [someone] who will say, "I can help you." And they want to hear that [their] mentor is firm in their helping. . . . I think a lot of students would choose that. I wouldn't want a mentor that wouldn't want to help me. I think they come in and hear my spiel about where they can go in clinical microbiology and they like it because obviously that's why they came here in the first place.*

The chair of Peterson's nursing program likewise noted that she used the advising process to mentor students. Early on she asked her advisees such open-ended questions as: "Where do you get the most benefit from what you're doing? Where do you picture yourself in five years? What do you want to be a specialist in?" With this information in hand, she then worked with students "to make a program . . . that [met] their professional and personal goals."

Along with mentoring students during formal advising sessions, many faculty and administrators tried to facilitate their students' professional development through various forms of individualized instruction. These included informal, one-on-one interactions with students outside of class, individualized tutorials, and independent readings and research courses.

By way of example, we spoke with a faculty member in Major State's microbiology program who told us that he "made a point" of mentoring students daily in the laboratory. "I like to see everyone, every day, just to know what's going on," he said. "The best professors I know are like that. . . . I've learned that just talking to students in the office isn't good enough. You actually have to see what they have in their hands, and you can help them interpret their experiments." An applied anthropology professor at City-State University similarly highlighted the individualized instruction that he and his colleagues provided to students: "We put a tremendous amount of energy into nurturing interactions between faculty and graduate students. This is a very labor-intensive program in terms of advising and supervising education outside the classroom—tutorials, individually-directed readings, taking students out for lunch, and simply being open to drop-by chats."

Faculty and administrators also mentored students in a third way: they provided students with regular and timely feedback on the development of their professional skills. At Phelps University, a theater professor—who described the modus operandi in their program as "do it, and critique"— said that he and his colleagues required students to complete ongoing projects which they, as a collective faculty, orally reviewed each week. A microbiology professor at Appleby State likewise noted that, in addition to "talking with [her master's] students every day," she scheduled weekly hour-long meetings with them to discuss their research projects. And at Helena State, a theater professor underscored the importance that faculty placed on providing honest, candid feedback to students: "We're very hard-assed and upfront with people about where they are in their own growth and development. You don't let people think that they're where they need to be if they're not. You level with them and then you help them move beyond. We are a very individualized program." In summary, providing students with frequent, constructive feedback on their learning and development was a major means by which faculty sought to mentor students.

## Consequences for Learning Experiences

Data from our study provided compelling evidence that students had more meaningful learning experiences when faculty and administrators invested in the mentoring process. Not surprisingly, when faculty made such investments, students received a considerable amount of individualized advice, guidance, and feedback that greatly facilitated and enriched their learning.

The individualized attention faculty gave to students took two major forms: faculty who shared their knowledge and expertise with students as they worked together on various projects, and faculty who met with students (formally and informally) outside of class to discuss and provide feedback on course work, research, and creative projects.

Many students and alumni spoke enthusiastically about the mentoring they received from faculty in the laboratory, field, and studio. An alumnus of Moore A&T's engineering program fondly recalled the guidance his advisor provided to students: "He always told us to come to the lab and he would work with us. . . . I saw some of our group working until midnight with him. . . . He really wanted to get students involved. He wanted to teach us how to do science. And he was always there, doing it right in front of you." An alumnus of Land-Grant's applied anthropology program similarly noted that the interactions he had with his advisor in the field had "really taught" him "how to be an anthropologist." And an NCC theater student described her professors as "coaches" who generously shared their professional expertise "so that we could become more independent, creative [theater] artists."

In addition to their mentoring experiences in the lab, field, or studio, students and alumni told us that faculty helped them to understand more fully the intricacies of their craft during one-on-one meetings held outside of class. Here, students raised questions or discussed problems in their research or course work with faculty who, in turn, offered advice and feedback. In Phelps' theater program, for instance, we learned that several of its playwriting students benefited from the mentoring they received during their weekly tutorials with faculty. One alumnus told us: "One of the things that was really great [about my master's] was the tutorial system that was built in [it]. Once a week I would have a tutorial with [my advisor] with specific goals and criteria that I worked on. . . . I'd say most of my 'a-ha' experiences were at those points—in the tutorials." An alumnus of Appleby State's program said that he had met weekly with his advisor to "talk about my research, how it was going, [and] the problems I was having": "My advisor was really helpful. She had high standards. I just couldn't regurgitate . . . [she helped me] to understand the concepts behind what I was doing. I had a lot of respect for her."

In many programs we visited, students and alumni also accentuated their informal, spur-of-the-moment interactions with faculty. A Major State microbiology alumna described the spontaneous mentoring she had received as follows:

> All the [medical micro] professors were very caring. If you had trouble with anything, and they could see you were having problems, they would say, "Please come and talk to me." And I did. They would take time out— I would be there for an hour, hour and a half. When I was an undergraduate, the classes were so big that I didn't have that. And the undergraduates here would find that, too. But the graduate program is smaller, you get to be more of a person to the professors. That [is one of the] biggest advantages [of the program].

In much the same way, a Middle State alumnus recalled how his professors "were always available": "We would have lunch together and we would sit down and they'd ask how the project was going, and I would say, 'I don't know how to separate this from this.' And one of the professors would say, 'Well, look, if you'll go over and get this publication and read about this paper, or if you'll find this method we'll go over it together.' All of it [the informal advising and guidance] really helped."

On numerous occasions, students and alumni told us how much they valued learning under the guidance of experienced professionals who kept students' educational and career goals squarely in mind. An alumnus of Land-Grant's applied anthropology program voiced this theme when he said of his advisor: "He taught me a lot about applied archaeology and [he] also encouraged me to do my very best. He would boost you up when you were down, but he always encouraged me to be independent, to pursue my own goals." A Major State nursing alumnus offered similar praise of her mentors, noting how their concern had immeasurably enriched the quality of her learning experience. "What I most appreciate[d] about them," she related, was that "they listened to me [and] they were interested in what I had to say":

> I really got a sense that they were interested in my learning and getting a good education. . . . I had a sense that there was commitment from them to facilitate my learning. I didn't get the sense that they had a very strict, clearly defined, and concise little goal that they wanted me to get to. They had some kind of goal but they also wanted me to reach my own goals. I had the sense that I was driving for my own goals.

By contrast, our sample also included some programs in which mentoring was conspicuously absent. Interviewees in these programs told us that faculty seldom took an active interest in students' professional goals and rarely provided students with individualized guidance. A Barrett State nursing student, for instance, made this pointed remark about the program's faculty:

> They're supposed to be aware of our program and our needs and they're supposed to help guide us in the construction of this individualized program. Well, my advisor is on campus one-and-a-half days a week and is unavailable for conference. I'm lucky that she and I see eye-to-eye on what I'm doing. . . . The master's student comes in about seven or eight on a scale of five as far as priority [to the faculty] sometimes. And so to get the guidance, to get the structure and assistance in putting things together, sometimes can be a real effort.

An employer associated with this program offered a similar perspective, criticizing faculty for spending too much time "travelling the international circuit" and not enough on advising and teaching master's students.

Barrett State was not the only program in our study where interviewees criticized faculty for failing to mentor students. In Major State's theater program, for example, several students and alumni scolded faculty for shirking their responsibilities to students. As one student put it: "Surprisingly, people do get lost in the shuffle [here]. . . . Even though you think it's a small program and you'll be taken care of, you can't assume that. You still have to take care of yourself. So, the size of the program doesn't necessarily mean that the faculty will see you and have your interests in mind." A theater student at Trafalgar College said disappointedly that faculty there seldom "made time to meet with students" or to provide them with "advising and feedback during the term."

Whether they described positive or negative experiences, stakeholders across the forty-seven programs in our study stressed the importance of mentoring to high-quality programs. Perhaps an alumnus of Phelps' theater program best summarized this point when he said of his faculty advisor: "He has been the world's most generous person to me. It feels like it's just me, but I know from my peers that it is everybody. . . . There are good playwrights and good educators and then there are both. He happens to be both."

## Effects on Students

Throughout our study, we found that mentoring had two positive effects on students' growth and development. First, the individualized feedback that students received from their mentors went a long way toward strengthening students' professional competence and confidence. Second, mentoring— in both direct and indirect ways—helped students to advance their careers in the university and non-university workplace.

Across the programs in our sample, interviewees indicated that mentoring contributed markedly to students' development as highly-skilled, self-assured professionals. A Peterson nursing alumna expressed this outcome:

> I guess I always felt that [before my master's] there was something so sophisticated and so special about being a therapist—like there was some special magic that you had and I didn't think I had it. . . . It's a very odd feeling to look around and say, "I'm as good, if not better, than some of the therapists that I see." That was such a hard thing for me to acknowledge. . . . The supervision, the feedback from my [advisor and clinical supervisor]— that kind of acknowledgement from them made me confident to do something that I always wanted to do but that I thought I would never have the magic to do.

In a similar light, a Moore A&T administrator told us that although many students entered the school's engineering program unsure of their abilities, the mentoring he and his colleagues provided helped to ensure that students graduated as "poised, self-confident professionals." He shared this anecdote to support his observation:

> We had a student who came here from [a very highly-regarded institution on the West Coast]. . . . He was talented enough to survive [his bachelor's],

*but he didn't put out his maximum until he came to us. He is very smart, but wasn't very motivated, and [faculty at his undergraduate institution] didn't do anything about that. He said he played basketball all the time . . . he barely got out of there! So, if he could do that, we knew he must have potential. He did very well here—we [his mentors] built up his confidence. I mean, he lost his confidence [at his undergraduate institution], and then he came here and got it back, and is now a Ph.D. student [at another well-regarded institution].*

Mentoring also positively affected students in another way: the skills and competencies that students developed under the guidance of experienced professionals contributed—directly and indirectly—to the advancement of their professional careers. An alumnus of Phelps' theater program spoke unambiguously of the impact that his mentor had on his professional success: "I think everything that has happened to me [in my career has] happened because I went to [Phelps]. That I won a Tony Award happened because I went to [Phelps]. . . . I started that play at [Phelps] under the direction of [his mentor] . . . and that launched the play, and [he helped me to] eventually bring it to Broadway."

An alumnus of Land-Grant's program related a similar story about how his mentor had helped him to "discover" what his "capabilities were [as an archaeologist]." This discovery, coupled with his mentor's professional contacts, had led him down a very different, and much more fulfilling, career track. As he explained: "Let me put it to you this way. Three years ago I was working for a backpacking store in Chapel Hill, North Carolina. Today, I'm working as a research scientist at a national laboratory. . . . I'm much more self-confident and I have a lot more self-esteem [now]. . . . I have this fabulous feeling that there is so much more out there to learn. It's very questing."

Many faculty and administrators also provided similar accounts. This anecdote from an Appleby State professor aptly communicated the positive, tangible effects that mentoring had on students' professional and career development:

*All of the faculty here probably can give you several instances where people have made it better for themselves. My favorite example is a husband and wife team who were medical technicians at [a local hospital], and they weren't very happy there. They kept their med tech jobs and they both came down here and went through this master's program. And they both happened to work for me. Both were very talented.*

*After they finished, the husband went on to get his Ph.D. and then did post-doctoral study. Now he's an assistant professor in microbiology. At one point we were talking when he was in his Ph.D. program—and he's not a competitive person at all—and he said to me, "Yeah, I want your job." Now he's got it. And his wife went to work in industry [for a while] and now works for him [as a research scientist in his university laboratory]. Here's an example where we were the first stepping-stone for people who were stuck in a hole and then they made a better life for themselves. . . .*

*As I understand our role here, I think, by and large, we do master's education right . . . and I think that role is to help people see their own potential as scientists . . . and to channel those talents. Our greatest pride is in facilitating people to make better lives for themselves.*

## Cooperative Peer Learning

Cooperative peer learning was yet another attribute of high-quality programs that we culled from our interview material. In a relatively large number of programs we visited, students actively contributed to and supported one anothers' learning through various in- and out-of-class group activities. These collaborative and social interactions consistently enhanced the quality of students' learning experiences and positively affected their growth and development.

## Actions

Faculty and administrators laid a foundation for peer learning in their programs in two ways. First, they used in- and out-of-class group activities to promote cooperative learning among students. Second, faculty themselves engaged in collaborative research and team-teaching activities, thus modeling peer learning for students and emphasizing its importance in their programs and professions.

In a number of programs we studied, faculty and administrators believed that students needed to learn how to work effectively with one another as team players. Accordingly, they required students to participate in various cooperative learning activities—including study groups, research teams, group projects, collaborative artistic performances, and group presentations.

The electrical engineering program at Prestige State serves as a model case where faculty and administrators actively promoted cooperative peer learning. As we learned from many interviewees, collaborative "teamwork" ran like a golden thread throughout this program. Faculty not only collaborated with one another on various research projects, but they also insisted that students learn how to interact effectively with one another as members of various research and study teams. The department chair particularly stressed this latter point, telling us that he let incoming students know that "go[ing] off alone and study[ing]in the library" was not what this engineering program was "all about." To the contrary, he told students "You're going to learn more than half of what you learn while you're here from your fellow students. It won't be from your classes or from your professors. . . . You have to work together in teams, and you're going to have to learn from each other." Toward this end, he stated that many faculty required students to complete group projects in their classes and encouraged students to become involved in one of the program's forty-plus collaborative research teams.

Prestige State faculty and administrators were not alone in promoting cooperative peer learning in their programs. During our site visit to Pierpont University, for example, several faculty members said that they required students to form out-of-class study groups to address complex business problems as members of corporate teams. These study groups, one professor explained, were "pivotal to students' experiences here [because] we try and emphasize a culture of shared learning and cooperation, rather than competition, among our students. Working in study groups on case studies helps to nurture teamwork skills in our students." A Phelps faculty member said that he and his colleagues required students to participate in collaborative theater productions for much the same reason. As he put it: "Theater is not a one-person activity. It's a group effort. People have to learn how to get along with one another to put on a successful production."

Faculty and administrators across our sample told us that they fostered cooperative peer learning in a second way: they personally engaged in cooperative research, teaching, and service activities and, in so doing, modeled for students how professionals learned from one another as colleagues.

Illustrating this point, a Prestige State engineering professor told us that the team-oriented approach to science that he and his colleagues practiced sent a clear message to students that "prima donnas" were not tolerated in their department. As he explained:

> Usually in top departments you have one god here and another god there, and the gods don't talk to each other. Everybody has this rose garden of their own and nobody intrudes. . . . [But] in this department, we're willing to share the research glory here. I think the era of "single hero change the world" has gone—at least as far as engineering is concerned. The products are very complex today and take a lot of people with different expertise working together. . . . Collaboration is a fact in our department.

Invoking the adage that "actions speak louder than words," a Helena State administrator said that faculty members' "cooperative" and "anti-territorial" interactions taught students much about the importance of collaboration in the school's theater program. Along the same lines, the chair of Southwest State's applied anthropology program told us that since he and his faculty colleagues "actively did things" together and "learned from one another," they served "as role models for our students [in] that way."

## Consequences for Learning Experiences

Faculty and administrators who promoted cooperative peer learning consistently enhanced the quality of students' learning experiences. Such efforts helped ensure that students had opportunities to participate in group activities in which they could contribute to and support one anothers' learning in ways that enriched their understandings of knowledge and professional practice.

Many students and alumni enthusiastically shared their cooperative learning experiences with us. A St. Joan's business student described the peer learning that occurred in one of her courses:

> I had a person in one of my classes who was working at a major record company, and the company had some advertising problems and were looking to go into some new areas. And one of the top executives at the company suggested that they put their label on a totally different kind of music than the label had been associated with previously. So this classmate of mine brought up this issue in class one day and asked us what we thought. All the students said, "Why are you going to do that? You have a solid issue with your label already. You're going to destroy your company's issue if you diversify like that." And then a few more students added, "Gosh, haven't you been in the class where we discussed strategic positioning in marketing?" Then he said, "Oh yeah, you're right." So we helped him and now he's trying to convince the top management that instead of ruining the image, they should create a new label.

An Appleby State alumnus was equally enthusiastic about the team research projects he had completed during his master's program. He eagerly described one of them for us:

> We approached [this particular] research project like we were out in the real world doing that research. All five or six of us worked on the project to achieve results. This was kind of nice—we bounced things back and forth and did a lot of group interaction. . . . We experienced successes and failures together. . . . We'd do whatever we could to insure the good of the group [and the success of the project].

We came to understand that, for the most part, a spirit of cooperative support enriched students' interactions in peer learning activities. Many students and alumni said that as they muddled through group assignments, puzzled through difficult problems in the laboratory, or worked together to mount successful theater productions, they became much more appreciative of the ways in which they could learn from their peers. This appreciation led many students to interact with one another less as competitive rivals and more as cooperative partners in a shared learning experience. A alumna of St. Joan's business program, for instance, told us that she and her fellow students "worked very closely with one another": "We weren't trying to compete with one another because we all really just wanted to see each other succeed." Two Southwest State students elaborated on the collegial spirit that animated peer interactions in their microbiology program:

> [Student 1]: I learn a great deal from the other students. No one is afraid to talk about their research, and nobody's going to stab me in the back if they find out what I'm doing.

> [Student 2]: Yeah, it's really different than when I was at [another university]. There students didn't enter each other's labs—everyone wanted to keep their work top-secret, and there was a lot of sabotage—ugly things like unplugging people's refrigerators, even in the cancer center. I didn't like that at all. At [Southwest State], the doors to the labs are always open. I like that.

Indeed, many faculty and administrators emphasized that students learned a great deal from and actively supported one another in their programs. A microbiology professor at Appleby State described their students as "quite close": "There is a cooperative spirit here," he observed. "Students help each other out. The equipment is limited, and so they borrow from each other . . . but they all share and they all do that very well. If there is a job out there, they share that information. They are all concerned that everyone get a fair shake." In much the same spirit, an administrator in Phelps' environmental studies program underscored the caring support that students provided to one another: "Students work very hard around here, but they are great human beings. They are well-rounded, and care for one another. It's competitive, in a sense, but not one-on-one, against each other. I see students get together and study for exams [and work on group projects], but there's no competition that's hard to take—none of this vying for place."

Throughout our study, students and alumni told us that they benefited in various ways from one anothers' teaching and learning. Referring to the study group of which he was a part, a Pierpont business student commented, "I've found that ninety percent of the exchange in the program is with other students. The raw brainpower is great. . . . These people bring so many perspectives and ways of thinking. The work is so much better. It's an excellent way to learn." An alumnus of Major State's engineering program expressed his appreciation for his group learning experiences in this way:

*Certainly a rewarding and significant aspect of the program for me was working with other students in the lab. . . . A lot of times we would be working together on a project in the lab and we'd find ourselves saying, "Gee, this is neat stuff" and there are "neat ideas here." We were just getting absorbed in the ideas. And . . . there was the case of finding—in our research—interesting connections to other fields and we formed a solution. . . . It was also the case that when I had a particular problem with my research, I could catch somebody else and say, "Hey, this is what's going on right now" and just have a sounding board, and I played that role for somebody else a few times. That was valuable.*

These positive accounts notwithstanding, some interviewees in our study sharply criticized the lack of peer learning in their programs. A second-year business student at Peterson University, for instance, made this pointed remark about the program: "A big part of your M.B.A. program should be interacting with your fellow students and the groups you work with as well as the time you devote to your studies. At [Peterson], you never learn how to work as a team. Instead, you really are forced to do things independently here." A Major State employer we interviewed offered a similarly damning comment about the school's computer science program: "You can graduate from [Major State] never having worked on a project with another person. This is scary, from our hiring perspective. . . . Knowing how people work together, [how to] apportion work, how to negotiate, [how to] be able to develop specifications that are not exclusively in your own head—all of those sorts of things turn out to be very important to us because that's our life here." Finally, an employer of United Tech's graduates criticized the school's engineering program for underemphasizing people skills, highlighting the importance of such skills:

*Dealing with conflict, learning how to recognize different people's needs and modes of operation, [and] how they communicate—learning those aspects of the profession are so important. Even in an engineering-only job, you still deal enough with people in R&D [research and development] that you need these skills. . . . There used to be much more reliance [in engineering] on the project manager to carry that load and the team worked around that person. That's no longer the case . . . it's much more the team carries the load, the team makes decisions. As such, teamwork skills and team effectiveness are a much greater part of [what we do in engineering].*

Anchored in this evidence, then, we identified cooperative peer learning as an important feature of high-quality programs. As many students, alumni, faculty, administrators, and employers told us, students had far richer master's experiences when they actively contributed to and supported one anothers' learning.

## *Effects on Students*

Cooperative peer learning positively affected students' growth and development in two important respects. First, cooperative learning experiences considerably improved students' interpersonal and teamwork skills. Second, since learning experiences of this sort challenged students to teach one another, they did much to strengthen and solidify students' confidence in their professional abilities.

Many interviewees stressed that the ongoing interactions students had with one another improved their interpersonal and teamwork skills. A Peterson nursing alumna, for example, explained how the collaborative projects she completed in the program greatly strengthened her group process skills:

> *You know, it's so much easier to pick a topic, go out and review the literature, and formulate an individual opinion. But it's a lot harder to collaborate with three or four people and to do it that way. And there was a lot of that here. I really think we learned so much from that. . . . You learned how to put up with a lot of people who didn't work as hard as others [as well as] people who presented information in different ways. And you learned how to tell a peer that they weren't pulling their weight--it's very hard to say something like that to somebody. These confrontation skills are very worthwhile down the road.*

An alumnus of City-State's applied anthropology program articulated a similar viewpoint. As he put it, his various team-related course projects had "taught him" how to "listen to people, hear the other person's point of view, and negotiate tensions [among people in a group]."

We spoke with many employers who echoed these student and alumni accounts. An employer of Walton State's environmental studies graduates, for instance, credited the program's emphasis on cooperative peer learning with cultivating students' teamwork skills. Elaborating on this point, she told us:

> *I feel that the program really does prepare the students very well for being able to come into an office-type environment where so much of what at least I do—and the jobs in the departments that I have been involved in do—is teamwork. In this organization we do a lot of teamwork across departments, and we do a lot of work with citizens. The whole nature of public sector decision making in the environmental arena means that you have to have an understanding of different values and perspectives, and you need to be able to work with people of different disciplines and technical expertise and understand them. . . . And this program does prepare people to do that. People come out of there, and they know how to sit down*

*in meetings and work with other people. They understand networking with people of different disciplines and how to work with others on projects.*

An employer of Pierpont's business graduates offered a similar assessment when speaking of the program's study groups and their impact on students: "That's one of the things that really sets their graduates apart from others. They have strong interpersonal and, especially, teamwork skills."

We also learned that as students shared their knowledge with one another in research teams, study groups, or professional ensembles, they became more confident in their professional abilities. A student in Major State's engineering program described how his research team experience boosted his self-confidence:

*The dealing . . . the back and forth with my advisor about my particular problem, thinking about it with my fellow students and stuff like that— just the continued interaction [was really valuable]. I would step back and say, "Hey, I'm doing this right. I'm raising interesting issues and I can see what their [his peers' and advisor's] concerns are." [It was] just this whole process of being on the edge and feeling like, "Hey, I can play this game."*

A Major State microbiology student similarly explained how her involvement in various peer learning activities had done much to cement her professional identity as a microbiologist. In her words:

*It's when you can help someone solve a problem that you think, "I'm not so dumb after all, I can think of that, I helped somebody." Doing that really makes you feel like you're a microbiologist. It's like you've learned all of this stuff, but deep down you don't know how much you know until somebody quizzes you, or tests you, or just asks you a question in the lab. And when somebody does that and you can actually answer them, and talk like a microbiologist, you think school really helped. I mean, you begin to believe you are a microbiologist!*

## Out-of-Class Activities

Taking a cue from a Southern State nursing professor—who described the curriculum as "everything that happens to students . . . not just the courses and the content . . . [but] the whole context of their educational experience"— we identified out-of-class activities as an important attribute of high-quality programs. In broad strokes, we learned that when faculty, administrators, and students actively participated in out-of-class activities, ranging from brown bag lunches and seminars to end-of-semester parties and picnics, the informal learning that took place greatly enriched students' overall learning experiences.

## Actions

Faculty, administrators, and students built a foundation for out-of-class learning in their programs in two ways. First, they developed and sponsored formal and informal out-of-class activities. Second, faculty and administrators supported—financially and otherwise—these activities as integral parts of their programs.

Faculty, administrators, and students across our sample took an active role in developing and sponsoring out-of-class activities that provided participants with opportunities to learn from one another in relaxed, informal settings. These activities included departmental brown-bag seminars, colloquia, and speaker series; journal clubs; laboratory and research team meetings; student clubs; internet user networks; faculty–student social hours; and end-of-semester social events.

In paging through a departmental newsletter at Prestige State, for instance, we discovered that faculty and administrators sponsored more than thirty-five weekly research seminars for engineering students. Business and industry representatives from around the world, as well as faculty members from other universities, were among the seminars' speakers. In Major State's sociology program, several interviewees told us that faculty hosted up to a dozen brown bag luncheon seminars each week in which visiting faculty, doctoral students, and departmental faculty discussed current research and mutual topics of interest. On a much smaller scale, administrators in Middle State's microbiology program coordinated a weekly "soup day" where faculty and students, in the words of the chair, "swapped ideas around."

Students often joined faculty and administrators in developing out-of-class activities for their programs. In Phelps' environmental studies program, for instance, students sponsored various extracurricular activities, including weekly forums on selected environmental topics, canoeing and backpacking trips, environmental education outreach seminars, and weekly T.G.I.F. ("Thank God I'm A Forester") parties. At Parks-Beecher University, business students oversaw the entrepreneur's, marketing, and toastmaster's international student clubs, and worked with administrators to plan conferences and seminars of mutual professional interest. Similarly, the M.B.A. student association at St. Joan's College created numerous opportunities for faculty, student, and employer interaction through various networking seminars, picnics, ski trips, and parties.

Grounded in their shared belief that meaningful learning often occurs outside of formal classroom contexts, many faculty and administrators indicated that they financially supported out-of-class activities as an integral part of their programs. To illustrate, the chair of Prestige State's electrical engineering program told us that he "made a point" of allocating funds for graduate student organizations and faculty–student social events as part of the department's annual budget. Administrators at Pierpont University likewise said that they generously supported corporate seminars and receptions, new student orientation meetings, and sundry faculty–student social gatherings in their M.B.A. program. Funding such events, they explained, was easily justified: Not only did they foster a "camaraderie" among program participants, but they also provided faculty, students, and employers with invaluable opportunities to learn from one another in settings that strongly emphasized "corporate culture."

Faculty and administrators also supported out-of-class program activities in other, less tangible ways. Some, for instance, regularly attended departmental brown bag luncheons, colloquia, and social events. Others dedicated time to supervising journal clubs or to interacting with students over lunch or coffee. In all cases, these actions sent a clear signal to all participants that faculty and administrators considered out-of-class learning experiences an important part of their programs.

## Consequences for Learning Experiences

In many programs we studied, faculty, administrative, and student engagement in out-of-class activities significantly enhanced the quality of students' learning experiences. In these programs, students—and occasionally faculty—participated in informal, out-of-class gatherings in which they explored and discussed topics of mutual interest that enriched one anothers' learning.

On countless occasions, students and alumni told us about their out-of-class experiences. Whether it was attending a brown bag luncheon, exchanging ideas over an internet users network, or debating the fine points of a research article in a journal club, these interviewees made it clear that they had woven out-of-class activities fully into the fabric of their learning experiences. We spoke with many business students at Parks-Beecher University, for instance, who indicated that they were so enmeshed in student life that they often had difficulty deciding "what to do at noon." In Phelps' theater program, students so enjoyed the experimental opportunities that their student-run cabaret offered that many spent the bulk of their late evening hours there. And, in Land-Grant's archaeology program, many students mentioned that they "swapped field stories" and "batted around ideas" with one another and faculty every Friday afternoon at a local pub.

We were surprised—sometimes even astonished—by how positively students and alumni regarded their out-of-class learning experiences. When we probed into why they valued these experiences, students and alumni offered two responses. First, many indicated that out-of-class activities helped them to stay in touch with current developments in their fields. Second, many others emphasized that the relaxed and informal nature of these activities provided rich opportunities to learn from others in ways that promoted free-flowing, reflective inquiry.

Many students and alumni told us that they greatly appreciated learning about new developments in their fields at extracurricular seminars and colloquia. A student in Major State's sociology program, for example, said that he benefited from the department's brown-bag seminars in this way:

> *It's a really valuable part about being [in this department] because you really see what people [faculty and doctoral students] are doing in their research. And if you don't know what's wrong with what you're doing you're going to hear it in there. . . . In the 'class analysis' specialization, they bring in guest lecturers [from universities across the United States]. They stay on campus for three weeks, and they give two brown-bag seminars a week. They're great . . . you really learn about cutting-edge stuff.*

In a similar fashion, an alumnus of Prestige State's engineering program valued the departmental seminars he attended as a master's student because, as he stated, "they gave you kind of a feel for industry": "A lot of industry people visited the campus frequently. And even though we were in the master's program, we knew what was happening outside."

Besides keeping students abreast of new developments in their fields, we learned that students and alumni also appreciated the opportunities that out-of-class activities provided for informal, free-spirited discussion and inquiry. Underscoring the valuable interactions she had with others in the program's "group lab meetings," a Major State microbiology student illustrated this point:

> *We have [these] meetings where we'll just get together and talk about what's going on in the lab at the current time. They're really casual and informal but some of the students and faculty who are in the other labs will get up and say, "I think you're doing that wrong; maybe you should try this or that." I know my department and my lab, in particular, really tries to get involved with other laboratories because they think that interaction is very important. I think the more interactions you have in journal clubs and in lab meetings, the better off you are. You learn so much from other students and faculty [in those meetings].*

Turning to a different example, a Phelps environmental studies graduate fondly recalled the reflective dialogue and inquiry that took place among students in the program's weekly T.G.I.F. ("Thank God I'm a Forester") parties:

> I remember sitting at one of our student-organized social events and lis-
> tening to my peers. The first-year students were so black and white—they
> thought that all foresters did was rape and pillage the land—and they were
> heavy into the conservation movement. Then I would listen to how the
> second-year students talked to them. They provided a more broadened view
> on things—they were more informed and less orthodox in their approaches.
> They spoke with a more holistic perspective on things. And I think that's
> where a lot of the real learning happened for us—in those informal discus-
> sions we had with each other.

Conversely, in some programs students did not participate actively in out-of-class activities. This lack of student involvement contributed to the individualistic student cultures rampant in most of these programs—cultures, we learned, that valued isolated or competitive student learning more strongly than cooperative peer learning. At Peterson University, for example, several interviewees criticized M.B.A. students for seldom participating in out-of-class program activities. One administrator stated, "These students take the subway to school, they attend classes, and then they go home. That's it." A student in the program made this pointed remark about the individualistic orientation of his peers: "Nobody wants to give of their time. I mean, we end up talking before class and then after class, and then, after that, everyone goes their own way."

A similar situation existed in the theater program at Trafalgar College. Many students there told us that they were so busy "doing their own thing" that they rarely interacted with their peers outside of class or participated in extracurricular activities. As a result, students who were eager to learn from their peers often were left wanting. As one student told us: "You know, I would meet people in class and start talking with them, and then they'd say that they had to run off to a job off campus or to work on their own show. . . . My sense is that students really didn't want to see much of each other in this program."

In light of these accounts, we came to understand that out-of-class activities are an important attribute of high-quality programs. Again and again, interviewees stressed that when students participated in various out-of-class activities, they made valuable contributions to one anothers' learning experiences.

## Effects on Students

Out-of-class learning experiences had two favorable effects on students' growth and development. First, students who actively participated in various out-of-class activities strengthened their oral communication and interpersonal skills. Second, the interactive learning that occurred in these activities raised students' awareness of and appreciation for collaborative approaches to inquiry, problem-solving, and leadership in their fields.

Many students and alumni emphasized that the ongoing interactions they had with others in various out-of-class activities improved their oral communication and interpersonal skills. A Major State microbiology student said, for example, that her involvement in a weekly journal club had "forced" her to "become a good speaker." As she told us:

> *You present at least once or twice and we interact. And the faculty usually asks you billions of questions. . . . And it builds up your confidence and it gets you interacting and acting at a research level. . . . It gets you up there presenting research, explaining things when someone doesn't understand a particular table or figure. And there are a lot of people in science that do not have good speaking skills. And being a good speaker in science is really one of the most crucial parts [of being a scientist]. I mean, you can be one of the best researchers in the world and go up and give a talk and look like a fool if your ideas don't come across. So, speaking skills are very, very important. Presenting in the journal club has really helped me with that.*

Many other students and alumni provided similar appraisals, ranging from that of a Parks-Beecher business student who said that his participation in the toastmaster's international club had made him a "more confident speaker," to a St. Joan's business student who remarked that her "communication" and "people skills" had improved considerably throughout her tenure as president of the M.B.A. student organization.

Interviewees informed us that out-of-class activities enriched students' growth and development in a second way: as students worked with and learned from one another and faculty in these activities, many noted that students developed a greater appreciation for the value of collaboration. This appreciation, particularly when coupled with students' improved social skills, often had a transforming effect on their professional practice. An alumna of Longmont's English program, for instance, said that the collaborative character of her interactions with others "during dinner," "in the dorms," and "out on the grass" helped her to grasp the importance of "speaking an idea as a first step in writing." She explained that this insight changed how she taught writing to high school students. Rather than requiring students to "go off on their own" and write, she now uses more interactive approaches that encourage students to explore their own and others' ideas as part of the writing process.

In much the same way, an alumna of Southern State's nursing program said that the collaborative experiences she had with other students over lunch, after class, and in departmental colloquia convinced her that "collegial interactions" produced a "better" and "more professional" nursing practice. "Because of those experiences," she remarked, "I now use a more collaborative approach at work." Finally, a Helena State alumna told us that the collaborative out-of-class experiences she had while "working on sets," "hanging lights," and "rehearsing lines" carried over into her professional practice as a drama teacher: she now invites students to work with her on all facets of school-sponsored theater productions.

# 7

# Connected Program Requirements

Connected program requirements is the fourth cluster of attributes in our engagement theory of program quality. In many programs we studied, faculty and administrators designed program requirements that challenged students to develop an integrated understanding of their professions. Faculty provided students with opportunities to bridge the worlds of theory and practice—the classroom and the workplace—through three sequential learning experiences. First, they required students to develop a solid grasp of the fundamental theories, practices, and skills of their fields through planned breadth and depth course work. With this foundational knowledge in place, faculty challenged students to apply and test their course-related understandings in a professional residency (such as a teaching or research assistantship, internship, or clinical placement). Finally, faculty required students to complete a tangible project—such as a thesis, project report, or creative performance—in which they were expected to demonstrate to themselves and others their abilities to make meaningful contributions to their professions.

As in the previous chapters, our treatment of each of these attributes—planned breadth and depth course work, a professional residency, and a tangible product—is separated into three parts. We begin by explaining how faculty and program administrators enacted the attribute in their programs, and then describe how these actions enriched the quality of students' learning experiences. Last, we consider the ways in which these learning experiences affected students' growth and development.

## *Planned Breadth and Depth Course Work*

Our analysis of interview material and program documents led us to identify planned breadth and depth course work as an important feature of high-quality programs. In many programs across our sample, faculty and administrators required students to complete a blend of core and specialized course work. The generalized and specialized knowledge that students acquired in these courses consistently enriched the quality of students' learning experiences.

### *Actions*

Faculty and administrators designed planned breadth and depth course work requirements via a two-step process. As a beginning point, they collectively determined the fundamental knowledge, skills, and practices they expected of all program graduates. In turn, faculty and administrators developed core and specialized course work requirements that dovetailed with these expectations.

In many programs we studied, faculty and administrators met periodically to determine the knowledge and skills they most wanted students to learn, often framing their decision making within the context of their program's direction and goals. The business program at Pierpont University provides an interesting case in point. During our visit there, we learned that faculty had recently examined their curriculum in light of stated program goals. This examination process, one professor told us, had prompted faculty to discuss and eventually agree on the fundamental knowledge they believed all students should know, including "the essential body of conceptual knowledge and decision tools from economics, behavioral science, and quantitative analysis on which business is based." Another professor mentioned that the process had also challenged faculty to "make hard choices" regarding specialized courses, leading them to offer only those courses that complemented and built upon "the fundamental base of generalized business knowledge" that students learned in the core.

Once faculty and administrators determined the knowledge and skills they expected students to learn, they turned to the task of designing curricula to convey this knowledge to students. More often than not, faculty and administrators planned curricula around core and specialized courses that provided students with both a breadth and depth of knowledge in their fields. Core, or foundational, course work generally included advanced theoretical, methodological, and professional knowledge and practices. Specialized course work addressed advanced disciplinary or interdisciplinary content in one or more subfields.

The environmental studies program at Major State is a model case in which faculty and administrators adopted a "planned breadth and depth" curricular design. As stated in the program's brochure, students were required to complete a core curriculum consisting of thirty "breadth credits in management and planning" distributed into the following categories: natural science and technology, water resources institutions and public decision-making processes, analytical and design tools in water resources, and synthesis and integration. In addition, students were expected to complete fifteen "depth" credits in an area specialty (such as aquatic biology, forestry, land use management, or urban and regional planning). As one administrator told us, this combination of generalized and specialized course work was a planned feature of the program:

> *One of the kinds of things we are trying to accomplish . . . is the [bridging of the] breadth–depth dichotomy. What you do is attempt to give people sufficient breadth about connecting together unlike things, and at the same time give them sufficient depth in an area or a couple of areas that they appreciate all about what is in a discipline and about what their limitations are. The more you know about how a particular field works—whether it's sanitary engineering, water chemistry, or agricultural economics—the smarter you are, yet the more you realize your own limitations.*

A similar curricular strategy was used in Peterson University's business program. There, faculty required students to take a core of "business foundation" and "advanced skills" courses as well as twenty-one credits of specialized course work in a subfield of business (such as marketing, accounting, and finance). This "breadth and depth" strategy, an administrator explained, not only provided students with a "solid grounding" in "general business," but it also went a step further, making each student, in his words, "somewhat of an expert in a particular area."

## Consequences for Learning Experiences

We came to understand that the efforts faculty and administrators put into designing breadth and depth course work greatly improved the quality of students' learning experiences. In many programs we studied, students completed a combination of core and specialized course work in which they learned both generalized and specialized knowledge in their respective fields.

Students and alumni often spoke at length about their core course work experiences. In particular, many indicated that while they initially resented having to take these courses, they eventually came to appreciate the generalized knowledge they acquired in them. Two Major State education students amplified on this point:

*[Student 1]: I have to say that when I started I didn't think that the educa-*
*tion credits would be that useful, but they have been.*

*[Student 2]: Yeah, for me, it has been the theory [in these courses] that has*
*been so practical. I would not be nearly as satisfied academically or profes-*
*sionally [without them]. . . . So, for me, the learning theory and the philo-*
*sophical and social-type [education] courses were very practical. . . . I know*
*exactly what I would do if I were going into an eighth grade mathematics*
*classroom—how I would structure it and so forth—but not because the*
*course showed me step one or step two. But because I can look at the theo-*
*retical things that I've done, and I can look at the research in cognition,*
*and say "I will teach this way."*

*[Student 1]: I agree with that. We describe them [the required education*
*courses] as theory courses, but that doesn't mean that they're not terribly*
*practical.*

A United Tech engineering student similarly told us that although he
originally pursued the master's to learn "really technical" knowledge in
one specialty area, he ended up relishing the required "breadth" credits in
his program. As he explained:

*If an engineer's education was just very focused and not into providing a*
*broad-based education, it wouldn't be providing everything that you need*
*[to be a productive engineer]. A fixed curriculum forces you into a re-*
*quired broad range of courses. . . . Without these courses, there are a lot of*
*parts of the discipline that you wouldn't take the time to learn—you'd just*
*work in those areas that you were particularly interested in or involved*
*with. And to become really well-rounded you need to take a full course of*
*study. Graduate education requires you to take courses you wouldn't oth-*
*erwise take, but end up being glad that you took.*

For the most part, students and alumni were equally positive about the
specialized course work they completed in their programs. A Parks-Beecher
business alumnus, for example, told us that his three advanced finance
courses taught him the "basics of becoming a financial engineer." An education student at Major State said that the four advanced genetics courses she
completed gave her "enough depth" to write a high school curriculum on
the subject. And a Peterson nursing alumna credited the program's specialty courses with giving her "expert knowledge" on mental health nursing concepts and practices.

Many interviewees stressed that a judicious blend of required core and
specialized course work benefited students by providing them with both
"broad" and "deep" understandings of major issues in their fields. As a

Peterson business alumnus put it, his required courses equipped him with both the "technical skills" and the "expertise to perform" in the workplace: "[They] gave me the basics [of the field] and the specialized knowledge." An alumnus of Land-Grant's applied anthropology program similarly noted that besides "gaining in-depth knowledge" in cultural resources management, his core courses had helped him to "see redundancies of information across fields. . . . It's this sharing of ideas and the thinking about them that's so valuable," he explained. "It provides the student with a recognition that there's a whole range of information out there that we can discover and learn from each other. It's this breadth—and the recognition of the broader view—that's really a strength of this program."

Many employers offered comparable perspectives. At Prestige State, for instance, an employer praised the program's engineering graduates for having, in his words, "sound fundamentals": "They have an understanding of the field and they can use the basics to solve problems. They have state-of-the-art skills." With like enthusiasm, an employer associated with Middle State's microbiology program paid this compliment to their alumni: "[Middle State's] graduates have good technical skills, superb knowledge background, are very well-read, and come with a highly-professional decorum. They are considered scientists in our company."

By contrast, interviewees in some programs indicated that their curricula lacked either sufficient breadth or depth. Many emphasized how this imbalance undercut the quality of students' learning experiences. Two Walton State environmental studies students, for example, panned the shallow, intellectual "dilettantism" of their required courses. As they explained:

*[Student 1]: It [the core course work] was too much like a conventional graduate program. For example, the books: We read hundreds of books and articles. But the time in which we went into depth, into the deeper vision—how to incorporate the vision into action plans—was never a part of it. We could never take the ideas [to] their next logical step: how to incorporate the ideas into some meaningful pursuit.*

*[Student 2]: The program covered a lot of issues in the core [classes]. But we didn't get a lot of depth on any particular issue.*

Referring to an imbalance in the opposite direction, a graduate of Major State engineering program criticized the highly specialized nature of his required course work:

*To some extent I feel like there are significant aspects of electrical engineering that I never touched. I had very little contact or experience with people in other areas of electrical engineering and certainly there are lots of other*

*areas you can get into—communication systems, processing, power engi-
neering, solid state devices, and things of that sort. So one aspect of the
program that I experienced was that it was [overly specialized]. I didn't
come out of that program with a lot of breadth in electrical engineering.*

Several faculty and employers confirmed a lack of symmetry between
breadth and depth in their programs, often saying that they erred on the
side of becoming too specialized. Several faculty and employers in Barrett
State's nursing program, for instance, described the curriculum as "hyper-
specialized" and "Balkanized." A Western State administrator said much
the same, noting that the pronounced tendencies for specialization among
nursing faculty had fragmented the school's program. In her experience,
efforts to "shift [the curriculum] toward broader courses" normally met
with "strong faculty resistance."

In light of these positive and negative accounts, we came to appreciate
that planned breadth and depth course work is an important feature of high-
quality programs. Time and again, many stakeholders in our study told us
that a well-designed curriculum of core and specialized course work helped
students to learn both generalized and specialized knowledge in their respective fields.

## Effects on Students

Planned breadth and depth course work positively affected students' growth
and development in two respects. First, and most obvious, the advanced
knowledge, skills, and practices students learned in these courses strengthened their professional competency. Second, they helped students to develop more holistic perspectives on their fields that, in turn, improved their
workplace effectiveness.

Many students and alumni talked about how the knowledge and skills
they learned in required courses enhanced their professional abilities. A
United Tech engineering graduate, for instance, told us that as he "completed each and every course" in his program, he became "much more theo-
retically-based in a particular area": "There was this progression of competency [and] feeling of accomplishment." Two business students at Peterson
University reached similar conclusions. One credited his master's courses
with transforming him into a "different kind" of "businessperson": "I know
my quantitative, data analysis, and business writing skills are much stronger." The other student concurred. "Yeah, I feel like I have the knowledge
now. I feel like I can really run spreadsheets, do cost-benefit analyses, and
write effective marketing strategies. This [the required course work] has
really given me the confidence to go out there and be a little more demanding about what I want. . . . I really feel like I can be very effective in the
business world right now."

Many employers also stressed that their master's-educated employees were highly-competent professionals, owing in no small measure to their course work experiences. An employer of Prestige State's engineering graduates, for example, said that the generalized and specialized knowledge students acquired in the program equipped them with the "tools to be effective" for his company. From a somewhat different angle, a United Tech employer referred to a survey he had conducted to show how this course work-only engineering program had improved his employees' on-the-job performance:

> *I couldn't believe the results [of the survey]. Most of these master's-trained engineers told me that they were more effective—usually by an average of 33 percent more than before the courses. I was hoping they would say maybe 5 percent more effective—but 33 percent more effective! I then interviewed their project supervisors and they all corroborated that [these master's-educated engineers] were more effective. . . . What really matters in the workplace is whether or not you can perform. Our [United Tech] grads perform. I'm really overjoyed with [United Tech's] program.*

Planned breadth and depth course work had another, albeit closely linked, effect on students: it helped students to develop a holistic perspective that enhanced their workplace effectiveness. An alumna of Major State's environmental studies program made this point as follows:

> *I went into consulting, and found that my training was extremely valuable. I ended up having to do policy work. I ended up having to go out and be able to interpret engineering and operations, and then go back and tell my client what risks were involved. . . . I found that I adapted very quickly, whereas the geologist never figured out what was going on with the engineering, and the engineers couldn't look past the flanges to understand what was going on from a practical point of view or from a hydrogeologic, or geologic, or land-use type perspective. Seeing past that narrow discipline—having a multidisciplinary background—makes it much easier to do that.*

Similarly, a Major State microbiology graduate said that as she progressed through basic and advanced courses in her program, she began to notice "a big difference" in her "contributions at work": "Things began to fall together for me. I began to integrate things, to see the big picture. I began to hold my head up in the scientific community. . . . I began to see myself as a scientist who could contribute to the field."

Many employers' comments mirrored those of program graduates. One, for instance, told us that while he valued the specialized expertise of Appleby State's alumni, he primarily hired the program's graduates because they had the "big picture": "They know how to think. Their approaches are more broad-based." An employer associated with Walton State's environmental studies program likewise said of program graduates: "They have a broader perspective and understanding of the system. They have a context for their technical work. And that's really valuable if I'm hiring for a job that is more policy-oriented. . . . Their graduates have an understanding of the big picture and how the pieces fit together." Finally, a St. Joan's employer praised the "global perspective" that program graduates brought to her organization. As she elaborated, their "ideas, creativity, and innovation" had helped to "change" her organization in new and exciting ways.

## Professional Residency

We found that a professional residency is also a vital component of high-quality programs. In many cases in our sample, students were required to complete at least one semester of graduate study in an applied setting of their choice. Typically, professional residencies took one of the following forms: university research and teaching assistantships for students pursuing academic careers; internships in government agencies, businesses, and human service organizations for students seeking professional careers in such fields as applied anthropology, business, and environmental science; practica in health care and educational settings for students interested in advanced positions in nursing and education; and residencies in theatrical companies for students aspiring to careers in the dramatic arts. We came to understand that the intensive, hands-on learning that took place in these residential experiences greatly enriched the overall quality of students' learning.

## Actions

Faculty and administrators developed and implemented professional residency requirements in three ways. First, they designed professional residency experiences with students' career interests in mind. Second, faculty and administrators maintained ties with employers, alumni, and community members that, in turn, helped them to identify and secure residency sites and supervisors for students. Third, once students were involved in their residencies, faculty members and site supervisors provided them with regular guidance and feedback.

In many programs, faculty and administrators designed professional residency experiences with students' career interests and goals in mind. Faculty not only met individually with students to explore their objectives, but they also worked with them to tailor residencies that met their specific needs. For instance, during our visit to Peterson University, an administrator told us that nursing faculty required students to "fill out clinical placement forms several months prior" to their culminating, eight-week long clinical practicum. Students were asked to respond to such questions as: "What are your career goals?" "What are your overall objectives for the clinical?" "What type of setting would you prefer for your clinical placement?" Once completed, faculty met individually with students to discuss their responses. These conversations often played a useful role in helping faculty design residency experiences that addressed students' needs. "We've had students tell us," said this administrator, "that they want to go to this hospital or they would like to work with a particular preceptor. We make every attempt to get a contract for these students there."

Along these same lines, the chair of Prestige State's engineering department detailed how he assisted master's students in finding research assistantship placements that complemented their professional interests. As he told us:

> *I encourage students to listen to faculty, doctoral students, and industry experts talk about their work [in the department's more than twenty-five weekly seminars] and to get acquainted with these people. I think this is really important because students begin to see what they're interested in. Once they find something, I tell them to go around to the faculty during their office hours and say, "I'm interested in project work in your area. This is my background and these are my interests. What do you suggest?" At that point, the student is assigned to a "shared laboratory area" and they become a member of a research team.*

Faculty and administrators also worked together to identify and secure residency sites and supervisors for students. Many did so by maintaining close ties with employers, alumni, and community members through advisory councils, alumni associations, and regional professional organizations.

At Southeast State, for instance, faculty maintained open lines of communication with regional employers in government, health care, and industry as well as stayed in contact with program graduates through a local applied anthropology practitioner organization. As a result of their efforts, students could select from more than 250 internship opportunities in the surrounding area. Similarly, in Peterson's nursing program, many faculty and administrators credited their ongoing involvement in nursing practice with helping the program maintain strong ties with local health care professionals. Along with the dean's regular contact with area hospital administrators, nursing professionals and school alumni, the program had more than 135 clinical practicum sites to offer its students.

Once faculty and administrators had secured residency sites, many met with site supervisors and students prior to placement. For the most part, these meetings focused on clarifying student and supervisor expectations for the residency, defining work responsibilities for the student-resident, and determining the frequency and extent of supervisory and faculty evaluation for the duration of the residency.

To illustrate, an administrator in City-State's anthropology program told us that prior to beginning a residency, each student was required to meet with his or her site supervisor and faculty advisor to draft a formal contract describing what the student would do at the site, what learning outcomes were expected, and who would evaluate the student's performance. Similarly, a teacher in Peterson's nursing program said that she met formally with students to discuss expectations and learning objectives prior to taking on new interns, and a Southeast State employer completed "internship contracts" outlining work responsibilities, salary, and evaluation methods before he supervised students from the applied anthropology program.

Faculty and administrators participated in one other activity associated with their program's professional residency requirement: they provided students with regular guidance and feedback on their performance. At Western State University, nursing faculty made at least three site visits during each semester-long practicum to observe and offer feedback to students on their skills development. In Land-Grant's applied anthropology program, an archaeology professor frequently "sat down" with his research assistants to "find out what they were doing" and to offer them guidance. And, like many other faculty we interviewed there, a professor in Southeast State's applied anthropology program said that she conscientiously provided her internship advisees with "regular and constructive feedback."

To be sure, designing and implementing meaningful professional residency requirements made additional time demands on faculty and administrators. When asked why they engaged in this particular learning experience, many cited the instrumental role that real-world, hands-on learning experiences played in helping students make vital connections between theory and practice. A professor in Land-Grant's applied anthropology program vividly conveyed this idea:

> *It may all sound real exciting [in the classroom], but until you get dirt in your teeth and you're sitting out there and its 110 degrees and you haven't found anything for three days and the wind is blowing a cyclonic force across the site and you're eating bad food and not getting a lot of sleep— it's then, and only then, that you can really appreciate what archaeology is. So, we get [our students] into the field [as research assistants or interns] as soon as we can. We know that they're just not going to really know what archaeology is [if they just learn it in the classroom].*

A nursing professor at Peterson University concurred. From her perspective, it was only when students became "actively involved in their clinical experiences [that] they learned to put it all together—to see the connections between theory and practice."

## Consequences for Learning Experiences

The commitments that faculty and administrators made to professional residencies greatly enriched students' learning experiences. As we learned, because residential experiences challenged students to build bridges between what they learned in class with what they encountered in the "real world," they helped them to develop deeper, more integrated understandings of their professions.

Time and again, students and alumni enthusiastically described the intensive, hands-on learning experiences they had in their professional residencies. An alumna of Southwest State's applied anthropology program, for instance, distinctly remembered the "cultural brokering" she did during her internship at a local community foundation, which included coordinating activities "designed to bring about a stronger community spirit" among various racial and ethnic groups in the area. She elaborated on one such "brokering" activity:

> One of the things I did was help to bring back [a city festival] that had [been discontinued] some fifteen years ago. That was a tough one, because everyone thought there would be drunk people everywhere, people sleeping in the streets. My job was to coordinate different groups—city officials, [ethnic group] representatives, corporate officials—to work with our board of directors. After two weeks of talking with people, I knew this thing wasn't going to work. Everyone [still] had a bad image of it [from fifteen years ago]. I told the director [of the foundation], but he said that we had already made the plans so we had to do it. And there I was. It did work out all right. . . . I learned how to be the intermediary between [different racial and ethnic groups], the foundation board, the city merchants, the city staff, and the city council. It was a good dose of real-world applied anthropology.

In much the same spirit, a Peterson nursing alumna fondly recalled the individual and group psychotherapy she conducted during her residency in a mental health counseling unit at a local hospital. The following anecdote vividly relates the real-world, hands-on character of her residency experience:

> I worked with a client who suffered from terrible anxiety attacks. I remember working with this patient [throughout my practicum] and we tried to

*explore the earliest memories that he had. And, sure enough, these anxious feelings went back to a very early age—to an age where those feelings belonged. . . . And [after working with this patient for a while] he was able to look at the feelings he was having now and say to me, "My god, it's exactly the same feeling, but those feelings don't belong here. They're from a long time ago." I remember the expression on his face, and the tears in his eyes, when he was thinking this through [one day in my office]. The following week he told me that he had been on a bus . . . and that he started to perspire and he felt his pulse rate quickening and he told me that he said to himself, "There's nothing to be frightened of here. These feelings are from a long time ago and they don't belong here." And that was the most wonderful thing for me—to actually [work with someone over a period of time and] see them gain some real insight into their problem and use that insight to actually change their present experience. . . . I was so impressed with him that I really felt like, "Wow, maybe I can do this [psychotherapy]." It [her practicum experience] was really positive for me.*

Most students and alumni benefited from their residency experiences in two interconnected ways. To begin with, students and alumni valued applying and testing their classroom-based understandings of knowledge and practice in real-world professional settings. An alumna of Atlantic State's applied anthropology program, for instance, "greatly enjoyed" her internship with the Select Committee on Hunger in the U.S. House of Representatives because it gave her a forum for "testing and revising" her "academic" understandings of policy development and decision making. A Middle State microbiology alumna—who subsequently received her M.D.—was equally positive about her research assistantship. She illustrated the value of this experience by contrasting it to other aspects of her medical education:

*In my master's, we really were doing research. That's where medical school was a let down because we were just going back to the memorization stuff. Memorize it, take the test, forget it. . . . It [the research assistantship] was very hard work and long hours, but I really feel that I learned so much that you don't learn by going through classes and reading books—that that experience couldn't be duplicated in any other way—getting into the lab, having things fail, having to start all over again, discussing your results, having to organize to present at national meetings, coming up with ingenious ways to test hypotheses. All of those things really make you learn better.*

A professional residency benefited students in another way: It provided them with valuable insights into the daily workings of their professions—insights, many interviewees suggested, that seldom could be developed solely through classroom study. A Phelps playwriting student expressed this point well, noting that his involvement in stage productions had made him keenly aware of the importance of "deadlines" in the professional theater. As he told us:

> *[It's important to have the] opportunity to practice interacting with other people in theater—understanding what it means to have a budget, what it means when a director wants a script now because the designers need to know things about the play. So it turns into knowing how to deal with that word "deadline." Nothing happens until the playwright does it. And if you don't do it, people get irate. You understand that part of the process because you have to do it in this program. And it's a* real *[his emphasis] part of the process in this field.*

No less telling, a City-State applied anthropology alumnus said that his practicum had provided him with many useful insights into the nitty-gritty realities of public urban planning. In his words:

> *The practicum, to me, was the strongest piece because you're out there in the real world. You act in a real-world setting. That's critical. . . . You're only getting half the story sitting here [at the university] learning about whatever it is you're learning about, because implementing it in the real world is a whole other ball game. There's not a textbook out there about what to do about the feud between the social workers and the planners. There's not a textbook about why the grants come down the way they do, how to handle competition, how to become competitive in your grant writing. To learn about competition, personalities, state and local government, institutions, who the players are—all those things are things you can only learn when you're in the practicum.*

For their part, many faculty, administrators, and employers also told us that residency experiences helped students to develop more "realistic" understandings of their professions. An Atlantic State applied anthropology professor made this point straightforwardly:

> *It [the internship] gives students that half of the experience that we academics can't give them. There they are, actually working on a day-to-day basis in an institutional setting and experiencing firsthand how different [from academe] the time rhythms are, the language, the discourse, the office politics. So there are lots of awareness shocks that come out of that experience. . . . Being a practitioner is about practical intelligence.*

Approaching this idea from a different vantage point, an employer of Major State's engineering graduates said that research and teaching assistants were his "hires of choice" because "they know what they were taught":

"It means they can apply it [and] they understand the boundaries and they have the intelligence to go beyond the boundary in a systematic way. . . . It's not just academic knowledge . . . it's 'walking knowledge.' "

By contrast, students and alumni from some programs in our sample said that their residency experiences would have been much improved with more faculty guidance and feedback. An alumnus of Peterson's nursing program, for instance, recalled the difficulty that he and many of his peers had with their clinical preceptors:

> They didn't have time [to spend with students]. Resources were just not available. . . . You went to the site. You saw patients, but there was no one there to provide the supervision, the peer review. You didn't have [video]tapes, you didn't have cameras, you didn't have observation rooms. And it's important to have that. . . . I don't feel like I'm enough of a clinical expert [because of this lack of professional feedback and supervision].

An alumna of Chester College's education program raised a similar complaint:

> I really care about [what my practicum] supervisor says—her feedback— because she is watching me all the time develop. So that [feedback] was helpful for me. But the people who come and supervise you from [Chester]— well, they're just going through the motions. . . . It's bullshit [sic]. They [the faculty advisors] just come out and watch you . . . for an hour three times [during the semester]. . . . That's not enough feedback. The faculty supervisors are useless.

Employers were quick to criticize programs that did not require students to complete a professional residency. An employer we interviewed in conjunction with Major State's business program made this pointed remark:

> Their curriculum would be improved by much more practical education, perhaps even some time spent on the firing line in jobs. I don't know if you could work out co-op [cooperative education] type jobs or not [but I think it would be a good idea]. . . . [Many of] the M.B.A.'s [we've employed] are always trying to fit problems into the textbook cases. You know, "We studied it in class and it's got to work like this." . . . And all of a sudden the real world comes crashing in and the M.B.A. says, "Now what am I going to do?" M.B.A. students are missing the nuts and bolts and are too much involved in theory of senior management. . . . They need more practical education.

Another Major State employer leveled a similar complaint against its theater program. Specifically, he faulted faculty for failing to require students to complete "internships in a [regional] theater like mine. That's really a concern of mine, and in the field in general. The students don't come out having the skills that we need and don't even have an understanding of the not-for-profit theater."

Based on a wealth of evidence, a professional residency emerged from our analysis as a key feature of high-quality programs. Throughout the study, many faculty, administrators, students, alumni, and employers helped us to understand that these intensive, hands-on, real-world learning opportunities considerably enriched students' learning experiences by challenging them to develop more complete and integrated understandings of their professions.

## Effects on Students

Completing a professional residency contributed to students' growth and development in three ways. First, students who successfully applied their knowledge and skills in real-world settings matured into more confident and competent professionals. Second, residency experiences further clarified and strengthened students' professional identities. Third, the confidence, knowledge, and professional networks students developed in their professional residencies enhanced their job prospects upon graduation.

Many students and alumni told us that they developed into more confident and competent professionals as they successfully tackled challenging tasks in their internships, practica, or assistantships. An alumna of Phelps' theater program, for instance, said that as she completed several demanding assignments during her internship—including casting, publicity, and budget forecasts—she began to feel "very confident that I could do these things and do them well." A Major State engineering student—who held a research assistantship—described the change in self-confidence he was experiencing:

> When I finished my undergraduate program, I didn't really feel qualified to do anything; I felt I was qualified to learn how to do something. But instead of learning how to do it in the workplace, I'm learning how to do it in the master's program [through my assistantship]. . . . I feel like I've gotten a much better handle on what I can do now as an engineer [as a result of the research experience].

Many students and alumni also indicated that their residency experiences further sharpened their professional identities. An alumna of Southern State's nursing program made this point powerfully:

> [When I was a staff nurse] you just kind of did what everybody does all the time. That was one of the reasons why I liked my clinical experience so much [because I got to think for myself]. Yes, it was hard, but it was

*refreshing. I remember thinking, "Wow, finally we can think and we can experience things differently." See, since nursing is such a new field, I think this has forced nurses with advanced degrees to have to do more thinking on our feet—reflecting—thinking about how we interface with the other professions, who we are in relation to other professions. We have had to do that because we're still so undefined in terms of how others see us. And since I was new to that, I was still undefined prior to my clinical experience. Now I would know what to say and how to do things. But then [before my clinical practicum] I was still struggling with the idea that nursing was more than just following doctor's orders.*

In much the same spirit, a Southwest State alumna said that her teaching assistantship had provided her with "a strong basis for discovering and strengthening" her identity as an author. "I don't think my master's experience without being a TA [teaching assistant] would have been very meaningful to me at all," she remarked. "Finding that creative voice—finding that expression and the way to apply it was one of those pushing points for me."

Finally, we learned that a professional residency positively affected students in one other way: Directly or indirectly, these learning experiences enhanced students' job prospects upon graduation. In terms of direct effects, some students received job offers from their site supervisors. An Atlantic State alumnus, for instance, said that his internship as a regional archaeologist with the National Park Service had resulted in a permanent placement. Similarly, at Peterson and Southern State, faculty and administrators indicated that many of their nursing students were offered advanced professional positions following the completion of their clinical assignments.

The confidence, professional contacts, and knowledge that students developed in their residencies also had important indirect effects on their job prospects. At Peterson University, a nursing professor said that the self-confidence students acquired during their clinical practicums sparked many to "move into new positions—[they] dare to do something different than what they did before." An alumnus of City-State's applied anthropology program confided that he had used the contacts he developed during his residency to obtain funding for a county-wide housing program, thereby also creating a job for himself. Finally, faculty in many programs told us that the on-the-job knowledge and skills students acquired in their professional residencies often made their graduates much more attractive to employers upon graduation.

## Tangible Product

In culling through our interview material, we identified a tangible product as still another attribute of high-quality programs. In our study, many faculty and administrators required students to complete a product—usually a thesis, project report, or creative performance—in which they demonstrated their abilities to connect knowledge and practice together in ways that contributed meaningfully to their fields. This culminating program activity consistently strengthened students' learning experiences and had positive effects on their growth and development.

## Actions

Faculty and administrators developed and implemented tangible product requirements in their programs in two ways. First, they designed this requirement in light of their program's overall direction and goals. Second, faculty and administrators supported students throughout this culminating activity, providing them with guidance and feedback as needed.

In many programs, faculty and administrators crafted tangible product requirements with their program's overall direction and goals in mind. In those programs aimed at educating advanced professionals for the nonuniversity workplace, for example, faculty required students to complete individual or, in some cases, collaborative, project reports that addressed real-world problems in their fields. In programs where faculty sought to prepare students for doctoral study or careers in research, a conventional scholarly thesis was the tangible product of choice. And in performing arts programs focused on training students for the professional theater, faculty frequently required students to undertake a special project—such as writing an original play or directing a full-length production.

Illustrating this point, we interviewed several faculty and administrators at Walton State College who said that, in keeping with the program's emphasis on preparing "broadly-trained [environmental] policy specialists," they required students to write a thesis or essay on a "real-world" policy issue for their final product. Similarly, at Lake College—a program that focused on preparing individuals as "master teachers"—an administrator told us that students completed a culminating "applied, relevant, practitioner-based research project" in which they "looked at and evaluated their own practice." And, with a slightly different twist, the chair of Helena State's performing arts department explained that faculty required students to produce a "professional project" that was "largely slanted toward production—whether it be in directing, producing, or acting. . . . The focus at this school is not so much detailed research in the field—we're not dramaturges here. Our focus is straightforward and honest: We are performance-oriented in this department."

In addition to designing requirements that complemented and reinforced the focus of their programs, faculty and administrators also supported students as they worked on their tangible products. Many faculty spent considerable time guiding students throughout the research process, discussing emerging problems with them, and critically reviewing and providing feedback on drafts of theses and reports.

A professor in Southwest State's applied anthropology program gave several examples of how she and her colleagues supported students throughout the thesis experience. To begin with, faculty sponsored a "pre-thesis" seminar to familiarize students with "how to do a large research project": "How to design it, how to outline a thesis, how to do a lit[erature] search, even how to put a committee together. . . . We break the research experience into units they can understand and feel confident about doing . . . so it [the thesis] is less of an initiation by fire." Once their research was underway, faculty not only met regularly with students to "keep them on the right track," but they also coordinated a weekly informal thesis seminar in which students could discuss their research and "help each other out."

The chair of Middle State's microbiology program likewise accentuated the intellectual support and feedback that he and his colleagues provided to students during the thesis process:

> *In a larger institution it may be as much as a week before a student can make an appointment with their major professor to find out why something [in their research] didn't work. As you just witnessed, a student just walked into my office—the chairman of the department—which is no big deal, but she's able to walk in the office, pop her head in and talk to me. . . . I think the encouragement part [in the thesis] comes when the kid says to his professor, "It didn't work. What did I do wrong?" And the prof answers, "Well, why don't you try this or that?" That's the personal touch. That's what's important.*

## Consequences for Learning Experiences

The investments that faculty and administrators made in designing and implementing tangible product requirements substantially enhanced the quality of students' learning experiences. In many instances, this culminating activity challenged students to draw upon and integrate various principles, practices, and skills they had learned in their studies into final products that were of value to their fields as well as to them personally.

Students and alumni from across our sample often enthusiastically described their tangible products to us. These products ran the gamut, from conventional research-based theses at Appleby State to innovative one-act plays at Helena State. Among the more unusual were a collection of original short stories that a Southwest State English alumna had written for her master's thesis, a comprehensive "lake clean-up" revitalization plan that several alumni had collaboratively developed as a concluding activity in Major State's environmental studies program, and a six-week environmental science curriculum that a Lake College alumnus had written and applied in his classroom for his final master's project.

We learned that students and alumni valued such tangible learning experiences for two reasons. First, a thesis, report, or professional project provided students with a beneficial, culminating opportunity that helped them to integrate and apply many of the theories and practices they had learned in their classes and to further refine their analytical, research, and written communication skills. A Western State nursing alumna nicely illustrated this theme when she said of her thesis experience:

> *It's gruelling in many respects, but it taught me to be a good writer. It taught me, in terms of research, how to do the whole thing . . . [to] think through this whole process. . . . Then I had to find out the statistical method I wanted to use, and I had to know my theory, and conceptual framework. So I'm really glad that I did it, and I still use things from it all the time. It really did pull it all together. It was a lot of hard work, but it was fun, too.*

Similarly, an alumna of Appleby State's microbiology program told us that being able to "do both—to have the knowledge and apply it" and "to communicate [ideas] in writing and verbally" was a valuable aspect of her thesis experience. "Sure," she said, the "struggle [is] different for each person—some people can't write, others aren't well organized, others can't communicate verbally, but in finishing a master's thesis, you have to do all of these things. You are forced to do it."

Many faculty and administrators reinforced these alumni views. An environmental studies professor at Vernon College, for example, observed that the thesis provided students with an opportunity "to take full responsibility for a project": "[It's] a chance to pick up a lot of technical skills. And usually there is a lot of intense practical learning mingled in with the science. It helps [them] translate all the stuff from classes and from work-based experiences into an independent project." Similarly, a Laramie education professor commented that the curriculum projects students completed offered them a "chance to integrate [the conceptual knowledge they were learning in the program] into their teaching style with students." In these and many other cases in our study, faculty and administrators emphasized that the integrative and applications-oriented nature of a culminating learning experience—such as a thesis, project report, or artistic performance—greatly benefited students.

Students and alumni also valued their tangible product experiences for a second reason: many strongly appreciated being able to create products that contributed in some way to their fields or to their own professional practice. As a Major State engineering student related:

*[With my thesis] I had to produce a finished product at the end—a product that worked and was useful and was original. And that was something I never did as an undergrad. As an undergrad I basically studied from a book. . . . You didn't work on something that was tangible, that you could point at and say "This thing works; this is something that is useful to somebody." That product—that's something that I now take a lot of pride in.*

An alumnus of Land-Grant's applied anthropology program likewise noted that "one of the most rewarding aspects" of his thesis was "contributing to the knowledge base in the field." As he put it, that was "a big bullet in the program."

In contrast, faculty in some programs in our study either did not require, or did not encourage, students to complete a tangible product. Students and alumni in these programs often commented that a thesis or a professional project would have significantly enriched their learning experiences. For example, we interviewed two Middle State engineering students who openly disapproved of the program's "non-thesis option." "I think the point of the degree is to do the research," one said. "The non-thesis option degrades the prestige of the master's degree. It's just an easy way out for faculty and students." The other concurred: "The non-thesis option distracts energy from where the program should be. What makes the master's significant is the thesis. That's what makes it good [to me] as a grad student." In much the same vein, a Peterson business student explained why he disapproved of a recent faculty decision to eliminate the program's thesis requirement. "Not that I'm a glutton for punishment, but I am doing a thesis now on a voluntary basis. I didn't know what I was getting myself into; it's a lot of work, but I've certainly learned a lot. To eliminate that requirement, [I think] that they're cutting out a whole section of experience that students should be accomplishing and doing at graduate school."

Within the context of these criticisms, some students and alumni reprimanded faculty for failing to provide them with adequate guidance when they chose to complete a tangible product. A Barrett State nursing alumna, for instance, told us that although she was only one of a handful of students who wrote a master's thesis, she had a "terrible time accessing" her faculty advisor and assembling a faculty committee. A Major State microbiology student voiced a similar complaint, describing how difficult it was for master's students to attract faculty attention in this heavily doctorally-oriented department:

*With the thesis, I feel we've [the master's students] gotten a little bit—I don't know, I shouldn't say—treated unfairly. But if they're going to treat us like we almost don't exist, then why have the program? . . . Do like the rest do—if you don't want to fool with it, then don't have one and go straight into the Ph.D. program. That has bothered me through my whole time in this program.*

The preponderance of affirmative and negative evidence in our study led us to conclude that a tangible product is an important hallmark of high-quality programs. Time and again, interviewees across our forty-seven case sample emphasized that the integrative nature of this culminating activity substantially enriched the overall quality of students' learning experiences.

## Effects on Students

Working on a tangible product had three important effects on students' growth and development. One, the research and writing associated with thesis and project work improved students' analytical and written communication skills. Two, because they often assumed major responsibility for their projects from start to finish, students further matured into more confident and independent professionals. Three, as a culminating—and often an integrative—activity, this experience helped students to develop a "big picture" perspective on their profession.

Many interviewees told us that students' analytical and written communication skills greatly improved as they researched and wrote theses and project reports. An alumnus of Walton State's environmental studies program spoke directly to this point when he remarked, "Before I entered the program I could barely write. But in writing my little fingers off on [my final essay], I finally learned how to write. I don't write that much anymore, but right now I'm doing a major writing project and it's just a wonderful skill to have." At Peterson University, an alumnus of the M.B.A. program credited his thesis experience with helping him to strengthen his research and writing skills. He used the following anecdote to support his observation:

> *For my thesis I wrote a 200-page paper. I did it on trusts and [after graduation] converted it into an eight-page article. I think having gone through that experience, I learned how to write. And my research skills were immense because of that experience. Now I could do what the [tax] lawyers did. I knew how to write cases. And there's no way I would have known that without doing the thesis.*

Faculty and administrators made similar observations. At Laramie University, for instance, an education professor pointed out that the curriculum projects students completed for their master's "honed their writing skills [and] their abilit[ies] to think and create and write curriculum." On a different note, a faculty member in Appleby State's microbiology program highlighted the positive effects that conducting thesis research had on students' analytical skills:

*Students have told me that the [specialized] knowledge they had just didn't matter as long as they had a scientific background. But what really did matter—and what gave them an edge over others—was their ability to solve problems, their analytical thinking. And students tell me they learned that during their thesis experience—by asking a question, setting up the experiment, collecting the data, and analyzing the results.*

Many interviewees also told us that, in the process of completing a thesis, report, or professional project, students matured into more independent, self-assured professionals. A Carver A&M environmental studies student made this point unambiguously: "The thesis is helping to make me more professional—I have to be more independent, I have to write well, I have to think. . . . I've become much more observant and I'm much more serious about what I'm doing. I feel a lot more confident because I think I have the skills to really do this stuff now." A Middle State microbiology alumnus voiced a similar sentiment:

*I think a lot of what I did [in my master's thesis] was independent learning. . . . In order to do research and to do a thesis, you have to know how to work by yourself and be creative. You had to make your own proposal, you had to make your own thesis up. They weren't going to say to you that "we have a problem here and it needs five experiments and so you do them and write a paper on them." A lot of people weren't ready for that. They wanted professors to tell them what to do. I'm glad it wasn't that way. I would have been bored. . . . The thesis taught me how to think on my feet and really bolstered my self-confidence.*

Faculty and employers in many other programs reiterated these student and alumni accounts. A professor in Middle State's microbiology program, for instance, remarked that the thesis experience frequently transformed students from "handholders" to "creative, innovative, confident self-starters who know that they can do it [research] themselves." A Major State engineering faculty member elaborated on the value of the thesis:

*I think the thesis is crucial to a good master's program. With that kind of a program, you have people leaving the program who have, first of all, a self-confidence in themselves because they have tackled a problem that they really didn't know the solution to and they solved it. They also have confidence that, by golly, there's a lot of different dimensions to solving problems and that sometimes some of those stones that look too difficult to turn over, well, when you turn them over you realize that there really was a beautiful solution waiting for you there. You need to have the confidence that that happens. So, I think these graduates leave here and can enter into strong leadership positions because they've had that experience. . . . The self-confidence that you need to have—that knowledge that solutions do exist and if you dig hard enough, you'll find them . . . [those are] skills that will potentially make that person the kind of person who can make significant contributions to the company.*

An employer of this program's engineering graduates strongly agreed. As he said of their alumni:

*They [the master's graduates] think of themselves in more creative ways than people with [their] bachelor's. I suspect it's the independent research [that they do]. I find that master's-level people can see the need to research something that needs to be done. Bachelor's-level people seem to need a little more pointing or direction. They [master's-prepared engineers] go forward on independent research; [they] create on a higher level—a systems level—rather than on a detail level.*

Similarly, an employer we interviewed in conjunction with Major State's environmental studies program described their graduates as "independent and confident professionals": "They generally have conducted a research project, so they know how to work independently and come to a conclusion, [how to] follow a systematic, scientific process. . . . [The project helps] students become more mature, more confident, more investigative professionals."

Finally, we came to appreciate that, as a culminating and oftentimes integrative activity, the completion of a tangible product helped students develop a "big picture" perspective on their professions. On numerous occasions, students and alumni told us that as they worked on their theses, project reports, and creative productions, they made connections across a wide range of field-related perspectives and practices that had earlier eluded them. These connections, in turn, helped them to view their professions from a new vantage point. An alumna from Appleby State's microbiology program provided compelling testimony to this aspect of thesis work when she described how her thesis experience had provided the "missing piece" that brought together her understanding of the field:

*This is the piece you need that makes all of this other information fit together. It was the piece I needed that applied to so many things that I had just been blocked from knowing before. It just fit things together. . . . That piece would be different for everybody, but in my case, it was how the structure of molecules is put together on a different level than in chemical interactions. It was the experience of realizing that most everything is held together by very weak hydrophobic interactions and hydrogen bonds—Van der Waal's forces—and that those are the weakest link. . . . It was at that point when I realized that all of biology is based on the weakest link, and this is it. And I teach this now—I teach biology based on the weakest link.*

She then said that she may have never grasped this point if she had not been required to connect theory with practice during her thesis work:

*It's like I suddenly saw it from the ground up, you know. . . . This wouldn't have happened had I not simultaneously been assembling research and doing things in the lab, and trying to figure out why one degree of temperature matters. If you are never forced to do that, I don't know if you can still put it in perspective. It's a struggle. I mean, I didn't* want *[interviewee's emphasis] to learn about Van der Waal's forces.*

# 8

---

# *Adequate Resources*

During the course of our study, we came to appreciate that adequate resources provide an important part of the foundation upon which high-quality programs are built and developed. Put simply, the driving idea in this cluster of attributes is that certain types of resource support—whether monetary, as in support for basic infrastructure needs, or nonmonetary, as in supportive faculty promotion and merit review policies—do much to enhance faculty and student investments in teaching and learning.

In this chapter, we elaborate on three attributes—support for students, support for faculty, and support for basic infrastructure—that make up this last cluster of attributes in our engagement theory of program quality. As in the preceding chapters, our discussion of each attribute is divided into three parts. First, we consider the actions that campus and program administrators, as well as faculty, took to enact the attribute in their programs. Second, we describe the ways in which these actions enhanced students' learning experiences. Third, we examine the positive effects of these experiences on students' growth and development.

## *Support for Students*

Throughout our study, support for students repeatedly surfaced as an important feature of high-quality programs. Interviewees emphasized repeatedly that support in the forms of financial aid, nontraditional course delivery formats, and career planning and placement assistance consistently elevated the quality of students' learning experiences and favorably affected their personal and professional development.

## *Actions*

Institutional and program administrators, as well as faculty, supported master's students in our sample of programs in three ways. First, they secured monetary resources for student assistantships, fellowships, and travel to professional conferences. Second, faculty and administrators designed nontraditional course delivery formats to support the educational needs of working professionals. Third, faculty and administrators provided career planning and placement assistance to help students prepare for and locate employment upon graduation.

In a substantial number of programs in our study, faculty and administrators made considerable efforts to provide various forms of financial support to their master's students. At Moore A&T, for example, a departmental administrator said that, besides successfully "lobbying" campus administrators for "teaching assistantships and tuition waivers," he secured corporate and governmental grants to finance ten full-time fellowships for engineering master's students. Similarly, at Appleby State, several faculty indicated that the department chair used "some ingenious strategies" to fund student assistantships in their small master's program in microbiology. These included reallocating part of the department's undergraduate student assistance fund to support four quarter-time graduate teaching assistants and attracting external grant support to fund another three students as half-time research assistants. No less impressive, a faculty member at Helena State told us that when a group of master's students earned a trip to the national finals of a major collegiate theater festival, his department chair convinced the university's president to award healthy travel stipends to all twenty members of the production's cast and crew.

In addition to securing financial resources, faculty and administrators designed nontraditional course delivery formats in response to the educational needs of working professionals in their programs. These formats included innovative off-campus delivery systems—such as long-distance satellite-based instruction and videotaped lectures—as well as on-campus "extended day" programs in which students completed their studies through evening, weekend, and summer courses.

The electrical engineering program at United Tech is a model case in which faculty and administrators relied exclusively on a nontraditional course delivery design. Constructed entirely around satellite-based and videotaped instruction delivered directly to participating worksites, this format allowed engineers to complete advanced engineering course work at their own pace and convenience without losing the benefits of full-time employment. A campus administrator described the rationale behind the program's format:

*In my experience [at a Fortune 500 company], I found that students weren't going to graduate school. They were very busy and they travelled a lot and they had heavy meeting schedules. Going to a conventional program that met every Tuesday or Thursday at a given time was not an option that was available to them. On top of that, they chaffed under the lost time. . . .*

*I think the convenience and flexibility of our [satellite delivery] approach meets a real need out there in the marketplace. Sure, I think if you took most of the students at [United Tech] and asked them, "Would you rather go off full-time to M.I.T. and get your master's or would you rather get it from [United Tech] on a part-time basis while you work?", I think most of them would say, "If I had a choice, which I don't, I guess I would like to go off and immerse myself in a graduate program at a prestigious university and get it that way. But I have a family, I'm six years into my career, and I'm not going to do that even if I could afford it. I will not sever myself from my job and go away to get a degree." So, I think most of them see it as a trade-off and they think that our program is a pretty good alternative for getting their master's degree.*

Along these same lines, a Peterson administrator told us that he and his colleagues designed their business program largely around evening courses to better serve the needs of a professional student body. As he put it:

*We realize that we're not a Harvard or a Wharton. We know what our target market is: we're a commuter-type school and we cater to a primarily evening population because there is a big demand for a part-time M.B.A. program in this market. Our students need the flexibility to come and go when they want and to buy into a system where they can take a semester off if they have to travel or they get an extra assignment at work. We try to be responsive to our student's needs.*

Many faculty and administrators in our study invested in a third activity to support master's students: they provided career planning and placement assistance—sometimes at the institutional level but more often at the departmental level—to help students prepare for and locate employment upon graduation. At Peterson University, the director of the campus-wide career planning and placement center said that they offered several services to M.B.A. students, including individualized career counseling, resume referral, and alumni mentoring. Such was also the case in many other business and education programs in our sample, where interviewing and resume-writing workshops, on-campus employer recruitment visits and job interviews, and individualized job-search referral services were tailored to meet students' needs.

More frequently, faculty and administrators indicated that they helped master's students prepare for and locate employment through personal efforts. During our visit to Moore A&T's engineering program, for example, we learned that the chair had assembled a book containing a complete listing of student resumes and distributed it to every company represented at an on-campus employers' fair. Similarly, in Major State's microbiology program, faculty assisted students in the job-search process by working their professional networks as well as inviting recruiters on campus to interview students for professional positions. Finally, at St. Joan's, we heard frequently that the M.B.A. faculty sponsored informal seminars and receptions that provided students with "golden opportunities" to network with prospective employers.

## Consequences for Learning Experiences

We learned that these investments enhanced students' master's experiences in two important respects. First, students who received financial aid for full-time study, or who completed their studies part-time in programs with nontraditional course delivery formats, were in a better position to concentrate on their learning. Second, students who took advantage of career counseling and placement services learned job-search strategies and developed professional networks that better prepared them for locating employment upon graduation.

In a substantial number of programs in our sample, students and alumni received some form of financial aid to support their studies. Many students in the engineering programs at Major State, Prestige State, and Moore A&T, for instance, had funded research assistantships. At Phelps University, several theater students received substantial grants to defray tuition expenses, while at Parks-Beecher, a combination of institutionally-based scholarships, grants, and work-study monies supported a sizeable number of business students.

Many interviewees observed that these forms of monetary support helped students to focus less on how they could continue financing their education and more on what they were learning in their studies. A student in Helena State's theater program spoke directly to this point, noting that the stipend and health benefits she received as a program assistant gave her the financial security to focus "first and foremost" on learning her craft. Likewise, a Moore A&T engineering student remarked that the money he earned as a research assistant helped him to "perform better in the classroom": "If I have pressure outside the classroom—like not having any money during the first couple months of school to pay for my rent—it's harder to study."

Students and alumni in other programs commented upon the negative impact that a lack of monetary support had on students' learning. In Southwest State's microbiology program, for example, a student told us that although he spent more than twenty-five hours a week working as a teaching assistant, the poor pay necessitated that he take an off campus job to "make ends meet." Worries over money, working too many hours off campus, and logging enough time in the lab doing research exacted a toll on this student. Angry and dejected, he remarked, "I can't take the stress anymore. It's degrading. And they make us pay tuition—which is a third of my teaching assistantship [salary]." A City-State alumnus voiced a similar complaint, stating that the insufficient financial support students received seriously undermined the quality of time and effort they could realistically devote to their studies: "Funding is a real problem here. There's so little money to go around. Students are asked to do too much—to keep up with their course work, to work on community-based projects without pay, and to work one or two part-time jobs in order to earn a living. . . . They don't have any time to reflect on things."

Just as adequate financial aid provided full-time students with the resources to focus more time and energy on their studies, nontraditional course delivery formats also provided an essential form of support to (primarily) part-time students. Students and alumni repeatedly told us that satellite-based and videotaped instruction—as well as evening, weekend, and summer courses—allowed them to focus intensely on their studies without interrupting their professional careers.

The Longmont English program serves as an example of the benefits of a nontraditional course delivery format. In this five-year, summer's-only master's program, teachers from across the United States gathered annually to explore writing, literature, and the teaching of English. This format, one alumnus commented, gave him "a chance to study intensely . . . with some really good scholar–teachers" in a way that enriched his "teaching and professional development." A student nearing completion of her master's also found the program's format particularly appealing, noting that it provided her with opportunities to learn "a great deal" from other teachers in the summer and then "to bring lots of creative ideas home" to share with her colleagues during the school year.

Longmont students were not the only individuals to benefit from a nontraditional delivery format. For instance, a United Tech engineering alumnus—who had completed his master's while working full-time for a major computer and electronics corporation—described how the program's videotaped lecture format supported his learning style: "It allowed me to watch the lectures when I was in the right frame of mind for learning. It also allowed me to rewind the tape and listen to parts of the lecture that were not clear during the first viewing. . . . There are some real advantages to tape delay." Likewise, a Lake education student spoke appreciatively about the condensed three-week summer courses he had completed. "We have a lot of intense discussions in those classes," he stated, "and, since it's the summer, I can really give my all to learning. There aren't the same pressures in the summer as there are in the school year."

Finally, we learned that career counseling and placement services also supported students in ways that contributed to their learning experiences. On many occasions, students and alumni emphasized that the career planning workshops and seminars they attended, as well as the individualized job placement assistance they received, helped them develop job-search strategies and professional networks that better prepared them for locating employment in their fields.

By way of illustration, several students in Parks-Beecher's M.B.A. program told us that the school's placement office sponsored workshops on such beneficial topics as "The Effective Job Search," "Dressing for Corporate Success," and "Improving Your Interviewing Skills." At Major State, an alumnus of the microbiology program said that faculty and administrators arranged seminars in which students learned from and networked with professionals in the field. And almost every student we interviewed in Phelps' theater program remarked that their instructors provided them with helpful pointers on how to prepare for, and land, professional auditions.

Not surprisingly, students and alumni greatly valued the support they received from career counselors and faculty. One Peterson business student, for instance, said that the university's placement staff had "really helped [her] understand how to go about getting a job." An applied anthropology student at Southwest State offered comparable words of praise for his professors: "They were really serious about helping students find jobs. They really work with you [and] network for you."

In light of these and other like accounts, we identified support for students as an important feature of high-quality programs. Across our sample, stakeholders repeatedly emphasized that financial aid, nontraditional course delivery formats, and career planning and placement assistance elevated the quality of students' learning experiences by providing them with the resource support necessary to invest more fully in their studies.

## Effects on Students

Monetary and non-monetary support for students had three salutary effects on their growth and development. One, students who utilized career planning and placement services were more likely to secure employment in their respective fields upon graduation. Two, since financial aid and nontraditional course delivery formats provided students with the support necessary to concentrate more fully on their learning, resources such as these indirectly assisted students in developing into more committed, lifelong learners. Three, and more broadly, since support facilitated student investment in many of the other attributes in our theory, it further intensified many of the effects associated with these attributes.

Many students and alumni told us that the career planning and placement assistance they received from counselors and faculty helped them a great deal in locating employment upon graduation. An education student from Chester College, for example, mentioned that her on-campus interviews with prospective employers had led to "a good placement," while a freshly-minted Peterson M.B.A. said gratefully of the institution's career placement staff, "They helped me to get some key interviews. They try to network you with lots of alumni and employers. So far, I've interviewed with many employers and have received a [good] job offer."

Faculty and administrators echoed these student and alumni accounts. At Appleby State, an administrator told us that faculty used their extensive professional networks to ensure that "100 percent" of their graduates found employment. Similarly, the director of Parks-Beecher's career planning and placement office said the resume-writing, job referral, on-campus interviewing, and alumni networking services they offered to M.B.A. students contributed, in part, to the program's "90-plus" percent placement rate.

Interviewees also stressed that since financial aid and nontraditional course delivery formats allowed students to concentrate more intensely on their learning, these resources indirectly helped students to become more committed, lifelong learners. An alumna of Longmont's English program—whose tuition expenses were covered, in part, by an institutional fellowship—said simply that the master's was "one of the best things that ever happened" to her. As she put it: "It stretched me intellectually in all kinds of new directions. Now I'm pursuing my Ph.D." With a somewhat different twist, an alumnus of Lake's education program—who now works as a middle school social studies teacher—told us that "being on the other side of the desk" had instilled in him "a love for continued learning." He added that he "probably wouldn't have pursued his master's"—and rekindled his passion for learning—if it had not been for the off-campus weekend and summer school courses Lake College offered in his community.

Finally, we learned that adequate monetary and non-monetary support provided students with the means necessary to invest more heavily in other attributes in our engagement theory. In particular, students who were awarded funding for full-time study, or who were able to complete their studies on a part-time basis through nontraditional formats, often were in a better position to participate more actively in their learning communities, to engage in critical dialogue and cooperative learning activities with their peers, and to concentrate more fully on their course work and tangible product learning experiences. In short, adequate support for students further contributed to and intensified many of the effects associated with these attributes.

150     Chapter 8

## Support for Faculty

Support for faculty stands out as yet another important attribute of high-quality programs. Not altogether surprisingly, we found that adequate monetary resources and supportive reward structures consistently led faculty to invest more fully in their teaching and learning. Such investments greatly enriched the overall quality of students' learning experiences and, in various ways, positively contributed to their growth and development.

### Actions

In our study, campus and departmental administrators supported faculty through two major actions. First, they allocated monetary resources for faculty salaries, sabbaticals, and travel to professional conferences. Second, campus and departmental administrators established tenure and merit review policies that rewarded faculty for their involvement in teaching and learning.

In numerous programs in our sample, administrators sought to support faculty investments in teaching and learning in a variety of ways. Institutional administrators at Peterson University, for instance, generously funded sabbaticals and professional travel for nursing faculty even though enrollment in the master's program had declined in recent years. At Lake College, a small, predominantly undergraduate liberal arts institution, campus administrators established a faculty development fund to support the research interests of graduate faculty, while institutional administrators at Prestige State sponsored an internal grants program to enhance the scholarly productivity of junior engineering faculty.

In addition to allocating monetary resources to support faculty, campus and departmental administrators established reward structures that supported faculty for their involvement in teaching and learning—including at the master's level. In particular, administrators crafted promotion, tenure, and merit review policies that recognized faculty not only for their scholarly accomplishments but also for their efforts in teaching master's courses, advising master's students, and coordinating master's programs.

Peterson University provides one such representative case. During our visit there, a senior campus administrator emphasized that their institutional tenure and promotion policies focused "primarily on teaching and scholarship that supports teaching." An administrator in the School of Nursing elaborated on this point, noting that faculty were rewarded not just for teaching, but also for their involvement in various other scholarly activities—including administering subspecialties within the master's program, coordinating clinical placements for master's students, serving on thesis committees, and conducting basic and applied research.

In a few programs in our sample, administrators broke with tradition and abolished tenure, developing reward structures that, in the context of their programs, more fully recognized faculty for their direct involvement in teaching at the master's level. Walton State's environmental studies program serves as an interesting example of this approach. There, all faculty received renewable two-year contracts. Such an arrangement prompted regular evaluations of every faculty member's teaching effectiveness—evaluations, we learned, that were based on elaborate portfolios consisting of peer and student teaching evaluations, syllabi, and course materials. A similar situation existed in the M.F.A. (master's of fine arts) programs at Phelps University and National Conservatory College (NCC). At both of these institutions, faculty were issued one-year contracts and were told that their renewal was contingent upon two factors: the professional contributions they made to each school's theater company and the quality of their teaching. Particularly at Phelps University, this system of evaluation recognized the unique scholarly contributions that theater faculty made to the program, university, and field and, as one administrator put it, "saved" them from the "academic publish or perish" reward structure typical of most research universities.

## Consequences for Learning Experiences

Not unexpectedly, we learned that administrative efforts to support faculty almost always helped to enhance students' learning. Again and again, stakeholders told us that when faculty were supported—monetarily as well as non-monetarily—for engaging in teaching and learning (especially at the master's level), they put considerable time and effort into teaching and mentoring students.

In contrast to most of the attributes in our theory, we identified the consequences associated with this particular attribute primarily through negative, rather than affirmative, evidence. For more often than not, faculty and administrators told us that they were not adequately supported for their involvement in teaching-related activities generally, let alone for teaching at the master's level. Many stressed that since teaching and mentoring master's students was seldom rewarded as generously in their institutional reward structures as was obtaining external research funding or publishing in peer-reviewed journals, they often chose to invest less in the former and more in the latter.[1]

A faculty member in Major State's engineering program illustrated this point well when he chronicled the frustration he experienced working at a flagship research institution. "What you need to understand," he said emphatically, "is that everything in this university is run on a shoestring. We're told [by institutional administrators] that they don't have enough money to pay our salaries, so we are told to bring in money from the outside. . . . It's like each faculty member is a small business bringing in grant money for the university. So, we're doing that. And our pay raises depend on that—far more than publications or teaching." He then elaborated on how this survival-of-the-fittest setting undermined the time that he and his colleagues could realistically devote to students:

> *I mean, faculty are on a conveyer belt here. Let me give you an example. Our Ph.D. qualifying exams reflect this conveyer belt quality—it's difficult to get a faculty member to stay for more than one hour at them. Just imagine what our master's program is like if the Ph.D. is like that. A master's student is hard-pressed to get a lot of attention from faculty. There definitely are some of us who do it—but we are not rewarded for it. . . . You have to remember that given the pressure to get grant money and publish here, teaching becomes a marginal activity. . . . There are no rewards for being a good teacher at this institution. It's not rewarded at all.*

Another Major State faculty member, in the M.B.A. program, reiterated this perspective:

> *Any faculty member who spends his time on teaching is going to get "had" at this institution. There are no incentives in the system for developing new courses or for teaching. None. You don't get paid for that. All people care about is that you're not bad. You get rewarded for one thing: what research you publish in which journals. The faculty that are responsible to students—you know what happens to them? Five years down the road they're denied tenure. An M.B.A. program needs high quality pedagogy and the institution isn't set up for that. We have to give a life raft to people who are taking risks to be involved in pedagogy and not just research.*

We also spoke with faculty who worked in institutions with historic teaching missions who felt unsupported as teachers. Representing the view of many of her colleagues, a senior faculty member in Appleby State's microbiology program expressed frustration and concern over the current lack of recognition given to teaching and other service-related activities in her institution's reward structure. "When I went through tenure," she remarked, "people didn't have this propensity for adding up numbers—how many publications you had. . . . Now, I think, the young people coming in will not have the luxuries I had. . . . [The message now is:] 'Don't spend your time on that [teaching and service] because you don't get any credit for that in P&T [promotion and tenure decision] and merit. That wasn't true when I went though the process." In fact, a high-ranking administrator at this institution made it very clear to us that faculty service to "teaching master's courses" or to "running a good master's program" had very little bearing on promotion or tenure decisions at this traditionally undergraduate teaching institution.

Many students, alumni, and employers reinforced these accounts. Two Barrett State nursing students, for example, said that the tenure and merit review policies under which faculty worked negatively affected the quality of their learning experiences in this way:

> [Student 1]: *Well, money is the almighty arbiter here. The faculty on this campus are hired because of their grant-producing and grant-getting ability and are tenured a lot on that. I think they pay lip service to "How did your students evaluate you in your classes?" . . . The professors are very outspoken about saying, "Look, I'm here because I publish, because I've gotten these grants, and I try to squeeze students in as best I can," but they really have a difficult time juggling student needs and this omnipresent push to get grant money into the university.*

> [Student 2]: *Yeah, it [understanding the grant emphasis and influence] is certainly not spelled out to you in black and white when you enter the door. You know, "Don't expect this professor to be here because she's applying for such and such grant" and it's something that you just discover as you muddle along. . . . I've had a lot of trouble getting the guidance—the structure and assistance—I need to put things together [in my program]. It's been a real effort [to get faculty attention].*

A Major State English alumna offered this explanation for the lack of attention she and many of her peers received from faculty:

> *I guess my problem is that, having survived this long, I tend to get more cynical about changing things. It's not cynical, it's seeing more of the picture, so it's very easy to say that professors should spend more of their time with the students, and I think that's true, but then the whole system needs to be changed so that's rewarded. Professors are trying to get tenure and so on. If they spend their time "pal-ling around" with M.A. students, then they couldn't get their books published. So in order to make the M.A. better, the whole institution would have to be changed.*

An employer of Pierpont's business students was not as gracious. As he put it, "Byzantine decisions" about tenure and promotion had seriously jeopardized the "quality of instruction" students received in this M.B.A. program. Like interviewees in many programs, he criticized administrators for evaluating faculty "too much on what journals they publish in and how much they publish" and not enough for their abilities as teachers. Such a practice, he observed, made "teaching a second-class activity" and led to the dismissal of "many good faculty" who were "passionate" about teaching.

By contrast, faculty in some programs we studied were supported for their involvement in teaching generally, and in master's education specifically. More often than not, faculty in these programs emphasized that tenure and merit review policies in their institutions recognized and rewarded the investments they made in their research and in teaching and mentoring master's students.

A Helena State theater professor, for example, spoke appreciatively about the broadened view of scholarship implicit in her institution's reward structure, noting how it supported faculty both for their involvement in professional theatrical performances and teaching. This situation, she said, made her "feel valued": "It's not the money [one earns] itself. It's whether or not you're valued. I know that the institution really values my contributions." On a somewhat different note, a microbiology professor at Southwest State told us that she left her tenured post at a major research university for her current position because, in her words, "I wanted to be rewarded for teaching well and doing good research." The following remarks indicate that she was delighted with her decision:

*I think it's just wonderful that I have the same teaching load that I had at the "Research I" that I came from. I have a lab that I absolutely love, I have as much if not more time to spend at research, and yet here I am supposedly at a teaching institution. And the really nice thing is that I can feel very proud and happy about the fact that I like to teach instead of having to cover it up—pretend that I really don't like it and that I really want to spend all my time in the lab. Here there is some reward for doing that [teaching] well. This is the perfect kind of institution for me.*

Supportive institutional reward policies for faculty enriched—if not directly, then at least indirectly—the quality of students' learning experiences in such programs. For as many of these students and alumni told us, their professors were committed teachers who "took a little bit of extra time" to teach them the intricacies of their crafts. A student in Southwest State's microbiology program said of her professors, for instance, "They are concerned with you learning the material. We have professors who care about us. . . . They take time to answer your questions and often go out of their way. So you really do have that [individual] contact, which is really important." An alumna of Helena State's theater program voiced a similar perspective: "This is a very nurturing program. There's a lot more opportunity at this school for individual attention. . . . [The faculty give] more encouragement to each individual—they help you discover where your talent lies." Finally, a Moore A&T student emphasized that the engineering faculty "really took time" with students: "They help you to develop your whole self versus just getting your degree."

Whether they offered affirmative or negative accounts, interviewees across the forty-seven programs we visited stressed that support for faculty is an important attribute of high-quality programs. Adequate monetary resources and appropriate reward structures provided faculty with the support they needed to invest more of their time and energy in teaching and learning and, in so doing, to enrich considerably the quality of students' learning experiences.

## Effects on Students

Monetary and non-monetary support for faculty had two positive—albeit indirect—effects on students. First, students who studied with faculty who were invested in their growth and development left their programs as more self-confident, self-assured professionals. Second, and more broadly, since support facilitated faculty investments in other attributes in our engagement theory, it further intensified many of the effects that these attributes had on students.

Many students and alumni emphasized that the individualized and personalized attention they received from faculty played a major role in bolstering their self-confidence. An alumnus of Southwest State's microbiology program, for instance, told us that the confidence his advisor had in him generated a like belief in himself:

> *When I entered the program, I knew I had a poor academic record and that my lab skills were very undeveloped. But my faculty advisor really helped— he taught me a lot. If it wasn't for him, I would have left the program. When I graduated, I really felt like I could play the game. I still felt like an outsider to the core movers and shakers, but I was able to understand what they were up to. I had more confidence in my abilities. I knew I could do this stuff.*

Shortly after receiving his degree, he entered a doctoral program at a major research institution and later accepted an assistant professorship at a doctoral-granting university. An English student, also at Southwest State, attributed a surge in her self-confidence to "the encouragement" she had experienced from her professors. "I don't know if it's quality of instruction, or [the] quality of the relationships between you and the faculty... [but they] encourage you and say you can do it." She added that while she had initially hoped to just "survive the M.A.," she now was ready to pursue a doctorate. "I can do it," she said, bursting with self-confidence, "that's no problem."

Faculty and administrators across our sample offered similar assessments. In City-State's applied anthropology program, for instance, an administrator told us that the "quality of interaction" students had with faculty was a key "turning point" for them, often helping students to "gain
self-confidence" and develop into "real movers and shakers." At Moore A&T,
an engineering professor said that although many students entered their
program "unsure of themselves," they consistently "left as confident professionals." He attributed this change, in large part, to the individualized
attention that he and many of his colleagues provided to students.

We also learned that adequate monetary and non-monetary resources
provided faculty with a base of support that encouraged their investment in
almost every other attribute in our theory. Put simply, when faculty were
rewarded for their involvement in teaching and mentoring students, they
almost always devoted more time and energy to developing program cultures and interactive learning activities that enriched the quality of students'
experiences. These learning experiences, as discussed in previous chapters,
had many positive effects on students' growth and development. In short,
adequate support for faculty further contributed to and intensified (again,
indirectly) many of these effects on students.

## Support for Basic Infrastructure

Support for basic infrastructure is the last attribute of high-quality programs
in our engagement theory. Across our sample, interviewees emphasized that
adequate facilities and equipment—such as laboratories, theaters, computers, library resources, and essential field-related equipment and supplies—
complemented and enriched students' efforts to learn advanced knowledge
and techniques in their fields.

### Actions

In our study, campus and departmental administrators, as well as faculty,
supported the basic infrastructure of their programs in one major way: They
secured monetary resources to purchase requisite equipment and supplies;
to ensure suitable laboratory, performance, and classroom facilities; and to
support institutional library and computer needs.

At Prestige State, for instance, administrators and faculty regularly
sought corporate, foundation, and government grant support to purchase
up-to-date equipment for its engineering program. In Southwest State's
applied anthropology program, several interviewees pointed out that besides securing ample budgetary support from campus administrators, their
chair was particularly effective at obtaining external grant money, includ-

ing funding for a new computer laboratory for students. Similarly, at Appleby State, the chair's efforts to acquire adequate resources did not go unnoticed by faculty. As one of them related:

> We've been very fortunate because we have [the department chair] and he's very ingenious at tapping little sources of money that other people don't know of and making money stretch for the department. I've never been turned down for money. If a student has a request for a serum that might be a little expensive, he might grit his teeth a little, but he always gets it for them. I don't know where he gets the money and I don't want to know. But [the department chair] is very supportive of the master's program.

In sharp contrast, there were few programs in our sample in which institutional administrators matched the efforts of departmental administrators and faculty to secure monetary support for their programs. Helena State University was one of the exceptions. There, campus administrators had been, in the words of one professor, "particularly supportive of bricks-and-mortar projects" for the theater program, raising funds to pay for a multimillion dollar renovation of a main performance hall and budgeting for the expansion of a smaller, 150-seat theater facility. The theater program at Phelps University provided another illustrative case. Interestingly, although the drama school was considered financially autonomous from its parent university, institutional administrators contributed much-needed financial support to help keep the school afloat, regularly picking up the small deficit that it ran each year and providing all of its physical facilities gratis.

## Consequences for Learning Experiences

The effort that departmental administrators and faculty, and to a lesser extent campus administrators, put into supporting program infrastructure needs had important consequences for students' learning experiences. When such resource needs were met, students had the "tools" they needed to learn advanced knowledge and techniques in their fields.

Like support for faculty, we identified the consequences associated with this attribute largely through negative, rather than affirmative, evidence. In the overwhelming majority of programs we studied, faculty and departmental administrators stressed that, despite their successes at attracting external grant support for equipment and supplies, the limited financial support they received from campus administrators consistently undermined the quality of learning experiences they could provide to students.

During our visit to Major State, for example, two departmental administrators discussed the impact that inadequate budgetary support for equipment, supplies, and facilities maintenance had wrought on its microbiology program. As we learned from one, institutional support per student for supplies and other expenses had declined by "50 percent" in recent years, thereby putting "tremendous strains" on what faculty could "realistically do for students." This administrator candidly told us, "There are times in which we simply cannot offer some of the laboratory courses we ought to offer. We don't have the resources necessary to provide the supplies and materials needed for lab activity." The other administrator brought a different concern to our attention. As he put it, institutional resources for facilities maintenance were so abysmal that he recently had to "use duct tape to keep pipes together" in his lab. Both emphasized that inadequate equipment and facilities thwarted their efforts to train students in state-of-the-art scientific research techniques.

In much the same vein, a Carver A&M administrator charged that insufficient institutional support for facilities, equipment, and supplies had greatly limited the scope and quality of learning experiences he and his colleagues could offer to students:

> We simply don't have the laboratory space and the equipment to provide our students with enough exposure to laboratory techniques that they'll need when they leave [Carver A&M] and go into industry or on to Ph.D. studies. You need labs and equipment to run an environmental toxicology master's program. We're severely lacking in both. In the past, some of our faculty have tried to get around this by bringing their master's students up to [a nearby public national university] to work in their labs. These students need to learn more about scientific techniques, how you go about solving problems in the lab, how you use state-of-the-art equipment. . . . We need more space for labs and better equipment in this master's program. And since this program receives absolutely no institutional funding at all—we have no graduate assets to speak of—I doubt that this will change.

We spoke to scores of students and alumni who stated unequivocally that poor facilities, inadequate equipment, and limited supplies adversely affected the quality of their learning experiences. In particular, they stressed that out-of-date equipment and facilities frustrated and discouraged their attempts to learn advanced—and, in some cases, basic—field-related knowledge and practices. As an alumna of Carver A&M's environmental studies program bluntly said: "The equipment is so old at [Carver A&M] that it is hard to learn good techniques on it. I really feel it put me at a disadvantage when I got into my doctoral program." A student in Southwest State's microbiology program made a similar observation: "Sometimes we don't even have the basic materials to complete our experiments. Sometimes the microscopes don't even work. I've been to a couple of the community colleges around here to use the stuff in their labs. It's much better than what we have here." And nearly every student we interviewed in Southwest State's English and applied anthropology programs described their library as "woefully inadequate," noting that they often had to use interlibrary loans to obtain pertinent journal articles and books. "And that's really frustrating," one applied anthropology student remarked, "because if I have a question I want to answer it. I don't want to wait four weeks for an interlibrary loan before I can move on with my research."

To be sure, campus administrators in some programs in our study allocated adequate budgetary and space resources to master's programs. More often than not, these resources complemented those that departmental administrators and faculty had already secured, thereby helping to broaden the range of learning experiences that these programs could offer to students.

Moore A&T University serves as a representative case in point. During our visit, many interviewees emphasized that the program's state-of-the-art research and instructional facilities greatly expanded students' opportunities to learn about new developments and practices in engineering. One campus administrator (who had been instrumental in securing these resources) told us that master's students had access to more than a dozen research and educational laboratories and to the College of Engineering's teleclass/teleconference facility. This facility served as a meeting area for faculty–student conferences, interactive collaborations with faculty and students at other universities, and satellite-transmitted courses, seminars, and colloquia from other institutions. This "wealth" of facilities and equipment provided students with multiple opportunities, in this administrator's words, to "tool-up" on their engineering skills and to keep abreast of "cutting-edge developments" in the field.

A comparable situation existed in Helena State's theater program. Many interviewees there said that campus administrators generously supported the fine arts, and regularly allocated monetary resources for equipment, supplies, and facilities. This kind of support, one student explained, provided those in the master's program with the pertinent resources necessary to develop and further hone their stagecraft, lighting, and costume design skills. Another student remarked: "These differences, while they might seem slight, make a difference in how you feel about being at a place and what you get from your teachers and from the rest of the university."

Across the forty-seven programs in our sample, many interviewees conveyed affirmative and negative stories that helped us to understand that support for basic infrastructure is an important attribute of high-quality programs. Many emphasized repeatedly that adequate facilities and equipment—such as laboratories, classroom, studios, computers, library resources, and essential field-related equipment and supplies—enriched the quality of students' learning experiences by providing them with the necessary "tools" to learn advanced field-related knowledge and techniques.

## *Effects on Students*

In our sample, programs that had up-to-date equipment, current materials for classroom and research activities, and adequate instructional facilities contributed to students' growth and development in two ways. First, in large measure because students learned advanced field-specific knowledge and skills in these programs, they developed into more technically-competent professionals. Second, since this kind of support indirectly complemented student investments in other attributes in our theory, it further intensified many of the effects that these attributes had on students.

Many students and alumni emphasized that, in completing projects on up-to-date equipment in the laboratory, field, or studio, they had become more technically-competent professionals. An alumnus of Prestige State's engineering program told us: "I had lots of opportunities to develop technical expertise—the facilities were state-of-the art. My master's prepared me well for the workplace." A Phelps theater student similarly noted that the wide range of equipment and facilities he had been allowed to experiment with helped him to learn various lighting designs and techniques.

Employers provided similar accounts. At Prestige State, for instance, we spoke with an employer who described the program's graduates as "technically-competent engineers": "They have state-of-the-art training, especially in hardware. . . . Their graduates can be productive for us right away." A Moore A&T employer was no less sanguine about their engineering graduates. As he told us, "I have no hesitations about hiring an [A&T] graduate. They are very well-prepared in the fundamentals."

Finally, adequate equipment, supplies, and facilities provided students with the resources they needed to invest more fully in other attributes in our theory. In particular, such resources were needed for many learning experiences in master's programs—including those associated with integrative learning, cooperative learning, and the completion of a tangible product. Adequate support for these infrastructure needs further contributed to and intensified many of the effects that these learning experiences had on students.

## *Endnotes*

1. In a number of cases in our study, faculty told us that while the reward structure in their institutions seldom supported their involvement in master's-related activities, they did not allow this to diminish significantly their investment in master's-related activities. Rather, these faculty indicated that their strong commitments to master's education and to teaching led them to allocate considerable time and effort to master's students. A microbiology professor in Appleby State's program made this point forcefully:

*You have to understand that what makes this program go is the faculty. We have a very strong commitment to students. . . . You see, the microbiologists always had this desire for a master's program. They wanted to do research and they wanted their students to have that research experience. So they took care of it on an overload basis and they didn't complain about it and they didn't ask for time off or extra pay for doing it. The reward was in the doing of it. Now I know that altruism is not a very popular thing anymore and people laugh at it, but it comes back in satisfaction.*

That said, this faculty member—and many others in this subset of programs—repeatedly stressed that a supportive institutional reward structure would have helped to strengthen and sustain their ongoing investment in master's education and master's students.

# 9

---

# *Developing and Sustaining High-Quality Programs*

As the previous chapters suggest, developing and sustaining high-quality programs is an organic process, not a mechanical one. The task requires those who have a stake in academic programs to engage in an ongoing process of organizational learning that takes as its focus improved teaching and learning. A high-quality program cannot be reduced to a handful of discrete items or benchmarks that faculty and administrators piece together: Quality demands the collective intelligence and commitment of many people who mutually invest in their own and others' learning. Thus, the metaphor of "assembling" a high-quality program is eclipsed by people "growing" and "cultivating" one.

With this in mind, in this chapter we turn our attention to the practical issue of developing and sustaining high-quality academic programs. In so doing, we propose a framework that is intended to help faculty, administrators, and others learn about, assess, and improve the quality of undergraduate and graduate programs. Anchored in our engagement theory of program quality, the framework also reflects insights from the total quality management, organizational learning, and higher education assessment literatures. Our discussion is divided into three parts: To place our ideas in context, we begin with a critique of how most faculty, administrators, and policymakers assess program quality in higher education and argue for an alternative approach. We then describe our framework and elaborate on its key features. Last, we explain the potential benefits of this framework for cultivating and strengthening the quality of academic programs.

## Toward a Learning-Centered Approach to Quality Assessment

In myriad ways, stakeholders both internal and external to academe are involved in examining the quality of academic programs in our nation's colleges and universities. Parents and students, for example, conduct their own quality appraisals during the institutional selection process, often relying on quality rankings published by *U.S. News and World Report* and *The Gourman Report* for assistance. Faculty and administrators frequently take up this task as part of larger institutional program review and accreditation processes. Many others—including alumni, employers, policymakers, state legislators, and members of the media—render quality judgments as they evaluate alumni performances in the workplace, scrutinize faculty productivity on campus, and critique the content and character of undergraduate and graduate curricula in our nation's colleges and universities.

Given that our interest is in improving the ways in which faculty and administrators evaluate academic program quality, we invite readers to reflect critically on the following questions:

- What is the overarching purpose of quality assessment in your program or institution? Is it to determine a program's relative quality in relation to others in the field? To satisfy calls for external accountability? To learn more about the impact of a program on students' learning experiences and outcomes to facilitate ongoing program improvement?
- How are assessment results used? To compare and rank-order programs to determine, in part, resource allocation and program reduction priorities? To meet external mandates (with results having little to no bearing on program improvement)? To inform and guide ongoing efforts to strengthen the learning experiences and outcomes of students?
- What criteria or standards are used to evaluate program quality?
- Who participates in quality assessment efforts? Is there broad participation among diverse stakeholders or does this responsibility rest primarily with a small group of faculty and administrators?
- How frequently is the quality of the program evaluated? Continuously? Every year? Every five years? Every ten years?

We raise these questions both to prompt reflection and to make a broader point. In surveying the higher education literature as well as numerous program review protocols, we have found that there is relatively little variation in how faculty, administrators, and policy-makers evaluate the quality of academic programs.[1] More often than not, such evaluations occur as part of a formal program review process in which a small group of faculty and administrators conduct a program audit, collecting data on a set of preestablished quantifiable "quality indicators" and, in some cases, inviting colleagues from other institutions to review the program. Faculty and administrators then compare their findings to other programs of like size and stature, thus providing a comparative perspective on the program's overall quality. In some cases, these results are used, in part, by institutional administrators and state-level policymakers for resource allocation or program reduction purposes. In the majority of cases, these efforts rarely culminate in reports that have a significant bearing on future program planning or improvement efforts.

While traditional approaches to quality assessment have their merits, they also raise a host of concerns. In particular, we believe they suffer from three major limitations:

First, traditional approaches tend to rely heavily on program comparisons to assess program quality. This practice often leads faculty and administrators to concentrate more on where their program stands in relation to others and less on examining how its inner workings enhance or diminish the quality of students' learning experiences and achievement (Schilling and Schilling, 1993, 171). As faculty busily compare themselves on various proxies of quality—such as faculty research productivity and educational resources—they frequently lose sight of what those proxies were originally intended to represent. The objective no longer becomes to study and understand how various features internal to their program—such as curricular practices and instructional approaches—strengthen student learning and development but, rather, to compete with others to ensure a high "quality ranking." From our perspective, a new approach to quality assessment is needed that redirects faculty and administrators' attention away from their competitors and more on the needs of their own students. Only then will significant improvements be made in academic programs that enrich the quality of students' learning experiences in ways that promote their growth and development.

Second, current quality assessment approaches are informed by a set of widely-shared evaluative criteria and standards—often referred to in the literature as "attributes of quality"—that are presumed to enrich student learning. Yet, as we discussed in Chapter 1, there is very little research that documents causal connections between traditional indicators of quality and their actual effects on students' learning experiences and student outcomes. If student learning and development is the touchstone of a high-quality program, then a new approach to quality assessment is needed—one that advances a new set of evaluative criteria and standards that systematically relate program attributes, learning experiences, and student outcomes.

Third, the infrequency with which faculty and administrators conduct quality assessments tends to undermine efforts aimed at meaningful program improvement. The reasons for this are twofold. To begin with, when quality assessment occurs on a five- or ten-year cycle, it often leads to one-shot data collection efforts that leave faculty and administrators functioning for years at a time with little knowledge of what is and is not working in their programs. Moreover, episodic assessment tends to generate an evaluative climate that is more summative and judgmental than formative and instructive, making faculty less likely to welcome, let alone utilize, assessment results for program improvement. We concur with several scholars in the assessment movement who believe that if quality assessment is to make a difference in academic programs, then it must be formative in character (AAHE 1992; Hutchings 1990; Schilling and Schilling 1993). Formative evaluation promotes the understanding that quality is not a static object to be achieved, but rather a dynamic process requiring constant attention, cultivation, and investment. From our vantage point, such an approach to evaluating program quality is all too rare in higher education today.

The intent of our critique is not to throw traditional approaches to quality assessment out with the proverbial bathwater. For these approaches have their merits, the most important (and, in light of our critique, paradoxical) of which is a fundamental insistence on self-study. Nonetheless, we remain fundamentally concerned about the invisibility of the learner and the learning process in most quality assessment efforts today.

Karl Schilling and Karen Maitland Schilling have stated that in order "to change or improve an invisible system, one must first make it visible" (1993, 172). We could not agree more. In our view, a new approach to quality assessment is needed that will shed light on how various learning experiences within programs intersect with and improve the daily lives of students. Faculty, administrators, and other stakeholders need to be challenged to peer inside their own programs to discover how learning environments, instructional practices, and curricular requirements enrich or diminish students' learning and development. In short, we believe that a learning-centered approach to evaluating program quality is necessary—one that will harness the collective intelligence and commitment of faculty, administrators, students, and other participants to invest in a continuous process aimed at improving the quality of students' learning.

## A Framework for Assessing and Improving Academic Program Quality

In light of the need for a learning-centered approach to quality assessment, we have developed a framework for assessing and improving the quality of academic programs.[2] Conceptually, this framework places continuous learning among program participants squarely at the center of the program improvement effort and underscores the integral roles that planning and evaluation play in this process. In so doing, it encourages faculty, administrators and other program participants to make their "working space a learning space" (Senge et al. 1994, 35) through an ongoing and dynamic process of study, feedback, modification, and improvement.

In broad strokes, our framework is comprised of a set of guiding principles, questions to inform assessment and improvement, and quality assessment criteria and indicators. We will describe each of these features in detail next, with an eye toward their applicability in program improvement efforts.

But before elaborating on the framework, we introduce three caveats. First, this framework is heavily informed by our engagement theory of program quality. As such, for individuals who disagree with either our definition of a high-quality program or the theory itself, our framework may be of limited value. Second, while our framework promotes a range of strategies for assessing and improving program *quality,* it is not intended to serve as a comprehensive approach to program review. Quality assessment is only one, albeit important, component of program review; our framework does not address its other common components, such as program productivity, student need/demand, or cost. Third, since planning and assessment activities are most effective when they are tailored to the local context in which they occur, we do not view the framework as an authoritative "recipe" for planning and evaluating academic program quality. We believe that readers will be best served if they use the framework as a "thinking device" to promote ongoing dialogues about the quality of undergraduate and graduate programs within their own settings.

## Guiding Principles

The framework is grounded in a set of four guiding principles that we believe are fundamental to effective quality assessment. In effect, these principles comprise a statement of "best practices" for evaluating and improving the quality of academic programs. We identified and developed these principles on the basis of what we learned from the nearly 800 interviewees in our study, as well as from a critical reading of the total quality management, organizational learning, and higher education assessment literatures. The four principles are:

- The Linking Pin: A Constant Commitment to Student Learning
- People Make Quality Happen: Inclusivity and Engagement
- Learning Never Ends: Continuous Program Improvement
- Thinking Multidimensionally: Multiple Methods of Assessment

*The Linking Pin: A Constant Commitment to Student Learning*
At its most fundamental level, improving the quality of academic programs requires faculty and administrators to give thoughtful consideration to their collective core purposes and values and how these, in turn, are reflected in the overall direction and daily practices of their programs. This is not an easy task: it challenges faculty and administrators to examine their beliefs about what their assumptions are, whom they should serve, and what they hope to accomplish in their programs.

Reflecting on the higher education assessment and total quality management literatures as well as findings from our study, we concur with many others that perhaps no "core purpose" is more fundamental to improving the quality of academic programs than a constant commitment to student learning and development (Association of American Colleges 1992; Bergquist and Armstrong 1986; Bowen 1977; Bruffee 1993; Chickering and Gamson 1987; Guskin 1994; Kuh, Schuh, and Whitt 1991; Sanford 1968; Southern Association of Colleges and Schools 1982, Study Group on the Conditions of Excellence in American Higher Education 1984). As a beginning point, such a commitment ensures that students—and their learning experiences, needs, and outcomes—receive appropriate attention, study, and appraisal in ongoing program development.

When faculty and administrators are committed to student learning and development, they take two tasks seriously. First, they know that learning—and attending to and enhancing students' learning, in particular—is fundamental to what they do and who they are as educators. This overriding clarity of purpose provides faculty and administrators with a linking pin that incorporates the learner and the learning process fully into program planning and evaluation efforts. Second, a clear and consistent commitment to students' learning keeps faculty and administrators attuned to the needs and expectations of those whom they directly serve: students and employers. This attention to the "beneficiaries" of higher education (Chaffee, 1992) encourages faculty and administrators not only to ask these stakeholders what they expect students to learn in their programs, but also to assess if the program is effectively meeting these expectations.

From our perspective, a constant commitment to student learning and development is essential to improving the quality of our nation's undergraduate and graduate programs. In contrast to traditional approaches to quality assessment, this guiding principle makes students and their learning the focal point of program evaluation and improvement efforts. In so doing, it ensures that faculty and administrators give full attention to the quality of students' learning in their programs while also recognizing the needs of those whom they serve.

*People Make Quality Happen: Inclusivity and Engagement*
The total quality management and higher education assessment movements
have reminded many of us in higher education that, like it or not, enhancing
the quality of a program, good, or service is fundamentally a human activity (AAHE 1992; Chaffee 1992; Mentkowski 1991; Seymour 1992; Sherr and
Teeter 1991). It takes human beings to recognize weaknesses in the quality
of a learning system, to consider alternatives for its improvement, and to
act on proposals for change. In a very real sense, people—not simply curricular requirements or educational resources as many now believe—make
quality happen.

With this in mind, and supported by findings from our engagement
theory, we understand that meaningful quality assessment demands the collective intelligence and commitment of all parties who have a stake in academic programs. Faculty and administrators need to talk to one another
about the salience and impact of various learning experiences in their programs, while also recognizing and including others—especially students,
alumni, and employers—in these conversations. The "outsider" perspectives contributed by these latter stakeholders, in particular, often shed considerable light on issues related to program quality (Conrad, Haworth, and
Millar 1993; Kuh, Schuh, and Whitt 1991).

Faculty and administrators who take this guiding principle to heart make
it a priority to listen to and dialogue with students, alumni, and employers.
They establish participatory governance structures (such as alumni councils, employer advisory boards, and open forums with students) and make
use of interactive evaluation mechanisms (such as focus group interviews,
exit interviews, student advising sessions, and classroom research) to in-
quire into and listen carefully to stakeholders' appraisals of their programs.
More specifically, faculty and administrators use these "feedback loops" to
ask students and alumni about their learning experiences—including why
they find some more enriching than others, how they promote or hinder
their growth and development, and how they would modify or improve
these learning experiences in the future. From employers they seek to learn
what employers expect of their graduates and if program alumni, in fact,
meet these expectations. In both instances, faculty take Ellen Earle Chaffee's
advice about listening seriously: "Listen to the people you serve," she writes,
for "they are why you care about quality and they will tell you what to do"
(1992, 104).

Engaging diverse stakeholders in quality assessment and improvement
efforts is important for two primary reasons. First, generating a diversity of
perspectives challenges faculty and administrators to question their own
assumptions and to delve into the inner workings of their programs in new
and creative ways. These forms of creative inquiry almost always provide

meaningful fodder for continuous program improvement. Second, when students, alumni, and employers are regularly invited to comment on their program experiences and to suggest improvements, their collective sense of ownership in the program rises dramatically. They begin to understand that they have a voice in the program and that their ideas really matter. They also develop a greater appreciation that faculty and administrators are not the only parties responsible for ensuring program quality, and they assume that mantle more willingly. The idea here is simple: inclusivity fuels stakeholder engagement which, in turn, secures their future investment in the program. For these reasons, the importance of this guiding principle should not be overlooked in program planning and evaluation efforts. Particularly since it is people who, first and foremost, "make quality happen," this principle is especially crucial for ensuring stakeholder investment in the continuing improvement of academic programs.

*Learning Never Ends: Continuous Program Improvement*
In the Chinese language, "learning" literally means to "study and practice constantly" (Senge 1990, xv). As self-proclaimed "learners" who work in "learning organizations," it is tempting to assume that faculty and administrators devote sustained attention and effort to studying how their programs affect students' learning. To be sure, the literature contains support for this assumption (see, for example, Banta, 1993; Light 1990, 1992; Wright 1990). On balance, however, we concur with Ted Marchese that faculty and administrators in the majority of our nation's colleges and universities lack a "collective sense of obligation toward or avidness about the improvement of student learning" (1993, 12). For too many, self-study has become a relatively meaningless, episodic process targeted primarily at satisfying external mandates rather than a useful, continuous one aimed at understanding and improving the quality of student learning. To be sure, our colleges and universities are chock full of learners. But how many of them are interested, let alone engaged, in studying and learning about themselves?

Like many others, we believe that meaningful quality assessment requires faculty and administrators to make their "working space a learning space" in which they constantly examine and seek to learn about the inner workings of their own programs (AAHE 1992; Chaffee 1992; Ewell 1991; Marchese 1993; Seymour 1992; Sherr and Teeter 1991). More specifically, faculty and administrators need to turn a watchful and discerning eye to how various "processes" within their programs affect the quality of students' learning experiences and learning outcomes. What instructional and curricular practices, for example, do students and alumni find most useful and challenging? Useless and boring? What learning experiences do stakeholders cite (and other forms of evidence confirm) as "adding the most value" in terms of student learning outcomes? How does the learning environment—and, in particular, students' engagement with one another and faculty—enhance or hinder students' learning? Where does the "real learning" take place for students in the program? Ongoing learning of this sort—not least when informed by and interpreted within the context of our engagement theory—is critical if faculty and administrators are to obtain the types of usable information that can lead to meaningful educational change.

Continuous learning and improvement is an important feature of any quality assessment process for two reasons. First, since it requires faculty and administrators to turn a mirror on what they actually do in their programs and to collect data on how these practices affect the quality of students' learning, it provides a crucial evidentiary foundation upon which to base proposals for quality improvement. Again, we invoke the wise counsel of Karl and Karen Maitland Schilling: faculty and administrators cannot improve the quality of a system until they make that system visible. How can quality be improved if we have no idea what needs improving? How can we provide enriching learning experiences for students that positively affect their growth and development if we have little to no knowledge of what we are doing and how it is affecting students? Continuous program improvement—because it is formative in nature and provides useful data on educational practices within the "black box" of academic programs—helps us to see how we look from the inside out, often providing us with strong incentives to improve our appearance. When practiced with the openness and flexibility required of any meaningful learning effort, it promises to reveal program strengths and limitations and to spark informed suggestions targeted at improving the quality of teaching and learning.

Second, continuous program improvement helps to develop in faculty and administrators a new understanding that quality in academic programs—and, in particular, those learning experiences within them that enhance students' growth and development—demands constant attention and investment. Importing more resources or new curricular requirements into a program is no longer a ticket to improving academic quality. Faculty and administrators must now become learners as well as teachers. Without their engagement in studying, understanding, and improving student learning, the overall quality of academic programs—and students' experiences in them—will suffer greatly. Once again, it is people that matter—people make quality happen.

There is wisdom in the old adage, "learning never ends." The principle of continuous program improvement reflects that wisdom. From our perspective, as well as that of many others (AAHE 1992; Chaffee 1992; Ewell 1991; Marchese 1993; Seymour 1992; Sherr and Teeter 1991), it is an important guiding principle that faculty, administrators, and others should heed in assessing and planning academic programs.

*Thinking Multidimensionally: Multiple Methods of Assessment*
In his novel, *Slaughterhouse Five*, Kurt Vonnegut (1969) paints a vivid image of Billy Pilgrim, the story's main character, lying on a train capturing his only view of the Rocky Mountains through a pipe. He uses the scene in the novel as an analogy to describe how human beings think about time in unidimensional terms; we use it here to caution readers about the hazards of assessing program quality from only one vantage point. As our engagement theory suggests, program quality is a complex phenomenon. To engage and understand that complexity, a broader view is necessary—one that requires faculty and administrators to think about quality in multidimensional terms by surveying the landscape of their programs from multiple points of reference.

Just as many scholars in the higher education assessment movement advocate the use of multiple methods in assessing student learning (Davis 1989; Mentkowski 1991; Prus and Johnson 1992; Sell 1989; Terenzini 1989; Thomas 1991), we strongly believe that faculty and administrators must use multiple methods to assess the quality of academic programs. By drawing upon different data sources through various data collection methods, this guiding principle helps ensure that a more accurate and holistic understanding of program quality will be achieved.

When faculty and administrators take this guiding principle seriously, they dismiss the myth that there is "one true method" for assessing program quality and incorporate a variety of assessment strategies into their programs. These include, among others, course-embedded assessment methods—such as student portfolios (Forrest 1990) and various classroom assessment techniques (Angelo and Cross 1993)—as well as alumni and employer surveys, focus groups with diverse stakeholders, exit interviews with graduating students, and document review.[3]

This guiding principle is important for two reasons. To begin with, when a combination of methods are used, faculty and administrators are far more likely to develop a more holistic understanding of the quality of their programs. For example, qualitative methods—such as portfolios, focus groups, and classroom research—not only help faculty and others to find out what learning experiences really matter to students, but they also allow them to explore how and why those learning experiences make a difference in students' growth and development. Particularly when coupled with larger-scale quantitative surveys of students, alumni, and employers, the resulting mix of information from these methods can create a dynamic and multifaceted empirical foundation for understanding and, in turn, making improvements in a program's overall quality. Multiple methods have another advantage as well. Since they build on the strengths of different approaches, they help to cancel out the weaknesses embedded in a solitary approach to assessment. In short, quality assessments that employ multiple methods tend to produce more accurate and trustworthy (valid) findings.

Billy Pilgrim knew that there was much more to the Rocky Mountains than what he could see through a pipe. Similarly, there is much more to program quality than what any single assessment method can reveal. We urge faculty, administrators, and others to recognize the salience of this guiding principle in their continuing efforts to assess and improve the quality of their own and others' programs.

In summary, we advance four simple principles to guide any quality assessment effort: Stay focused on students and their learning. Involve and engage multiple stakeholders in quality assessment and improvement efforts. Constantly question how program "processes" hinder or promote student learning, and make every effort to improve them. Finally, use multiple methods to learn about and document quality. These principles suggest a process—or a set of "best practices"—for assessing and improving program quality. They are intended to help faculty and administrators understand *how* to assess and improve the quality of undergraduate and graduate programs. The question of *what* to assess still looms large. This is the question to which we now turn.

## Informing Questions and Quality Standards

Effective program evaluation requires, at a minimum, two key components. First, it must be informed by a set of questions that will call attention to the pertinent issues under study. Second, it must clearly articulate stated standards or criteria against which the answers to those questions can be interpreted and judged. Without either component, the evaluation "will lack focus, and the evaluator will have considerable difficulty explaining what will be examined, how, and why" (Worthen and Sanders 1987, 210).

With this in mind, we propose a range of evaluative questions and quality standards to assist faculty, administrators, and others in assessing and improving the quality of their programs. Grounded in our engagement theory of program quality, these questions and standards provide faculty and administrators with a theoretical basis to guide their quality assessment efforts as well as a theoretical framework through which to interpret their findings. That is, faculty and administrators can use these questions to examine the quality of their program in light of the theory's seventeen attributes and then, on the basis of the evidence collected, they can draw upon these standards to evaluate program strengths and limitations. From our perspective, this is a significant improvement over traditional quality assessment approaches in which faculty and administrators have tended to collect and interpret data on any number of evaluative questions and standards that lacked a firm basis in a theory of quality.

Table 9.1, at the end of this chapter, is a template that consists of guiding questions, quality criteria, and methods of assessment that faculty, administrators, and others may find useful in assessing the quality of their own programs. We are aware that by dividing the template into seventeen components—one for each attribute in the theory—readers could form the impression that program quality can be understood in terms of discrete parts. Such an impression would be a false one, as our engagement theory suggests.

As with any template, we caution readers to use their judgment and to adapt this template to the particularities of their own settings. Not all of the questions we raise can or should be addressed, nor is it feasible to use all of the assessment methods we propose. We believe that the template will be most useful to faculty and administrators if they meet with key stakeholders in their programs to prioritize questions of interest, to develop additional questions as warranted, and to select assessment methods that are most appropriate for collecting data on the questions they seek to answer.

This template—especially when combined with the aforementioned four principles of quality assessment—helps to translate our engagement theory into a useful framework for understanding, assessing, and improving program quality. We invite faculty, administrators, and others who have program planning and evaluation responsibilities to consider the framework as they continuously seek to improve and better understand the quality of their own undergraduate and graduate programs.

## Benefits of the Framework

What are the potential benefits of using this framework? In our view, the framework promises to benefit faculty and administrators in at least four ways as they seek to develop and sustain high-quality academic programs.

First, the framework—with its clear and consistent focus on student learning and development—provides faculty, administrators, and others with a guide for improving teaching and learning in academic programs. Unlike previous approaches to quality assessment, the framework draws attention to—and offers a template for discovering and understanding—how various instructional, curricular, and cultural practices affect the quality of students' learning. It not only supplies faculty and administrators with a new focal point for understanding program quality, but it also provides them with a guide for making visible those processes within the "black box" of academic programs that promote and enrich student learning. With this information in hand, faculty and administrators can engage in meaningful planning and improvement efforts aimed at enhancing the overall quality of teaching and learning in their programs.

Second, and closely related, the framework proposes a number of principles, guiding questions, criteria, and assessment methods that place continuous quality improvement squarely at the center of the quality assessment process. It challenges faculty, administrators, and others to engage in the kinds of organizational learning that can nurture and promote a culture in which teaching and learning—and its constant improvement—is highly valued (Chaffee 1992). Program participants begin to talk to one another about teaching and learning, to ask questions about student learning in the program, and to voice creative suggestions for change. In a very real sense, ongoing assessment and improvement becomes an important part of organizational life in these programs—a development, no doubt, that can be of obvious value to faculty and administrators in sustaining the quality of academic programs.

Third, the framework has the potential to provide faculty, administrators, and others with useful data on which to base program planning and improvement decisions. In contrast to traditional approaches to quality assessment, this framework makes use of a wider range of data sources and data collection methods by which to compile evidence of program quality. Moreover, it recommends that faculty and others collect evidence in reference to criteria that are directly linked to a theory of quality. On both of these accounts, the framework offers those who have program planning and evaluation responsibilities with a template for collecting relevant and trustworthy evidence that can better inform decisions related to ongoing program improvement.

The framework has potentially salutary consequences for planning and improving the quality of academic programs in one final way: it is likely to enhance stakeholder ownership and investment in ensuring the quality of academic programs. When students, alumni, employers, and other stakeholders are regularly asked to participate in planning, assessment, and improvement efforts, they begin to feel like their ideas and efforts matter in the program. They begin to take more responsibility for sustaining the quality of the program: alumni offer to sponsor interns or to share their perspectives with students in class; students are more likely to initiate out-of-class conversations with their peers and faculty or to put extra effort into their studies; employers take an active interest in mentoring students or working with faculty on collaborative projects. Put simply, an ethic of mutual accountability develops where, in the words of Robert Galvin, Motorola's chairman of the board, quality becomes "very first person" (Seymour 1992, 14). From student to employer and everyone in between, ensuring the future quality of the program becomes a shared responsibility in which everyone has a vital stake.

To be sure, the framework we propose is a demanding one. It requires all stakeholders to devote time and energy to quality assessment and improvement. That said, we believe the benefits that can accrue to students, faculty, and other stakeholders more than justifies these demands. Chapters

4 through 8 provide compelling evidence of how students (and employers, indirectly) stand to benefit from continuing efforts to develop and sustain high-quality programs. Faculty can gain from this process as well: not only are they likely to develop new and richer insights that will revitalize them as teachers and learners, but they will also experience the satisfaction of engaging in teaching, learning, and assessment activities that make a difference in their own and others' lives.

# Endnotes

1. A notable exception to this general trend is found in a recent document published by the Association of American Colleges entitled, *Program Review and Educational Quality in the Major* (1992). Its authors argue that program review should take as its primary focus "the quality of learning and achievement in the major" (1992, vi). In turn, they offer a protocol for assessing program quality in the major with this particular focus in mind.

2. Our framework for developing and sustaining high-quality academic programs is informed both by what we learned in our study of program quality and by recent developments in the assessment movement. Yet, while our work emphasizes the underlying value of improving students' learning—as others do in the assessment movement (AAHE 1992; Hutchings 1990; Light 1990, 1992; Schilling and Schilling 1993)—it has a distinctive focus on the evaluation of academic program quality, rather than on the assessment of individual learners.

3. A number of resources are available on various methods of assessment and evaluation. For a general overview, see Banta (1993), Prus and Johnson (1992), Worthen and Sanders (1987). Regarding faculty and student portfolios see, for instance, Centra (1993), Seldin (1993), Courts and McInerney (1993), Forrest (1990), and Knight and Gallaro (1994). For information on individual and focus group interviews, see Guba and Lincoln (1981), Krueger (1994), Morgan (1988), Patton (1987), and Seidman (1991). Also see Angelo and Cross (1993) for information on classroom assessment techniques.

**TABLE 9.1  A Template for Assessing Program Quality**

*Attribute: Diverse and Engaged Faculty*

| Questions to Guide Assessment | Criteria and Indicators of Attribute | Suggested Methods of Assessment |
|---|---|---|
| 1. How do faculty and administrators define a "good" faculty member? What personal and professional characteristics do they look for in new faculty members?<br>2. What criteria are reflected in the program's hiring policy for faculty? Which criteria are given the most emphasis in the faculty recruitment and selection process?<br>3. How diverse are faculty in terms of race, ethnicity, gender, and socioeconomic background? Are faculty diverse in terms of educational and professional workplace experience?<br>4. Are faculty involved in a range of scholarly activities? Do faculty share their scholarship with students?<br>5. Is there a good representation of different theoretical, applied, and methodological perspectives among program faculty? Do faculty members infuse these different perspectives into their teaching? If so, how?<br>6. What effect (if any) does faculty diversity have on students' growth and development?<br>7. How committed are faculty to students? Where, when, and how do they demonstrate their commitment? | 1. Scholarly Diversity of Faculty<br>  • A variety of "ways-of-knowing" are represented among program faculty.<br>  • Differing modes of scholarship are represented among program faculty.<br>  • Faculty infuse a range of methodological, theoretical, and experiential perspectives into classroom lectures and discussions.<br>2. Faculty Engagement in Teaching<br>  • Faculty share a commitment to student learning and development.<br>  • Faculty invest in various teaching-related activities.<br>3. Educational Background and Professional Experience of Faculty<br>  • Faculty possess appropriate graduate degrees.<br>  • Individuals with professional, non-university workplace experience are represented among the program's faculty.<br>4. Departmental and Institutional Policies<br>  • Faculty hiring policies emphasize criteria such as educational background, research productivity, scholarly diversity, professional expe- | • Faculty portfolio assessment<br>• Peer evaluations of teaching<br>• Student evaluations of teaching<br>• Focus group interviews with faculty, administrators, students, alumni, and employers<br>• Document review (for evidence of supportive hiring, merit, promotion, and tenure policies) |

8. How do students describe program faculty? Do they believe that faculty are personally interested in their learning? Disinterested? What effect does faculty engagement (or disengagement) have on students' growth and development?

9. What kinds of instructional approaches do faculty members use in their classes? How frequently do faculty members revise the content of their courses to reflect new developments in their field?

10. Do department and institutional merit, promotion, and tenure policies recognize and reward faculty for their involvement in a broad range of scholarly activities? Are each of these activities comparably "weighted" in the departmental and institutional reward structure?

11. How important is teaching—and a demonstrated commitment to student learning and development—in merit, promotion, and tenure policies and practices?

rience in the non-university workplace, teaching and advising competence, and dedication to student learning.

• Departmental and institutional promotion, tenure, and merit review policies recognize and reward faculty for their participation in a range of scholarly endeavors as well as for their involvement in teaching-related activities.

*(Continued)*

**TABLE 9.1** (*Continued*)

*Attribute: Diverse and Engaged Students*

| Questions to Guide Assessment | Criteria and Indicators of Attribute | Suggested Methods of Assessment |
| --- | --- | --- |
| 1. How do faculty define a "good student"? What personal and professional characteristics do they look for in student applicants?<br><br>2. What criteria are reflected in the program's admissions policy? Which criteria are given the most emphasis by faculty in the student selection process?<br><br>3. How much emphasis is placed on matching student goals and interests with those of the program and faculty in the admissions selection process? Do faculty intentionally strive to ensure a "good fit" between students and faculty in this respect, admitting only those who will be well-served by the program?<br><br>4. How diverse are students in terms of race, ethnicity, gender, and socioeconomic background? Are a variety of educational, workplace, and life experiences represented in the student body?<br><br>5. How willing are students to share their life and workplace experiences with others in the program? Do faculty members encourage students to share their experiences and views in class?<br><br>6. In what ways (if any) do students' perspectives and views on knowledge and | 1. Student Diversity<br>• Students with a variety of educational, life, and professional workplace experiences are represented in the program.<br>• Male and female students from a variety of racial, ethnic, and socioeconomic backgrounds are represented.<br><br>2. Engagement in Teaching and Learning<br>• Students actively contribute diverse perspectives on knowledge and practice to class discussions.<br>• Students demonstrate a visible commitment to their own and others' learning (via their participation in classroom discussions, cooperative learning activities, individual and group projects, independent studies and research).<br><br>3. Departmental Policies and Practices<br>• Departmental student admissions policies emphasize a variety of criteria, including educational background, life experience, professional non-university workplace experience, cultural diversity, academic achievement, | • Focus group interviews with students, alumni, and faculty<br>• Student portfolio assessment (for evidence of engagement in learning via individual and collaborative reports, projects, and other products of learning)<br>• Document review (for evidence of supportive admissions policies) |

practice affect one anothers' learning and development?

7. Are students generally active or passive in their approach to learning?

8. How committed are students to their own and others' learning? Where, when, and how do they express their commitment?

9. How does students' commitment (or lack thereof) to one anothers' learning affect their learning and development?

and motivation for learning.
- Admissions decisions are based heavily on the "goodness of fit" between student goals and those of faculty and the program.

## Attribute: Engaged Leaders

| Questions to Guide Assessment | Criteria and Indicators of Attribute | Suggested Methods of Assessment |
|---|---|---|
| 1. How do diverse stakeholders, especially faculty and students, describe the chair of the program? Hierarchical or participatory? Invitational or off-putting? An advocate? Adversary? Disinterested bystander?<br>2. How committed is the chair to "championing" the program? Where, when, and how does he or she demonstrate his or her commitment?<br>3. Does the program chair make leadership opportunities available to faculty, students, and others? If so, how does he or she support faculty and students for their involvement in these leadership roles? How are students affected by these leadership experiences? | 1. Participatory Leadership<br>• The program director or chair invites a broad range of stakeholders—such as students, alumni, faculty, and employers—to participate in the governance of the program.<br>• The chair provides faculty, students, alumni, and others with opportunities to assume informal leadership roles in the program.<br>• The chair is instrumental in developing a culture that values teaching and learning.<br>2. Administrative Effectiveness<br>• The chair is effective at promoting the program and building support for it | • Focus group interviews with faculty, institutional administrators, students, alumni, and employers<br>• Faculty survey of administrative effectiveness |

(Continued)

181

**TABLE 9.1** (*Continued*)

*Attribute: Engaged Leaders* (*Continued*)

| Questions to Guide Assessment | Criteria and Indicators of Attribute | Suggested Methods of Assessment |
|---|---|---|
| 4. Does the program chair invite faculty, students, alumni, and employers to discuss and make decisions regarding program policies and practices? If so, in what ways does he or she do this? | with internal and external audiences. • The chair is adept at securing monetary and non-monetary support for the program. • The chair is effective at recruiting new faculty and students whose goals and interests are congruent with those of the program. | |
| 5. What messages does the chair send to faculty and students, in particular, about the importance of teaching and learning in the program? | | |
| 6. How effective is the chair at promoting the program and its mission to institutional administrators, prospective students, and other external audiences? How does the chair go about this task? | | |
| 7. How effective is the chair at securing monetary and non-monetary support for the program from institutional administrators? External parties (such as alumni, employers, private foundations)? | | |
| 8. How effective is the chair in recruiting faculty and students who share a commitment to their own and others' teaching and learning? | | |

## Attribute: Shared Program Direction

| Questions to Guide Assessment | Criteria and Indicators of Attribute | Suggested Methods of Assessment |
|---|---|---|
| 1. What is the overall direction or focus of the program? What do faculty and administrators intentionally hope to accomplish in the program?<br>2. How do different stakeholders—faculty, program administrators, institutional administrators, students, alumni, and employers—describe the program's overall direction? To what extent do they share similar understandings of the program's direction?<br>3. How was the program's overall direction determined? Who was involved? Was it a collective process?<br>4. When, where, how and to whom is the program's overall direction communicated? Is the content of what is communicated consistent with the overall direction of the program and actual practices within it?<br>5. How frequently are the overall direction and goals of the program reviewed? Who is involved in this process? Is student, alumni, and employer feedback solicited?<br>6. What kind of graduates are faculty and administrators in the program trying to develop? What kinds of curricular requirements and learning experiences does the program offer to ensure that graduates achieve this goal? | 1. Stakeholder Involvement in Program<br>  • Program leaders involve faculty, students, alumni, and employers in developing and sustaining a shared program direction.<br>  • Program leaders involve faculty, students, alumni, and employers in continuous program planning and evaluation efforts in which they examine the congruence between the program's teaching and learning experiences and its overall direction.<br>2. Shared Support for Program Direction<br>  • Diverse stakeholders share broadly similar understandings of the program's overall direction and are supportive of it.<br>3. Fitness-to-Purpose<br>  • Teaching and learning experiences in the program are congruent with its stated direction. | • Focus group interviews with faculty, administrators, students, recent program graduates, and employers<br>• Document review of promotional materials, mission statement, student handbooks, course syllabi, and self-studies |

*(Continued)*

**TABLE 9.1** *(Continued)*

*Attribute: Shared Program Direction (Continued)*

| Questions to Guide Assessment | Criteria and Indicators of Attribute | Suggested Methods of Assessment |
|---|---|---|
| 7. How does the program's overall direction inform the content and character of teaching and learning in the program? More specifically, how does it inform what knowledge, skills, and practices are taught to students and in what ways? Are curricular requirements and learning experiences congruent with the program's overall direction? | | |
| 8. How does a shared program direction (or lack of one) promote or hinder student's learning and development? | | |

*Attribute: Community of Learners*

| Questions to Guide Assessment | Criteria and Indicators of Attribute | Suggested Methods of Assessment |
|---|---|---|
| 1. How do faculty define their roles as teachers? Students' roles as learners? What words do they use to describe their relationships with students? | 1. Collegial Relations among Program Participants<br><br>• Program participants de-emphasize traditional hierarchical relationships (between faculty and students, senior and junior faculty, administrators and staff) and interact with one another more or less as colleagues. | • Focus groups with students, alumni, faculty, and administrators<br>• Exit interviews with graduating students<br>• Student and alumni surveys<br>• Document review (for evidence of an emphasis on collaborative learning in promotional materials, mission statement, syllabi) |
| 2. How do students define their roles as learners? Faculty members' roles as teachers? What words do they use to describe their relationships with faculty? | | |

3. How do students view one another? As competitive rivals? Disinterested bystanders? Knowledgeable peers? Colleagues? To what extent do students believe that they learn from one another?

4. To what extent do faculty collaborate with one another in their teaching or research? To what extent do they collaborate with students in these areas?

5. To what extent do students feel a camaraderie with one another? To what extent do faculty feel a camaraderie with one another?

6. What words do faculty, students, and administrators use to describe the general "feel" or "ethos" of the program?

7. Which is more pronounced in the program's learning environment: competition or collaboration? What effect does this dominant theme—and the way it is enacted in the program—have on student learning?

8. What is the general tenor of interactions among faculty in the program? Collegial? Indifferent? Antagonistic? Among students?

9. What opportunities exist in the program for students to engage in cooperative or team-based learning? Do faculty encourage cooperative learning? If yes, how? In what ways do these group-centered, interactive learning experiences affect students' growth and development?

- Faculty and students regularly collaborate between and among themselves on various research, teaching, and service-related projects.

2. Sense of Shared Identity and Membership

- Program participants share a common identity with the program that generates a positive camaraderie among all.
- Program participants feel like—and treat one another as—contributing members in a learning community.

3. Cooperative, Interactive Learning Environment

- An ethic of cooperation and interaction, rather than competition and isolation, characterizes the program's learning environment.
- The program has structured curricular requirements (such as required field school, laboratory, or core course work requirements) and various teaching and learning activities (such as collaborative research projects, journal clubs, and assorted out-of-class social events) that promote cooperative and interactive learning among program participants.

(Continued)

**TABLE 9.1** (*Continued*)

*Attribute: Risk-Taking Environment*

| Questions to Guide Assessment | Criteria and Indicators of Attribute | Suggested Methods of Assessment |
|---|---|---|
| 1. What messages do faculty and administrators send to students about the expectations they hold for their learning? How do students interpret these messages? In what ways, if any, do faculty and administrators develop a learning environment in which students feel "safe to fail"? | 1. High Expectations for Student Learning and Development<br>• Faculty and administrators hold high expectations for learning and articulate them clearly to students. | • Focus groups with students, alumni, faculty, and administrators<br>• Exit interviews with graduating students<br>• Student and alumni surveys<br>• Student portfolio assessment (for examples of creative and "risky" projects, papers, and so forth) |
| 2. To what extent do faculty encourage students to take risks in their own learning? How frequently do they provide them with opportunities to do so? | 2. Faculty Support for Risk-Taking<br>• Faculty model risk-taking to students and encourage them to follow their lead.<br>• Faculty provide students with frequent opportunities to take risks in their own learning without penalty. | |
| 3. Do faculty describe themselves as risk-takers? What kinds of risks do they take? Do they freely and willingly share their failures as well as their successes with students? Are they willing to take risks with new instructional approaches in their classes? | 3. Open and Hospitable Learning Climate<br>• The program has an open, hospitable, and "safe" learning environment in which students feel supported to take risks in their own learning. | |
| 4. What words do students use to describe the learning climate in the program? Do they believe it is an invitational or an intimidating place to learn? Do students feel challenged and supported to do their best? | | |
| 5. What words do faculty, students, and administrators use to describe the program's learning environment? | | |

6. Do students believe it is "safe" for them to question assumptions, engage in "risky" projects, and take other kinds of risks in the program? Do they fear penalty or reprisal from faculty?

7. To what extent do students take risks in their learning? What effect does risk-taking (or lack thereof) have on students' growth and development?

8. What is more pronounced in the program's learning environment: conformity or creativity? What effect does this dominant theme—and the way it is enacted in the program—have on student learning?

## Attribute: Critical Dialogue

| Questions to Guide Assessment | Criteria and Indicators of Attribute | Suggested Methods of Assessment |
|---|---|---|
| 1. How do faculty describe themselves as teachers? What words do they use to describe their overall approach to teaching and learning? Do students offer similar descriptions? <br><br> 2. What kinds of instructional activities (e.g., lectures, discussions, role plays, simulations, student-led seminars, Socratic dialogues) do faculty use most frequently in their classes? Least frequently? <br><br> 3. What is the character and frequency of faculty–student interaction in class? What | 1. Interactive Approach to Teaching and Learning <br> • Faculty utilize a two-way, interactive approach to teaching and learning that emphasizes ongoing dialogue and reflection with students. <br> • Faculty use a variety of interactive instructional activities, including small and large group discussions, role-playing exercises, and student-led seminars. <br><br> 2. Critical Inquiry | • Focus groups with students, alumni, faculty, and administrators <br> • Classroom research <br> • Exit interviews with graduating students <br> • Student, alumni and employer surveys <br> • Peer evaluations of teaching <br> • Student evaluations of teaching <br> • Student portfolio assessment (for examples of creative and "risky" projects, papers, and so forth) <br> • Faculty portfolio assessment (examination of syllabi and statement of philos- <br> *(Continued)* |

**TABLE 9.1** *(Continued)*

*Attribute: Critical Dialogue (Continued)*

| Questions to Guide Assessment | Criteria and Indicators of Attribute | Suggested Methods of Assessment |
|---|---|---|
| metaphors do faculty and students use to describe these interactions?<br>4. What kinds of opportunities are provided to students to share their ideas, views, and experiences with faculty? How frequently are these opportunities offered?<br>5. Are faculty respectful of students' views and opinions? How do they evaluate the contributions that students make to class discussions?<br>6. In what ways do faculty challenge students to examine assumptions, scrutinize theory and practice, and critically evaluate their own and others' ideas? What skills do students hone through discussions such as these?<br>7. Which is more pronounced in the program: active or passive student learning?<br>8. How do students describe their involvement in class? Do they believe faculty challenge them to "think aloud" in new and demanding ways?" What effect does active engagement in dialogues of this sort have on students' analytical and problem-solving skills? Professional confidence? | • Faculty and students engage in disciplined and mutually-enriching discussions in which they critically question and scrutinize knowledge and practice in the field.<br>• Students are actively engaged in the learning process, questioning their own and others' assumptions, discussing alternative points of view, and generating critically-informed understandings of knowledge and practice. | ophy of teaching to assess, in part, commitment to and use of critical dialogue in classroom teaching) |

*Attribute: Integrative Learning*

| Questions to Guide Assessment | Criteria and Indicators of Attribute | Suggested Methods of Assessment |
|---|---|---|
| 1. How do faculty describe themselves as teachers? What words do they use to describe their overall approach to teaching and learning? Do students offer similar descriptions?<br>2. What kinds of instructional activities (e.g., lectures, discussions, role plays, simulations, case studies, field research) do faculty use most frequently in the program? Least frequently?<br>3. How does the program, in terms of curricular content, connect with the lives of students? Important problems in the "real world"?<br>4. To what extent do faculty model "connected" understandings of theory and practice to students?<br>5. How frequently do faculty members invite professionals from the non-university workplace to "bridge the gap" between what students are learning in the program with "real world" issues, problems, and concerns of the profession?<br>6. What kinds of opportunities are provided to students to connect what they are learning in their classes to complex problems, issues, and situations in the real world? How frequently are these opportunities offered? | 1. Integrative Instruction<br>  • Faculty tie the knowledge and skills they present in their lectures or class discussions to tangible issues and "real world" problems.<br>  • Faculty use hands-on instructional activities—such as role-plays, case studies, simulations, field trips, artistic performances, field research, and laboratory experiments—that involve students directly in making connections between theory and practice. | • Focus groups with students, alumni, faculty, and administrators<br>• Classroom research<br>• Exit interviews with graduating students<br>• Student, alumni, and employer surveys<br>• Performance assessment<br>• Student portfolio assessment (for examples of integrative practice in course papers, projects, and other assignments)<br>• Peer evaluations of teaching<br>• Student evaluations of teaching |

*(Continued)*

189

**TABLE 9.1** (*Continued*)

*Attribute: Integrative Learning* (*Continued*)

| Questions to Guide Assessment | Criteria and Indicators of Attribute | Suggested Methods of Assessment |
|---|---|---|
| In what ways do learning opportunities of this sort enhance students' growth and development? | | |
| 7. How do students describe the knowledge and skills they are taught in the program? Theoretical? Applied? A judicious blend of both? Overly-academic? Too practical? | | |
| 8. In what ways do faculty challenge students to blend theory with practice in the program? What skills do students hone through activities such as these? | | |

*Attribute: Mentoring*

| Questions to Guide Assessment | Criteria and Indicators of Attribute | Suggested Methods of Assessment |
|---|---|---|
| 1. Do faculty actively seek to learn about students as individuals? Do they express an interest in learning about students' career interests and goals? | 1. Engaged Advising<br>• Faculty learn about students' career interests and goals and develop individualized program plans consonant with them.<br>• Faculty meet with advisees on a regular basis to discuss their academic progress and performance. | • Focus groups with students, alumni, faculty, and administrators<br>• Exit interviews with graduating students<br>• Student and alumni surveys<br>• Student portfolio assessment (for evidence of collaborative work with faculty)<br>• Faculty portfolio assessment (for evidence |
| 2. How seriously do faculty take their advising responsibilities? How do they advise students? | | |
| 3. How frequently do faculty meet with | | |

of collaborative work with students, for listing of advisees)

- Faculty assist students in locating employment upon graduation.
2. Individualization
  - Faculty mentor students through various forms of individualized instruction, including informal, one-on-one interactions with students outside-of-class in the lab, field, or studio; individualized tutorials; and independent readings and research courses.
  - Faculty provide students with regular and timely feedback on their professional development.

advisees to discuss their academic progress and performance in the program? Who initiates these meetings?

4. Are advising responsibilities equally shared among faculty in the department?

5. Are faculty generally on campus and available to meet with students outside of class?

6. What kinds of opportunities are provided to students for individualized study with faculty? To what extent are faculty willing to offer individualized learning opportunities to students? How frequently do students take advantage of such opportunities? In what ways do learning opportunities of this sort enhance students' growth and development?

7. Do faculty members view mentoring as an important professional responsibility? If so, who do they mentor and how?

8. Do students believe that faculty mentors are available in the program? Do they feel like they have been mentored in any way by faculty? How do they describe these experiences and their effects on their development?

9. How does mentoring positively affect students' knowledge and skills development? Professional confidence?

10. When, where, and how do faculty provide students with individualized feedback on their academic performance and skills development? How often is feedback provided to students? What form does this feedback take?

*(Continued)*

191

**TABLE 9.1** *(Continued)*

*Attribute: Cooperative Peer Learning*

| Questions to Guide Assessment | Criteria and Indicators of Attribute | Suggested Methods of Assessment |
| --- | --- | --- |
| 1. What is more pronounced among faculty in the program: individualism or cooperation? Among students? In the instructional approaches of faculty? | 1. Team-Oriented Teaching and Learning<br>• Faculty engage in collaborative research and team-teaching activities.<br>• Faculty use a number of instructional approaches that emphasize team-oriented approaches to learning, including small and large group discussions, role plays, study groups, research teams and group presentations. | • Focus groups with students, alumni, faculty, and administrators<br>• Classroom research<br>• Exit interviews with graduating students<br>• Student, alumni, and employer surveys<br>• Peer evaluations of teaching<br>• Student evaluations of teaching<br>• Student portfolio assessment (for evidence of collaborative work with peers)<br>• Faculty portfolio assessment (for evidence of the use of cooperative peer learning in courses as documented in syllabi, instructional materials, videotapes of instruction) |
| 2. What kinds of instructional activities (e.g., lectures, discussions, role plays, simulations, case studies, field research) do faculty use most frequently in the program? Least frequently? | • Faculty require students to complete collaborative assignments and projects, including group presentations, case studies, research projects, and artistic performances. | |
| 3. What opportunities are available to students to learn from one another as members of a team? How frequently do faculty provide students with these opportunities, and how often do students take advantage of them? How do learning opportunities of this sort enhance students' growth and development? | 2. Collaborative and Social Learning<br>• Students actively seek to learn from and support one another in the program, both in and out of class.<br>• An ethic of cooperation and interaction, rather than competition and isolation, characterizes students' interaction in the program. | |
| 4. Are students required to complete team-based projects, papers, or presentations as part of their courses? | | |
| 5. What words do students use to describe their interactions with one another? | | |
| 6. To what extent do students feel like they learn from their peers? Do they actively seek out one anothers' knowledge, ideas, and views? | | |

7. How frequently do students interact with one another in the program? How often do they participate in various out-of-class activities?
8. To what extent do students compete with one another over grades, scholarships, and other "limited goods" in the program? In what ways do faculty members and program policies promote or diminish competition among students?
9. How does cooperative peer learning positively affect students knowledge and skills development? Professional confidence?

## Attribute: Out-of-Class Activities

| Questions to Guide Assessment | Criteria and Indicators of Attribute | Suggested Methods of Assessment |
| --- | --- | --- |
| 1. Who initiates planning for out-of-class activities in the program? Who assumes primary responsibility for designing and promoting out-of-class activities? <br><br> 2. What opportunities are available for faculty, students, and administrators to learn from and socialize with one another outside of class? <br><br> 3. How frequently do faculty and administrators attend out-of-class activities in the program, such as colloquia, brown bag lunch | 1. Active Engagement in Out-of-Class Activities <br> • Faculty, administrators, and students design and sponsor an assortment of out-of-class activities, including brown bag seminars, journal clubs, colloquia, and informal social events. <br> • Faculty and administrators frequently attend out-of-class functions. <br> • Students frequently attend out-of-class functions. | • Focus groups with students, alumni, faculty, and administrators <br> • Exit interviews with graduating students <br> • Student, alumni, and employer surveys <br> • Document review (for evidence of student clubs, organizations, departmental financial support) |

*(Continued)*

**TABLE 9.1** (*Continued*)

*Attribute: Out-of-Class Activities* (*Continued*)

| Questions to Guide Assessment | Criteria and Indicators of Attribute | Suggested Methods of Assessment |
|---|---|---|
| seminars, departmental parties, and other informal social gatherings? <br> 4. How frequently do students participate in out-of-class activities such as study groups, journal clubs, colloquia, or other informal social gatherings? <br> 5. What words do students use to describe "student life" in the program? <br> 6. To what extent do students feel like they learn from their peers? Do they actively seek out one anothers' knowledge, ideas, and views outside of class? <br> 7. How does student participation in out-of-class activities positively affect their knowledge and skills development? Their attitudes toward collaboration? <br> 8. To what extent do departmental administrators support—financially and otherwise—out-of-class learning activities in the program? What kinds of support do they provide and why? | 2. Departmental Support <br> • Departmental administrators provide adequate financial support to support to sponsor various out-of-class activities. | |

## Attribute: *Planned Breadth and Depth Course Work*

| Questions to Guide Assessment | Criteria and Indicators of Attribute | Suggested Methods of Assessment |
|---|---|---|
| 1. What knowledge, skills, and practices do faculty and administrators most want students to learn in the program? To what extent are these expectations reflected in the program's curriculum? In their courses? | 1. Shared Agreement on Curricular Objectives | • Focus groups with students, alumni, faculty, and administrators |
| 2. To what extent do faculty and administrators share common understandings regarding their expectations for student learning in the program? How do they communicate these expectations? | • Faculty and administrators share common understandings of the knowledge, skills, and practices they expect all program graduates to learn. | • Exit interviews with graduating students |
|  | • The program's curriculum reflects these expectations. | • Student, alumni, and employer surveys |
| 3. Are curricular goals and objectives consistent with the larger goals (or direction) of the program? What processes are in place for monitoring their achievement? | 2. Coherent Sequence of Required Course Work | • Document review (for evidence of clearly stated curricular goals and objectives, descriptions of course work required and its sequencing) |
| 4. How frequently do faculty and administrators meet to review and discuss curricular goals and objectives? What modifications have been made to the curriculum as a result? | • A core of required course work is required in the program that provides students with a broad understanding of foundational knowledge in the field. | • Transcript analysis |
| 5. What is the overall design of the curriculum? How and by whom was it determined? | • A set of specialized courses are required in the program that provide in-depth instruction in one or more sub-areas of the field. | • Comprehensive examinations (for evidence of student learning in required courses) |
| 6. Are foundational, or breadth, courses a part of the curriculum? How many of these courses are required and how are they sequenced? What is the rationale for their inclusion? |  | • Student portfolio assessment (for evidence of student learning in required courses) |

*(Continued)*

**TABLE 9.1** *(Continued)*

*Attribute: Planned Breadth and Depth Course Work (Continued)*

| Questions to Guide Assessment | Criteria and Indicators of Attribute | Suggested Methods of Assessment |
| --- | --- | --- |
| 7. Are a set of specialized, or depth courses a part of the curriculum? How many of these courses are required and how are they sequenced? What is the rationale for their inclusion? | | |
| 8. What is the blend of "core" and "specialized" course work in the program? Is it balanced? Does the curriculum emphasize breadth at the expense of depth or vice versa? | | |
| 9. Are students aware of the connections between "core" and "specialized" courses? How do they describe the kinds of knowledge taught in each? | | |
| 10. How do students' learning experiences in core courses affect their knowledge and skills development? Specialized courses? The combination of the two? | | |

*Attribute: Professional Residency*

| Questions to Guide Assessment | Criteria and Indicators of Attribute | Suggested Methods of Assessment |
|---|---|---|
| 1. Is a professional residency of some sort—an internship, practicum, clinical, or teaching/research assistantship—required of students in the program? What rationale do faculty and administrators provide for requiring, or not requiring, a professional residency? | 1. Professional Residency Requirement | • Focus groups with students, alumni, faculty, and administrators |
| 2. If a residency is required, what is its overall design? How and by whom was it determined? | • Students are required to complete at least one semester-long, hands-on learning experience—such as an internship, practicum, clinical, or teaching/research assistantship—in an applied setting of their choice. | • Exit interviews with graduating students |
| 3. What professional residency opportunities are available to students through the program? How frequently are these opportunities offered? | 2. Supportive Departmental Practices | • Student, alumni, and employer surveys |
| | • Faculty and administrators maintain an up-to-date listing of residency sites and supervisors. | • Document review (for evidence of up-to-date listings of residency sites and supervisors; "residency" contracts that clearly describe expectations and responsibilities of students, site supervisors, and faculty; policy statements/handbooks that describe the residency and outline procedures for securing one) |
| 4. Are professional residency requirements tailored to meet the career goals and objectives of each student? How so? | • Faculty and administrators assist students in identifying and selecting residency experiences that complement their professional goals and interests. | • Performance assessments (for evidence of student learning during the residency) |
| 5. What are students expected to learn and do during their professional residencies? How are these expectations developed and by whom? How are they communicated to students, site supervisors, and faculty? | • Faculty members and site supervisors provide students with regular guidance and feedback throughout their residency. | • Student portfolio assessment (for evidence of student learning in residency via required papers, projects, and journals) |
| 6. What words do students use to describe their residency experiences? How do they benefit from this learning experience? How does it affect their knowledge and skills development? Professional confidence and identity? | | • Job placement data |
| 7. To what extent do students make meaningful connections between what they learned in their classes with what they are learning in | | |

*(Continued)*

197

**TABLE 9.1** (*Continued*)

*Attribute: Professional Residency (Continued)*

| Questions to Guide Assessment | Criteria and Indicators of Attribute | Suggested Methods of Assessment |
|---|---|---|
| the residency? How do these connections benefit students? | | |
| 8. To what extent do faculty and administrators assist students in locating residency sites? Does the program maintain a current listing of residency sites and contact persons? | | |
| 9. Do faculty and administrators maintain close ties with employers, alumni, and community members through advisory councils, alumni associations, and regional professional organizations that help them to identify and secure residency sites for students? | | |
| 10. Do faculty meet with site supervisors and students prior to placement in order to clarify student and supervisor expectations for the residency, define work responsibilities for the student-resident and determine the frequency and extent of supervisory and faculty feedback to student-residents? | | |
| 11. When, where, and how frequently do faculty, site supervisors, and student-residents meet to review and discuss the resident's performance? What kinds of feedback are provided to students throughout their residency? | | |

*Attribute: Tangible Product*

| Questions to Guide Assessment | Criteria and Indicators of Attribute | Suggested Methods of Assessment |
|---|---|---|
| 1. Is a tangible product of some sort—either a thesis, project report, or artistic performance—required of students in the program? What rationale do faculty and administrators provide for requiring, or not requiring, a tangible product? | 1. Tangible Product Requirement <br> • Students are required to complete a tangible product—usually a thesis, project report, or artistic performance—in which they demonstrate their abilities as knowledgeable and skilled professionals in the field. | • Focus groups with students, alumni, faculty, and administrators <br> • Exit interviews with graduating students <br> • Student, alumni, and employer surveys <br> • Document review (for evidence of policy statements/handbooks that describe the requirement and outline procedures for completing it) |
| 2. If a tangible product is required, what form does it take (e.g., thesis, project report, artistic performance). How does this requirement fit in with the overall direction and goals of the program? | 2. Individualized Guidance and Feedback <br> • Faculty members provide students with individualized guidance and feedback as appropriate while completing tangible product requirements. | • Oral examination on the tangible product (for evidence of students' understandings of what they learned as a result of their experience and how this knowledge connects to previous learning in the program) |
| 3. What kinds of projects do students produce? How do faculty and other external examiners evaluate their overall quality? | | • Student portfolio assessment (for examples of students' tangible products) |
| 4. What are students expected to demonstrate—in terms of knowledge, skills, and attitudes—to others in completing their tangible product? When and how are these expectations communicated to students? | | • Faculty portfolio assessment (for evidence of faculty involvement in advising students on their theses, project reports, and other culminating projects) |
| 5. How do students describe their tangible product learning experiences? How do they benefit from this experience? In what ways does the experience enhance their knowledge and skills development? Professional confidence and identity? | | |
| 6. To what extent do students meaningfully apply and connect knowledge and skills learned in the program to what they are | | |

*(Continued)*

199

**TABLE 9.1** (*Continued*)

*Attribute: Tangible Product* (*Continued*)

| Questions to Guide Assessment | Criteria and Indicators of Attribute | Suggested Methods of Assessment |
|---|---|---|
| completing for their culminating tangible products? How do these connections benefit students? | | |
| 7. Are faculty on campus and available to provide students with guidance and feedback on issues or concerns related to their tangible products? How often do faculty meet with students to review and discuss their progress? What kinds of feedback do they provide to students? | | |

*Attribute: Support for Students*

| Questions to Guide Assessment | Criteria and Indicators of Attribute | Suggested Methods of Assessment |
|---|---|---|
| 1. What forms of financial support are available to students in the program? What percentage of students who request financial support receive it? | 1. Financial Support for Students<br>• The institution and department provides funding to support an adequate number of student scholarships, fellowships, and assistantships. | • Focus groups with students, alumni, faculty, and administrators<br>• Exit interviews with graduating students<br>• Student, alumni, and employer surveys<br>• Document review (for evidence of financial support to students, flexible course scheduling) |
| 2. What efforts do program administrators and faculty make to secure financial support for students? | • The institution and department provides funding to support student travel to professional conferences. | |
| 3. Are courses offered on a flexible schedule and via different formats (such as evening/weekend or satellite-based/videotaped | 2. Flexible Course Delivery Formats<br>• The program utilizes flexible course | |

formats? How frequently are courses offered utilizing these formats?

4. In what ways does the university's career planning and placement office assist students in the job search process? How frequently do students take advantage of these services?

5. To what extent do faculty and administrators assist students in preparing for and locating professional employment upon graduation?

6. How do students describe and assess the financial support they receive in the program? Do they believe that the program seeks to accommodate students' needs, particularly in terms of where, when, and how it delivers course-based instruction? How do these forms of support help to facilitate or hinder students' learning?

7. How do students and employers describe the job placement services offered by the university's career counseling and placement center?

delivery formats—such as evening, weekend, and intensive summer courses and satellite-based or video-taped instruction—that allow students with different schedules and responsibilities to pursue their studies at convenient times.

3. Career Placement Services
- Faculty and program administrators assist students in preparing for and locating employment upon graduation.
- Staff in the university's career planning and placement office assist students in preparing for and locating employment upon graduation.

(Continued)

**TABLE 9.1** *(Continued)*

*Attribute: Support for Faculty*

| Questions to Guide Assessment | Criteria and Indicators of Attribute | Suggested Methods of Assessment |
|---|---|---|
| 1. Is financial support available for faculty research, travel to professional conferences, sabbaticals, and professional development opportunities? If so, how much support is available? How is this support distributed among faculty in the program? | 1. Financial Support for Faculty <br> • The institution provides competitive salaries to sustain a critical mass of faculty. <br> • The program provides adequate funding for faculty travel to professional conferences. | • Focus groups with students, alumni, faculty, and administrators <br> • Student, alumni, and employer surveys <br> • Document review (for evidence of financial support to faculty, supportive departmental and institutional merit, promotion, and tenure policies) |
| 2. What efforts do program and institutional administrators make to secure financial support for faculty? | • The institution and department provide adequate financial support for faculty research, sabbaticals, and professional development opportunities. | |
| 3. How do departmental and institutional reward structures encourage and promote faculty engagement in teaching? | 2. Supportive Institutional and Departmental Reward Structure <br> • Institutional and departmental merit, promotion, and tenure policies recognize and reward faculty for their involvement in a broad range of scholarly activities, including teaching, advising, and mentoring students. | |
| 4. Do faculty feel supported for their investments in teaching, mentoring, and advising students? Why or why not? Do they believe that departmental and institutional reward structures value teaching as much as other forms of scholarly activity? | | |
| 5. Do students believe that faculty are supported for their investments in teaching, mentoring, and advising students? Why or why not? Do they believe that departmental and institutional reward structures value teaching as much as other forms of scholarly activity? | | |

6. Is there evidence that faculty investments in teaching, course development, student advising, collaborative research, and program administration and coordination activities are valued in the department? Institution?

7. How does financial support promote or hinder faculty investments in teaching and learning? What impact does a supportive departmental and institutional reward structure have on the time and energy faculty devote to students, their learning, and program improvements?

*(Continued)*

**TABLE 9.1** (*Continued*)

*Attribute: Support for Basic Infrastructure*

| Questions to Guide Assessment | Criteria and Indicators of Attribute | Suggested Methods of Assessment |
|---|---|---|
| 1. What financial support is available to support basic infrastructure needs in the program? Is this support adequate? | 1. Financial Support for Basic Infrastructure | • Focus groups with students, alumni, faculty, and administrators |
| 2. Is laboratory, classroom, computing and other program equipment up to date and in good repair? | • The program receives adequate funding from the institution and elsewhere to purchase requisite equipment and supplies. | • Student, alumni, and employer surveys |
| 3. Does the program have adequate supplies to support instruction and research? | • The program receives adequate funding from the institution to maintain suitable laboratory, classroom, office, and performance facilities. | • Document review (for evidence of financial support for basic infrastructure needs in the program) |
| 4. Are classrooms, laboratories, studios, performance areas, and other program facilities suitable to meet the instructional and research needs of students and faculty? Are they in good repair? | • The institution provides adequate funding to support the college or university's library and computing facilities. | |
| 5. What efforts do program and instructional administrators make to secure financial support for the basic infrastructure of the program? | | |
| 6. Are institutional resources, especially in the library and computing center, adequate to support the instructional and research needs of program faculty and students? | | |
| 7. How do adequate resources—in terms of equipment, supplies, and facilities—help to facilitate and enrich students' learning? Faculty teaching and research? | | |

# 10

Engaged Teaching and
Learning: Staking a Claim
for a New Perspective
on Program Quality

In this chapter we stake a claim that the engagement theory advances a new
perspective on program quality—one that not only builds on and brings
together disparate literatures but also extends and deepens current understanding of program quality. We do this by first examining various writings
and studies in the program quality and other higher education literatures
that support the engagement theory. We then discuss the major ways in
which the theory extends and re-envisions current understandings of program quality.

## The Engagement Theory Builds On, and Brings
## Together, Current Views of Program Quality

The engagement theory finds some support in the literature on program
quality. Other higher education literatures—notably those on teaching and
learning, college impact, adult education, leadership, and organizational
culture—supply additional support for it as well. Following, we build upon
and integrate selected studies and writings to document the broad range of
support for the engagement theory. We begin with the literature on program quality and then turn to other relevant higher education literatures.

## Support from the Program Quality Literature

Support for some of the attributes in the engagement theory exists in the program quality literature. Regarding the first cluster of attributes—diverse and invested participants—few scholars have emphasized the significance of diverse faculty and diverse students to program quality (Association of American Colleges 1992). Several, however, have stressed the importance of faculty commitment and student involvement and effort, which are clearly encompassed within our concept of engagement. For instance, in their study of more than two hundred chemistry, history, and psychology programs, Mary Jo Clark, Rodney Hartnett, and Leonard Baird (1976) identified faculty concern for students and student commitment (motivation) as two key features of high-quality doctoral programs. In other major national studies, Alexander Astin (1977, 1980, 1993) and George Kuh (1981) found that students who become actively involved in their learning have higher-quality experiences in college, and C. Robert Pace (1980, 1986) found that the quality of student effort significantly enhances students' learning experiences. Moreover, two groups of researchers have identified administrative leadership as an attribute of high-quality academic programs (Clark, Hartnett, and Baird 1976; Young, Blackburn, Conrad, and Cameron 1989).

Two studies in the program quality literature support the importance of participatory cultures, the second cluster of attributes in our theory. George Kuh (1981) lends support to our findings that a shared program direction and a community of learners are important features of a high-quality program. In his monograph, *Indices of Quality in the Undergraduate Experience,* Kuh (1981) concluded that both a "clarity of purpose" (at the institutional, rather than the program, level) and a "generative learning community" enrich the quality of students' experiences in undergraduate education. Similarly, in their review of educational quality in the major, the Association of American Colleges (1992) identified clearly stated program goals and a "supportive community" as two key elements of "strong" undergraduate programs. We found no support in the program quality literature concerning the importance of a risk-taking environment.

Support for the third cluster of attributes in the theory—interactive teaching and learning—is likewise thin in the program quality literature. Only out-of-class activities enjoys direct empirical support in the published discourse on program quality in higher education (Kuh 1981). However, critical dialogue and mentoring receive indirect support in various studies and writings that emphasize the importance of informal faculty–student interaction in maintaining high-quality programs (Association of American Colleges 1992; Kuh 1981; Student Task Force on Education at Stanford 1973).

Several reports and scholarly writings provide support for the fourth cluster of attributes in our theory: connected program requirements. C. W.

Minkel and Mary P. Richards (1986) identified a core of planned course work and a culminating experience (a thesis, project, or internship) as important attributes of high-quality master's programs. Similarly, the Council of Graduate Schools (1981, 3) stated that "quality" master's programs require students to complete a "pre-planned and coherent sequence" of courses as well as a "component demonstrating creativity" such as a thesis or internship. Other scholars have also argued for the salience of these requirements (Association of American Colleges 1992; Ames 1979; Glazer 1986).

Finally, adequate resources—the fifth cluster of attributes in the engagement theory—has an extensive base of support in the program quality literature. Since the early 1960s, many scholars have conducted studies that have established empirical relationships between institutional and program resources—such as expenditures per student, faculty salaries, research funds, and physical facilities (including institutional library holdings)—and programs considered to be of high quality (Abbott and Barlow 1972; Astin and Solmon 1981; Beyer and Snipper 1974; Cartter 1966; Clark, Hartnett, and Baird 1976; Conrad and Blackburn 1985a, 1986; Janes 1969; Jones, Lindzey, and Coggeshall 1982; Jordan 1963; Lavendar, Mathers, and Pease 1971; Morgan, Kearney, and Regens 1976; Perkins and Snell 1962). Also, many scholars have argued that financial and physical resources are critical to maintaining high-quality programs.

More broadly, the engagement theory builds on all five of the major views of program quality that we derived from the literature and discussed in Chapter 1. The first cluster of attributes—diverse and invested faculty and students—finds selective support in the Faculty View, the Student Quality-and-Effort View, and the Multi-Dimensional/Multi-Level View. The fourth cluster of attributes—connected program requirements—enjoys support in the Curriculum Requirements View as well as the Multi-Dimensional/Multi-Level View. The fifth cluster of attributes in the theory—adequate program resources—finds strong support in the Resources View of program quality.

## Support in Other Literatures

In broad strokes, there is considerable support for our engagement theory in the higher education reform, teaching and learning, college impact, adult education, leadership, and organizational theory literatures. In particular, research and scholarship in these literatures strongly supports several clusters in the theory—notably participatory cultures and interactive teaching and learning—that have not received widespread attention in the literature on program quality.

The first cluster of attributes—diverse and invested participants—finds selective support in the teaching and learning, college impact, and leadership literatures. These literatures are replete with scholarly writings and empirical studies that emphasize the importance of faculty and students who bring diverse scholarly, educational, and professional experiences to the higher learning (see, for example, Astin 1993; Conrad, Haworth, and Millar 1993; Gamson 1992; Minnich 1990; Pascarella and Terenzini 1991). In particular, authors of several major college impact studies have identified numerous positive effects that accrue to students who interact with faculty and other students from backgrounds different than their own (Astin 1993; Newman and Newman 1978; Pascarella and Terenzini 1991).[1] Moreover, the teaching and learning and college impact literatures provide considerable evidence supporting the importance of faculty and student involvement—and, by implication, engagement—in the teaching and learning process (Astin 1980, 1984, 1993; Chickering and Gamson 1987; Conrad, Haworth, and Millar 1993; Feldman and Newcomb 1969; Pace 1984; Parker and Schmidt 1982; Pascarella and Terenzini 1991).

In the extensive literature on leadership in higher education, we also found support for the critical role that engaged leaders play in developing and sustaining high-quality programs. This literature supports our proposition that engaged leaders not only champion their programs to internal and external audiences, but that they also tend to view leadership as a team effort in which they encourage and support faculty, student, alumni, and employer participation in various informal program leadership roles. Some scholars provide exhortatory as well as empirical support for the effectiveness of a "team-oriented" or "participatory" approach to leadership (Bensimon and Neumann 1993; Chaffee and Tierney 1988; Eisenstat and Cohen 1990; Gabarro 1987; Seymour 1992).

The second cluster of attributes in the theory—participatory cultures—also enjoys a broad base of support in the teaching and learning, college impact, and organizational theory literatures. To begin with, several works buttress our finding that a shared program direction is, in the words of Arthur Chickering and Zelda Gamson (1987), important to "good practice" in academic programs. Moreover, many scholarly publications emphasize the value of learning communities at both the undergraduate and graduate levels (Carnegie Foundation for the Advancement of Teaching 1990; Chickering and Gamson 1987; Conrad, Haworth, and Millar 1993; Gabelnick, MacGregor, Matthews, and Smith 1990; Gaff 1991; Gamson 1984; Hill 1985; Palmer 1983; Spitzberg and Thorndike 1992; Study Group on the Conditions of Excellence in Higher Education 1984). For example, in their monograph on learning communities, Faith Gabelnick and her colleagues identified a number of student outcomes associated with learning communities that dovetail with our findings. These outcomes include higher levels of academic achievement (as measured by college grade point averages), a greater appreciation for collaborative approaches to learning, improved self-confidence and self-esteem, a stronger appreciation for other students' perspectives in the learning process, and an improved ability to make "intellectual connections" across disparate texts and courses (1990, 63–71).

In sifting through these diverse literatures, we identified only a few works that highlighted the importance of a risk-taking environment. To wit, Parker Palmer (1983) underscores the need to create "open" and "hospitable" learning spaces in which students feel free to receive each other's "newborn ideas with openness and care" as well as to "make the painful things possible, things without which no learning can occur—things like exposing ignorance, testing tentative hypotheses, challenging false and partial information, and mutual criticism of thought" (74). In their studies of effective teachers, Joseph Lowman (1984) and Ken Macrorie (1984) also provide empirical support for a risk-taking environment. Lowman (1984), for example, identified a number of behaviors that "superb" college professors use to build rapport and encourage risk-taking in the classroom, while Macrorie (1984) found that "exemplary" teachers consistently built classroom climates in which students were enabled "to take chances that sometimes result[ed] in failure" and were encouraged "to use their mistakes productively" (229).

Feminist literature also includes publications that directly or indirectly emphasize the importance of learning communities and a risk-taking environment (Belenky, Clinchy, Goldberger, and Tarule 1986; Katz 1985; Klein 1987; Schneidewind 1987; Shrewsbury 1987). More broadly, there is a considerable quantity of feminist literature that advocates a pedagogy that is anchored in empowerment, collaborative learning, and "creative community" (Shrewsbury 1987, 8).

Many scholarly writings and empirical studies also provide a wide range of support for integrative teaching and learning, the third cluster of attributes in the theory. In the teaching and learning, higher education reform, college impact, and adult education literatures, we identified many publications that supported all five of the attributes in this cluster. Moreover, we identified numerous writings that support the value of an interactive approach to teaching and learning (Boyer 1987; Bruffee 1987, 1993; Chickering and Gamson 1987; Cross 1987; McKeachie 1969; Palmer 1983; Study Group on the Conditions of Excellence in American Higher Education 1984).

Referred to throughout the teaching and learning literature as "critical awareness" (Gamson 1984), "reflective dialogue" (Schön 1987), or "dialogical interaction" (Freire 1970), there are myriad writings and studies that emphasize the importance of critical dialogue among faculty and students (Brookfield 1987; Bruffee 1993; Conrad, Haworth, and Millar 1993; Gabelnick, MacGregor, Matthews, and Smith 1990; Kurfiss 1988; Shor 1980, 1987; Shrewsbury 1987). For the most part, these writings stress the need for faculty and students to engage in ongoing conversations in which they question their own and others' assumptions in order to enhance and expand their awareness of complex issues. For example, in their case studies of "liberatory" undergraduate programs, feminist classrooms, and "exemplary" teachers, Gamson (1984), Belenky et al. (1986), and Macrorie (1984) sketch portraitures of faculty and student engagement in critical dialogue and emphasize the positive effects that such dialogues have on student learning and development.

In reviewing the higher education reform, teaching and learning, and college impact literatures, we also identified many articles and books that underscored the value of integrative learning. For instance, in *Seven Principles for Good Practice in Undergraduate Education,* Arthur Chickering and Zelda Gamson highlight the need for active learning, an integral component of integrative learning: "Learning is not a spectator sport. Students do not learn much just by sitting in class listening to teachers, memorizing prepackaged assignments, and spitting out answers. They must talk about what they are learning, write about it, relate it to past experiences, apply it to their daily lives. They must make what they learn part of themselves" (1987, 3). We also took note of many other authors who share Chickering and Gamson's assessment, most of whom provide empirical support to back up their position (Association of American College's Task Force on General Education 1988; Astin 1993; Bonwell and Eison 1991; Conrad, Haworth, and Millar 1993; Cross 1987; Fisher 1978; Gamson 1984; Light 1990; Macrorie 1984; McKeachie 1969; Meyers and Jones, 1993; Palmer 1983; Pascarella and Terenzini 1991; Sorcinelli 1991; Study Group on the Conditions of Excellence in American Higher Education 1984; Wulff and Nyquist 1988).

We found considerable support for mentoring, the third attribute in this cluster, in the teaching and learning and college impact literatures (Blackwell 1989; Hoyte and Collett 1993; Jacobi 1991; Light 1992; Lipschutz 1993; Lyons, Scroggins, and Rule 1990; Merriam, 1983; Pascarella and Terenzini 1991; Schön 1987; Sorcinelli 1991). Numerous college impact studies, for example, emphasize the positive effects that frequent and informal interactions with at least one faculty member have on student learning and development (Astin 1993; Hoyte and Collett 1993; Pascarella 1980; Snow 1973; Terenzini, Pascarella, and Lorang 1982; Wilson, Gaff, Dienst, Wood, and Bavry 1975). Among others, these effects include greater satisfaction with the college experience (Astin 1993; Pascarella 1980), enhanced certainty of career choice (Astin 1993; Wilson et al. 1975), and increased self-confidence and self-esteem (Astin 1993; Hoyte and Collett 1993). For example, in their longitudinal study of the impact of college professors on students, Robert Wilson and his colleagues accentuated the importance of mentoring and concluded that "the relationships that faculty and students develop outside the classroom may well be the part of teaching which has the greatest impact on students" (107).

There is considerable exhortatory and empirical support for cooperative peer learning in the elementary and secondary as well as the higher education literatures (Astin 1993; Bouton and Garth 1983; Chickering and Gamson 1987; Johnson and Johnson 1989, 1991; Johnson, Johnson, and Smith 1991; Kagan, 1988; Light 1990; McKeachie, Pintrich, Yi-Guang, and Smith 1986; Palmer 1983; Romer 1985; Slavin 1980, 1983, 1990; Sorcinelli 1991). To wit, in their review of 137 studies on cooperative learning methods at the college level, Roger Johnson, David Johnson, and Karl Smith (1991) found that cooperative learning groups enhanced productivity, fostered more committed and positive relationships among students, increased peer social support, and improved students' self-esteem. Along these same lines, Johnson and his colleagues (1981) conducted a series of meta-analyses in which the weight of the evidence confirmed that cooperative learning approaches surpass competitive or individualistic learning methods in promoting achievement among students. Other scholars, including Robert Slavin (1980, 1983, 1990) and James Cooper and Randall Mueck (1990), have also documented the effectiveness of cooperative learning.

Moreover, several studies have highlighted the importance of out-of-class activities in students' undergraduate and graduate experiences (Boyer 1987; Kuh 1993; Wilson 1966). In one of the most comprehensive qualitative studies ever conducted on the topic in American higher education, George Kuh, John Schuh, and Elizabeth Whitt (1991) found that participation in out-of-class activities had a number of favorable effects on students' growth and development. Among others, these included enhanced social competence, self-awareness, and self-worth. Other college impact studies have likewise shown that student involvement in out-of-class activities produces similar outcomes (Astin 1977, 1993; Baxter Magolda 1992; Pascarella, Ethington, and Smart 1988).

Several publications offer strong support for the fourth cluster of attributes in the engagement theory—connected program requirements. Alongside the voluminous literature on undergraduate education that emphasizes the importance of planned breadth and depth course work (American Association of Colleges 1985; Bennett 1984; Carnegie Foundation for the Advancement of Teaching 1977; Conrad 1978), a number of writers have stressed the advantages of experiential learning—such as internships or practica— at both the undergraduate and graduate levels (Jacobs and Allen 1982; Keeton 1976, 1980; Keeton and Tate 1978; Kolb 1984; Maehl 1982; Panel on Alternate Approaches to Graduate Education 1973).

Finally, while support for the last cluster of attributes—adequate resources—is abundant in the program quality literature, it is sparse in other higher education literatures. Indeed, aside from studies on the effects of financial aid on students (Leslie and Brinkman 1988; Pascarella and Terenzini 1991) and various higher education reform reports calling for broadened definitions of faculty scholarship and greater financial investment in faculty development programs (American Association of Colleges 1985; Boyer 1990; Study Group on the Conditions of Excellence in American Higher Education 1984), there seem to be few publications outside the program quality literature that emphasize the importance of monetary and non-monetary resources for students, faculty, and program infrastructures.

While the engagement theory finds considerable support in extant literatures, the theory does more than simply build on current views of program quality and related attributes: It also brings together many attributes of high-quality programs that, in one form of another, have been identified in disparate literatures (at both the undergraduate and graduate levels) but have not been brought to bear directly on program quality. In so doing, the theory at once builds on and connects these literatures in ways that contribute to a more comprehensive and holistic perspective on program quality in higher education than currently exists.

## *How the Engagement Theory Extends and Re-envisions Current Views of Program Quality*

While the engagement theory clearly builds on and integrates current conceptions, it also moves significantly beyond existing studies and writings in ways that invite reexamination of traditional views and assumptions about program quality. From our perspective, the theory extends and re-envisions current understandings of program quality in five major ways.

First, the engagement theory highlights the pivotal role that people—faculty, administrators, and students who engage in mutually supportive teaching and learning—play in fostering enriching learning experiences for students that promote their growth and development. In accenting the commitments of time and energy that program participants make to their own and others' learning, the engagement theory builds on and moves beyond conventional views of high-quality programs. These views tend to perceive high-quality programs as being more narrowly fueled by students—whether through active student learning (Meyers and Jones 1993), student involvement (Astin 1977 and 1993), or student effort (Pace 1980 and 1986)—or by non-human factors such as curriculum requirements and resources. Of particular note, both Alexander Astin and C. Robert Pace—along with many people who have written on active learning—have emphasized the importance of student involvement and effort in enhancing students' learning. While the engagement theory is anchored in part in this insight, it goes far beyond it to emphasize the importance of students' investments in teaching as well as the dual roles of faculty and administrators.

Second, the theory extends and deepens current understanding of program quality by advancing a number of new attributes, and clusters of attributes, that have not been integrated into the literature on program quality. In particular, two of the five clusters of attributes in the engagement theory (participatory cultures and interactive teaching and learning) identify attributes that are not currently included in the program quality literature—such as critical dialogue, integrative learning, and a risk-taking environment. In short, the engagement theory provides people with new insights into those characteristics that are most important to the quality of their programs.

Third, by defining high-quality programs as those which provide enriching learning experiences for students that have positive effects on their development, the theory provides people throughout higher education with a new vantage point for understanding program quality. Not only does this vantage point recognize student learning and development as the primary purpose of the higher learning (Astin, 1985), but it also embraces a complementary conceptual template that is organized around understanding and exploring relationships among program attributes, learning experiences, and student outcomes.[2]

Fourth, through connecting and extending current conceptions, the engagement theory provides a comprehensive and integrated theory of program quality. Anchored in a large body of empirical research along with supporting explanations as to how and why specific program attributes enhance students' learning, our work systematically identifies and integrates program attributes into a unified theory of program quality. Indeed, the engagement theory represents the only formal theory of program quality in the literature. For the first time, practitioners and scholars alike are invited to consider an inclusive and integrated theory of program quality.

Fifth, as a comprehensive new perspective for enriching our understanding of quality, the engagement theory provides a new framework for assessing and improving academic program quality. As elaborated on in the previous chapter, this theory can help stakeholders throughout higher education in their efforts to assess and improve the quality of students' learning in undergraduate and graduate programs.

## A Final Note

We stake a claim that the engagement perspective can appreciably enhance the way that people think about program quality in higher education: not only does the theory build on and bring together current views, but it extends and re-envisions them as well. Thus, the theory offers new insights into program quality—in essence, a new perspective—that may be as applicable to undergraduate and doctoral education as they are to master's education.

In closing, it is our hope that the engagement theory will contribute to the ongoing discourse about program quality in higher education and serve as an impetus for strengthening program quality within colleges and universities. To that end, we invite stakeholders to reexamine traditional assumptions and beliefs about academic program quality in higher education in light of our findings and conclusions.

## *Endnotes*

1. In his national study of more than 45,000 faculty and students, for instance, Alexander Astin (1993) found that undergraduate students who socialized with someone from another racial or ethnic group reported gains in cognitive and affective development (especially increased cultural awareness) and were more satisfied with their college experiences.

2. For the most part, individuals writing on program quality have identified and studied attributes of program quality without systematically examining their consequences for students' learning experiences, much less the effects of these learning experiences on students' growth and development. The program quality literature, for example, is replete with studies that identify faculty research productivity as a key attribute of program quality. Yet none of these studies provide empirical evidence to establish that faculty research productivity contributes to enriching learning experiences for students that positively affect their growth and development.

# Technical Appendix: Research Methods and Procedures

As described in Chapter 2, we used an open-ended, multicase study design that placed the perspectives of six groups of stakeholders at the center of our research. In this technical appendix we elaborate on the sampling strategy and procedures that we used in our multicase study design, discuss our data collection procedures, and provide an overview of the constant comparative method that guided our development of a theory of program quality.[1] We conclude with a discussion of trustworthiness, that is, how we sought to ensure the integrity of our findings.

## Sampling Strategy and Procedures

We used a multicase study design that was anchored in a representative sample of forty-seven cases (programs) and 781 interviewees. Our overall sampling strategy, including the selection of programs as well as interviewees within programs, was informed by an assumption in multi-case study design: if a credible claim is to be made that our findings can be generalized from individual interviewees to each case as a whole, and from a sample of cases to master's programs in this country, then the sample must be "substantively representative" of the population it claims to represent. To provide substantive representativeness in a multi-case study design, contextual characteristics of the population which may be theoretically relevant must be represented in the sample. There is no need, however, as David Greene and Jane David have emphasized, to "require adequate representation on every conceivable variable, parameter, or factor that one might think of. In particular, there is no reason to prefer—let alone require—a sample that includes all the principal selection factors in every combination with each other (i.e., a 'fully-crossed' design). If there is a substantive reason for a particular combination of factors to be included in the sample, that is sufficient; otherwise, no particular combination of factors is more essential than any other" (1981, 30).

Following this reasoning, we used a sampling strategy in which we selected cases from across the nation, and interviewees within each case, that were representative of program and interviewee characteristics we believed might be theoretically relevant. Thus, at the program level, we selected programs that differed in characteristics such as field of study, institutional type, and type of control, along with other characteristics such as geographic location and instructional delivery system. Within each of these programs, we selected individuals representing six stakeholder groups: institutional administrators, program administrators, faculty, students, alumni, and employers of alumni. We elaborate below on our selection of the forty-seven cases and our within-case interviewees.

## Selection of Cases (Programs)

To provide for heterogeneity (substantive representativeness) in academic discipline, we selected eleven different fields of study in the professions and liberal arts and sciences. We selected five programs in each of nine fields and one program in each of two fields (sociology and computer science), for a total sample of forty-seven programs. (Our original sample included five programs in each of eleven fields, but early in our fieldwork we decided to drop two of these fields—sociology and computer science—for the remainder of the study. Since we had already completed single case studies in them, we retained these two programs in the sample.[2])

Our forty-seven-case sample was distributed across the eleven fields of study as follows: five established professional fields, four emerging professional fields in the liberal arts and sciences (including one interdisciplinary field), and two traditional fields in the liberal arts and sciences. From established professional fields, we selected business, education, engineering, nursing, and theater. We chose business, education, and engineering because, in recent years, over one-half of all master's degrees awarded each year were in these three fields. Given the range of specializations offered within each, we chose subfields that have granted the largest number of master's degrees within the respective field: in business, business administration; in education, teacher education; and in engineering, electrical engineering. We selected nursing not only as a professional field but also because it grants the largest percentage of master's degrees in the health sciences. We chose theater as a representative field in the performing arts.

In emerging professional fields, we chose applied anthropology, computer science, environmental studies, and microbiology as representative of traditional liberal arts and sciences fields because a non-university job market demand has developed for master's graduates in recent years. Environmental studies was also chosen because it is an interdisciplinary field in which a growing share of master's degrees have been awarded in recent years. Applied anthropology and microbiology were chosen as representative fields in the social and biological sciences. In the traditional liberal arts and sciences, we selected English and sociology as core disciplines representing the humanities and social sciences.

To represent the diverse institutions offering master's programs in the United States, we also selected programs that differed in terms of institutional type and type of control. With respect to the former, we chose the forty-seven programs from among four types of institutions: national universities, regional colleges and universities, liberal arts colleges, and specialty institutions.[3] The forty-seven programs, which reflect national data on master's degrees awarded, were distributed as follows: national universities, 18 programs; regional colleges and universities, 21 programs; liberal arts colleges, five programs; and specialty institutions, three programs.[4] The 31 institutions represented in the sample include seven national universities, 16 regional colleges and universities, five liberal arts colleges, and three specialty institutions.[5] In terms of type of control, two-thirds of the forty-seven programs in the sample (31 programs) were located in public institutions and one-third (16 programs) were located in private (independent) institutions.[6] (Table A.1 shows the distribution of programs by field of study and institutional type. Table A.2 shows the distribution of programs by institutional type and type of control).

As indicated in Chapter 2, we also chose programs that differed on other characteristics, such as geographic location, student attendance patterns, type of delivery system, and program prestige. To provide for broad geographical representation, we distributed the forty-seven programs in the sample across four geographic sectors: East, West, South, and Midwest. We selected eleven programs in the Eastern United States, including the Mid-Atlantic, Tri-State, and New England areas. In the West, we chose fourteen programs spread across the Western coastline, Rocky Mountain, and Southwest desert states. We chose nine programs from the South and thirteen programs from the Midwest. Nineteen states were represented in our sample.

To provide for representative student attendance patterns, we included twenty-four (mostly) full-time, nineteen (mostly) part-time, and four "mixed" student enrollment programs. For the same reason, we included some

**TABLE A.1   Distribution of Case Studies: By Field of Study and Institutional Type**

| Field of Study | Institutional Type | | | |
| --- | --- | --- | --- | --- |
| | National | Regional | Lib. Arts | Specialty |
| Established Professional | | | | |
|   Business | 2 | 2 | 1 | |
|   Education | 1 | 3 | 1 | |
|   Engineering | 2 | 2 | | 1 |
|   Nursing | 2 | 2 | | 1 |
|   Theater | 2 | 2 | | 1 |
| Emerging Professional (Arts and Sciences) | | | | |
|   Applied Anthropology | 2 | 3 | | |
|   Computer Science | 1 | | | |
|   Environmental Studies | 2 | 1 | 2 | |
|   Microbiology | 1 | 4 | | |
| Traditional Arts and Sciences | | | | |
|   English | 2 | 2 | 1 | |
|   Sociology | 1 | | | |
| Total | 18 | 21 | 5 | 3 |

*Source:* From Clifton F. Conrad, Jennifer Grant, and Susan Bolyard Millar, *A Silent Success: Master's Education in the United States,* 1993, p. 32. Reprinted by permission of the Johns Hopkins University Press.

*Note:* Four predominantly black institutions and one predominantly women's college were represented in the sample. A total of 31 institutions were included in the sample.

programs in our sample in which the master's was the only degree offered in the department (7 programs), and other cases where the master's was offered either with the bachelor's (22 programs) or with both the bachelor's and doctoral degrees (18 programs).

In light of the rapid growth of innovative instructional delivery systems in master's education, we included nine programs with this particular characteristic. We chose, for example, seven in which the master's degree could be completed by either taking a combination of intensive evening, weekend, and summer courses (two programs in business and three programs in education) or in which the master's program was offered only during intensive summer sessions and required a three- to five-year summer residency for completion of the degree (one program each in English and environ-

**TABLE A.2** **Distribution of Case Studies: By Institutional Type and Type of Control**

| Institutional Type | Type of Control | | |
| --- | --- | --- | --- |
| | Public | Private | Total |
| National Universities | 14 | 4 | 18 |
| Regional Colleges and Universities | 15 | 6 | 21 |
| Liberal Arts Colleges | 1 | 4 | 5 |
| Specialty Institutions | 1 | 2 | 3 |
| Total | 31 | 16 | 47 |

*Source:* From Clifton F. Conrad, Jennifer Grant, and Susan Bolyard Millar, *A Silent Success: Master's Education in the United States*, 1993, p. 32. Reprinted by permission of the Johns Hopkins University Press.

mental studies). Additionally, we chose two programs in engineering where satellite-based instructional technology was used to deliver degree programs to students at off-campus locations.

We also included programs in the sample that varied in terms of "prestige" within their respective field of study. We used field-specific reputational rankings to help identify these programs. (With the exceptions of business and engineering, only reputational rankings on "graduate programs"—not master's programs—were published in the literature. In the other nine fields, we used rankings of graduate programs to identify "high-prestige" programs.) Across the eleven fields included in the study, we selected at least one "top five"-ranked program in each; there were a total of 12 high-prestige programs in the sample.

## Selection of Interviewees Within Programs

As discussed in the second chapter, we interviewed individuals who differed in terms of a variety of characteristics, such as stakeholder group, race, ethnicity, and sex. To identify individuals to interview we relied on a program liaison from each of the forty-seven programs included in the study. These individuals chose interviewees on the basis of written criteria we described in a formal request for assistance.[7] For the most part, program liaisons were able to select interviewees according to these criteria.

We acknowledge that our interview selection method has a positive, or at least a systematic nonnegative, bias that is linked to using program liaisons to select interviewees. Although we ran the risk that program liaisons might select individuals who would describe their programs in a highly favorable light, we used this procedure for two reasons. First, selecting interviewees ourselves would have been impossible given our time constraints; we were unable to spend more than three days visiting each program. Second, we suspected, on the grounds that this would have been intrusive, that many programs would have declined to participate if we had insisted on selecting interviewees ourselves.[8]

## Data Collection Procedures

After completing interviews in each program during our original field study, we summarized each interview and, using our tapes, transcribed long sections of many. One member of our four-person team then developed a program summary (80 to 170 pages in length) that included summaries of individual interviews. The format we used for program summaries included one section on stakeholders' views of the overall outcomes and value of the program, and another on stakeholders' views of program characteristics that enhanced or diminished the quality of students' learning experiences. These program summaries allowed us to retain the individuality of different stakeholders' voices while, at the same time, helping us begin to understand and describe those themes shared by interviewees both within and across stakeholder groups within a given program.

Once we completed all forty-seven program summaries, we conducted an extensive cross-program analysis in which we identified key decisions that shape master's experiences and developed a typology of master's programs.[9] These findings are published in *A Silent Success: Master's Education in the United States*. We also devoted a chapter in the book to attributes of high-quality master's experiences. We identified fourteen such attributes and grouped them into four clusters: culture, planned learning experiences, resources, and leadership and the human dimension.

After completing our book on master's education, we decided that our work on program quality was unfinished for four reasons. First, in focusing primarily on key decisions and program types, we had not provided a comprehensive treatment of program quality.[10] Second, despite having at hand one of the most comprehensive qualitative databases ever assembled in a study on higher education, we had hardly tapped our rich vein of interview material on program quality. Third, the analysis we used in preparing our chapter on program attributes for *A Silent Success: Master's Education in the United States* had been limited in several important respects. In our analysis of attributes we had reviewed our interview material without partitioning the forty-seven programs, and systematic cross-program comparisons were clearly needed to advance our earlier work. Moreover, we had relied primarily on our program summaries in our analysis—except in a handful of instances, we had not gone back and reviewed the tapes and interview summaries of each of the nearly 800 people that we interviewed. Had we adequately identified the most salient attributes of high-quality master's programs? Had we missed important attributes? Had we organized attributes into meaningful clusters? Fourth, many faculty, administrators, and students from throughout higher education told us that they wished we would extend our earlier work and write a book on program quality that elaborated on attributes of high-quality programs. For these reasons, we decided to revisit all our original transcripts and interview summaries and, through comparative analysis on a program-by-program basis, extend our earlier work. We turn now to an overview of the constant comparative method that guided our development of a theory of program quality.

## Overview of the Constant Comparative Method

The constant comparative method, a grounded theory approach to theory generation, guided our process of data analysis (Glaser and Strauss 1967; Glaser 1978; Strauss 1987; Strauss and Corbin 1990). This inductive approach blends systematic data collection, coding, and analysis with theoretical sampling into a comprehensive research strategy that is designed to "generate theory that is integrated, close to the data, and expressed in a form clear enough for further testing" (Conrad 1982, 241).

In *The Discovery of Grounded Theory*, Glaser and Strauss identified four stages in the constant comparative method: 1) "comparing incidents applicable to each category; 2) integrating categories and their properties; 3) delimiting the theory; and 4) writing the theory" (1967, 105). The first stage involves the collection and coding of data incidents. As the researcher compares data incident with data incident, he or she develops categories that are theoretical abstractions or symbolic representations based on these data. As categories are supported further by the data, the researcher begins to discern the theoretical properties—or attributes—of each category, as well as its dimensions and the conditions under which it is supported or minimized. In effect, this first stage requires the researcher to "take apart the story" and, according to Glaser and Strauss, is necessary if a "clear integration of the theory" is to take place in the next two stages (1967, 108).

While the first stage "takes apart the story," the second stage puts it back together. In this stage, the researcher focuses on emerging attributes within each category and the conditions which support or fail to support them. Using relational and variational sampling, the researcher will often pose questions aimed at facilitating the identification of relational patterns between attributes and categories. These relational patterns are subject to continuous scrutiny and verification throughout the research process, and must be consistently supported by new data incidents to be retained or modified in the emerging theory. As relationships between categories and their attributes and conditions are better understood, the emerging theory becomes more fully integrated.

During the third stage, the emerging theory is gradually delimited in two interrelated ways. First, as the researcher explores relationships across categories, he or she may begin to see uniformities in the data that previously went unnoticed. These uniformities can lead to the development of a smaller set of more abstract categories. Identifying uniformities within and across categories is advantageous not only because it delimits the emerging theory, but it also contributes to parsimony and broadens the scope of the theory (Glaser and Strauss 1967, 111). Delimitation also occurs in a second way. As categories become more clearly defined, the researcher engages in further testing. Categories that are not supported through this verification process are dropped, thus further delimiting the theory. When the comparisons of data incidents no longer yield new—or embellish existing—categories and properties, the theory is considered "saturated" or delimited. Once the researcher is satisfied that the theory is integrated and has met the requirements of theoretical saturation, he or she can move on to the fourth and final stage: writing the theory.

Throughout this four-stage process, theoretical sampling is closely linked to the development of the theory. Theoretical sampling is an iterative approach to selecting data incidents on the basis of their "theoretical relevance to the evolving theory" (Strauss and Corbin 1990, 177).[11] Three steps are involved in theoretical sampling, each of which involves a different "type" of sampling that builds upon the working categories and properties developed in the previous step (see Strauss and Corbin 1990, 57–175). "Open sampling" guides the initial selection of data. That is, any data that the researcher believes may be theoretically relevant to the phenomenon under study is included in the open sampling process. Once the researcher has developed working categories and their properties, he or she then moves to the second step in theoretical sampling: maximizing opportunities to explore developing concepts under different conditions. Using "relational" and "variational" sampling techniques, the researcher again samples on the basis of theoretical relevance, but does so with a focus on delimiting the working categories and properties identified in the previous step. Finally, in the third step, the researcher uses "discriminate sampling" to test further previously developed properties, categories, and relationships across categories. Sampling at this point becomes a "very directed and deliberate" activity and "conscious choices" [are made] about who and what to sample in order to obtain the needed data" (Strauss and Corbin 1990, 187).

## *Trustworthiness*

Maintaining fidelity to "trustworthiness" was a touchstone throughout our study. We defined trustworthiness as those measures that we, as qualitative researchers, took to safeguard the accuracy, consistency, and validity of the research findings during the data collection process.[12] In keeping with this definition, we ensured trustworthiness primarily through what researchers in the social sciences commonly refer to as "triangulation," namely, collecting and analyzing data across multiple and different data sources and using multiple methods of data collection. We used three basic strategies to enhance trustworthiness throughout our data collection, analysis, and interpretation.

First, we built triangulation into our sample by selecting stakeholder groups (institutional administrators, program administrators, faculty, students, alumni, and employers) who stood in different positions with respect to their master's programs. Faculty and program administrators held the most permanent and interior positions, since they were responsible for the program and often had long-term "insider" perspectives. Current students and alumni held partly interior and partly exterior standpoints: they were significantly involved in their program, yet they were also "visitors" who passed through it within a few years. Employers and institutional administrators, meanwhile, tended to represent exterior standpoints and, while generally less informed than other stakeholders, provided a valuable check on "insider" perspectives as well as another source of understanding.[13]

Second, just as triangulation was built into our design in the way we selected interviewees, it was also built into the analysis process we used in our fieldwork. Since at least two people conducted interviews in the same program at the same time, we continually engaged one another while we were in the field.[14] We frequently exchanged notes and observations on our interviews. These meetings helped us both to identify the occasional interviewee whose perspective seemed out of kilter with those of other interviewees and to listen and react more independently of any personal biases.[15] Moreover, our frequent interactions in the field helped us develop a fuller understanding of our interview data, thereby enabling us to explore some topics in greater detail during subsequent interviews—all as part of our ongoing efforts to triangulate. Finally, while completing our program summaries, we continued to "triangulate" and learn from each other's perspectives by critiquing one another's summaries.

Third, throughout the extensive data analysis process that accompanied the writing of this book, we made concerted efforts to ensure that all findings were based on the data and that the inferences drawn from the data were supported. In each of our three stages of data analysis, we jointly reexamined our inferences and the evidentiary basis for each and every finding by continually asking one another questions about both the processes and the products of the study. In turn, in line with Yvonna Lincoln and Egon Guba's (1985) advice, we developed an audit trail made up of: 1) raw data, including tapes, interview notes, and documents; 2) products of data reduction and analysis, including program summaries and a codebook; 3) products of data reconstruction and synthesis, including revisions of the codebook and analytic summaries of findings and conclusions; and 4) process notes, including notes on major methodological decisions as well as trustworthiness.

## Endnotes

1. The discussion of our sampling strategy and procedures draws upon material previously published in *A Silent Success: Master's Education in the United States* (see pp. 28–41).

2. After completing intensive case studies of master's programs in ten of these eleven fields at a national university, we reconsidered the necessity of including two traditional arts and sciences fields—sociology and computer science—in our study. Since only about 15 percent of the master's degrees conferred are granted in these fields (including professional fields in the arts and sciences) and we had strong representation in several emerging professional fields in the arts and sciences (applied anthropology and environmental studies), we decided to reduce our representation in the traditional liberal arts and sciences by eliminating sociology. Moreover, since many stakeholders interviewed in the computer science program suggested that their program was similar to a master's in engineering, we decided to drop computer science. With these adjustments, our sample was reduced to forty-seven cases—five programs in each of nine fields plus the programs in sociology and computer science.

3. Because we believe that the Carnegie classification inadequately distinguishes between universities serving national audiences and universities serving regional audiences, we designed a new institutional type classification scheme that differs from the Carnegie classification insofar as it incorporates the criterion of "audience served." For our purposes, "national" universities are institutions that are heavily committed to research and graduate education and serve a national and international audience. "Regional" universities are institutions that are involved in research and graduate education and, in some instances, offer doctoral as well as master's programs. In contrast to national universities, regional institutions are oriented largely to serving regional audiences through both their faculty research and program offerings. "Liberal arts" colleges are institutions that place a major emphasis on undergraduate education in the liberal arts and sciences, although many offer master's programs in a limited number of fields. Liberal arts institutions, for the most part, tend to serve regional or local audiences, though some attract students from throughout the nation. Finally, "specialized" institutions are those that offer degree programs ranging from the bachelor's to the doctorate, with at least one-half of all degrees awarded in a single field. These institutions often serve a national or a regional audience through faculty research and program offerings.

4. Our selections were guided, in part, by data for 1985–86 that were provided to us by the National Center for Education Statistics (NCES 1987). (NCES does not use the institutional classification scheme developed by the Carnegie Foundation for the Advancement of Teaching (1987), the most widely-used institutional classification scheme in higher education in the United States.) These data indicated that approximately 85 percent of all master's degrees in recent years have been granted by "doctoral" and "comprehensive" institutions, with the remaining 15 percent awarded by "general baccalaureate" and "specialty" institutions. Thirty-nine (83 percent) of the forty-seven programs in the sample are located at national universities and regional colleges and universities, and the remaining eight (17 percent) are located in liberal arts colleges and specialty institutions.

5. The forty-seven programs were distributed within these four types of institutions as follows: seven national universities (one program at five institutions, three programs at one institution, and 10 programs at one institution); 16 regional colleges and universities (one program at 13 institutions, two programs at two institutions, and four programs at one institution); five liberal arts colleges (one program at each of five institutions); and three specialty institutions (one program at each of three institutions).

6. According to estimates by the National Center for Education Statistics, slightly more than three-fifths of all master's degrees have been awarded by public institutions in recent years.

7. In addition to asking each program liaison to arrange interviews with individuals in each of the six stakeholder groups, we also requested that they select males and females within each stakeholder group who represented diverse racial and ethnic backgrounds. Furthermore, we specified other types of diversity which we hoped would be represented. In the faculty stakeholder group, for instance, we sought interviews with both senior and junior, tenured and non-tenured, and "research-oriented" and "practitioner-oriented" faculty. In terms of students, we asked to speak with individuals who differed in terms of part- and full-time status, level of financial support for graduate study, years of professional experience, and time in the program (from beginning to nearing completion of the degree). Within the alumni group, we requested interviews with alumni who were actively engaged in professional activities—as well as those who had pursued doctoral study—and asked to interview alumni who were at various stages in their careers. For employers of alumni, we asked to speak with individuals who represented both the public and private sectors and who represented a diversity of employment opportunities for program graduates.

8. We have been asked why we did not interview at least a few stakeholders who were not selected by the program liaison. We decided against this to avoid undermining our efforts to establish trusting relationships with program liaisons. While cognizant of the trade-offs involved, we believe that the congenial relationships we developed with program liaisons encouraged both them and the people whom they selected as interviewees to be open in their interviews. Our retrospective judgment is that we learned more this way than we might have by insisting that we interview people whom the program liaison did not choose. As it turned out, we occasionally interviewed one or two people in a program who had not been selected in advance.

When interviewees cancelled or did not show up, either we or the program liaison found substitutes.

9. Our original cross-program analysis, which mirrored the process we used in analyzing individual programs, began early in the study as we became attuned to themes, or patterns, in our fieldwork. Periodically, after several new program summaries had been completed, we paused to discuss them. These discussions helped us discern patterns across programs, but we avoided drawing conclusions so that we would remain open to emerging themes throughout the duration of our fieldwork. As a result, we had a vast amount of relatively unanalyzed information by the time all the program summaries were completed and we were ready to begin our cross-program analyses. Once all our program summaries had been completed, we began the process of developing themes across the forty-seven programs in our sample by reading and discussing individual summaries on a program-by-program basis. Over time, we began to piece together various themes that helped us to understand both similarities and differences across programs. For a more extended discussion of the analytic process we used in our original study, see *A Silent Success: Master's Education in the United States.*

10. We had scarcely looked at the actions that stakeholders had taken to develop and sustain individual program attributes that contribute to high-quality master's experiences, nor had we thoroughly explored the ways in which certain program attributes enhanced students' learning experiences or examined the effects of these learning experiences on students' growth and development. Moreover, we had not gone on to develop a theory of program quality which, in our view, was especially needed given the absence of any theory of program quality in the literature.

11. In contrast to more conventional sampling approaches that focus on selecting samples in terms of their statistical representation in the target population, theoretical sampling focuses instead on the representativeness of concepts in the sample population (Strauss and Corbin 1990, 190).

12. We do not mean to suggest that qualitative researchers share a common definition of trustworthiness. For example, LeCompte and Goetz (1982) provide a definition that is closely linked with a traditional positivist orientation. For alternative, post-positivist views, see Lincoln and Guba (1985) and Lather (1986).

13. While we did not rely extensively on documents in our analysis as a primary source, we collected documents from each program, including catalogs and brochures. In turn, we used these materials to check on the accuracy of stakeholders' statements and interpretations as part of our ongoing efforts to enhance trustworthiness.

14. In most cases, three of the four interviewers worked together on a program, while in the other cases either two or four people conducted the interviews.

15. While reviewing and analyzing the perspectives of these multi-positioned stakeholders, we sometimes noted one or two interviewees associated with a particular program whose experiences were clearly idiosyncratic compared with those of the other interviewees. We used these "outlier" perspectives in our analysis with great caution.

# References

Abbott, Walter F. "University and Departmental Determinants of the Prestige of Sociology Departments." *American Sociologist* 7 (November, 1972): 14–15.

Abbott, Walter F., and Henry M. Barlow. "Stratification Theory and Organizational Rank: Resources, Functions, and University Prestige in the United States." *Pacific Sociological Review* 15 (October, 1972): 401–424.

American Association for Higher Education. *Principles of Good Practice for Assessing Student Learning.* Washington, D.C.: 1992.

Ames, Russell. "Issues in the Development and Use of Appropriate Measuring Devices." In *Proceedings on the Conference on the Assessment of Quality of Master's Programs,* by Council of Graduate Schools. College Park: University of Maryland, 1979.

Anderson, Martin. *Imposters in the Temple: American Intellectuals are Destroying Our Universities and Cheating Our Students of Their Future.* New York: Simon & Schuster, 1992.

Andrews, Grover J. "Traditional vs. Nontraditional Master's Programs and Their Relationship to Quality Standards." *In Proceedings on the Conference on the Assessment of Quality of Master's Programs,* by Council of Graduate Schools. College Park: University of Maryland, 1979.

Angelo, Thomas A., and K. Patricia Cross. *Classroom Assessment Techniques: A Handbook for College Teachers* (Second Edition). San Francisco: Jossey-Bass, 1993.

Association of American Colleges. *Integrity in the College Curriculum: A Report to the Academic Community.* Project on Redefining the Meaning and Purpose of Baccalaureate Degrees. Washington, D.C.: Association of American Colleges, 1985.

Association of American Colleges Task Force on General Education. *A New Vitality in General Education.* Washington, D.C.: Association of American Colleges, 1988.

Association of American Colleges. *Program Review and Educational Quality in the Major.* Project on Liberal Learning, Study-in-Depth, and the Arts and Sciences Major. Washington, D.C.: 1992.

Astin, Alexander W. *Four Critical Years: Effects of College on Beliefs, Attitudes, and Knowledge.* San Francisco: Jossey-Bass, 1977.

Astin, Alexander W. "When Does A College Deserve To Be Called 'High Quality?'" *Current Issues in Higher Education: Improving Teaching and Institutional Quality.* Washington, D.C.: American Association for Higher Education, 1980.

Astin, Alexander W. "Why Not Try Some New Ways of Measuring Quality?" *Educational Record* (Spring, 1982): 10–15.

Astin, Alexander W. "Student Involvement: A Developmental Theory for Higher Education." *Journal of College Student Personnel* 25 (July, 1984): 297–308.

Astin, Alexander W. *Achieving Educational Excellence.* San Francisco: Jossey-Bass, 1985.

Astin, Alexander W. *What Matters in College: Four Critical Years Revisited.* San Francisco: Jossey-Bass, 1993.

Astin, Alexander W., and Lewis C. Solmon. "Measuring Academic Quality: An Interim Report." *Change* 11 (September, 1979): 48–51.

Astin, Alexander W., and Lewis C. Solmon. "Are Reputational Ratings Needed to Measure Quality?" *Change* 13 (October, 1981): 14–19.

Astin, Helen S., and Laura Kent. "Gender Roles in Transition: Research and Policy Implications for Higher Education." *Journal of Higher Education* 54 (May/June, 1983): 309–324.

Banta, Trudy and Associates. *Making A Difference: Outcomes of A Decade of Assessment in Higher Education.* San Francisco: Jossey-Bass, 1993.

Barwise, Jon, and John Perry. *Situations and Attitudes.* Cambridge: Massachusetts Institute of Technology Press, 1983.

Baxter Magolda, Marcia B. "Cocurricular Influences on College Students' Intellectual Development." *Journal of College Student Development* 33 (May, 1992): 203–213.

Beilock, Richard P., Polopolus, Leo C., and Mario Correal. "Ranking of Agricultural Economics Departments by Citations." *American Journal of Agricultural Economics* 68 (August, 1986): 595–604.

Belenky, Mary Field, Clinchy, Blythe McVicker, Goldberger, Nancy Rule, and Jill Mattuck Tarule. *Women's Ways of Knowing: The Development of Self, Voice, and Mind.* New York: Basic Books, 1986.

Bennett, William J. *To Reclaim a Legacy: A Report of the Humanities in Higher Education.* Washington, D.C.: National Endowment for the Humanities, 1984.

Bensimon, Estela Mara, and Anna Neumann. *Redesigning Collegiate Leadership: Teams and Teamwork in Higher Education.* Baltimore: Johns Hopkins University Press, 1993.

Bergquist, William H., and Jack L. Armstrong. *Planning Effectively for Educational Quality.* San Francisco: Jossey-Bass, 1986.

Beyer, Janice M., and Reuben Snipper. "Objective Versus Subjective Indicators of Quality." *Sociology of Education* 47 (Fall, 1974): 541–557.

Blackburn, Robert T., and Paul E. Lingenfelter. *Assessing Quality for Doctoral Programs: Criteria and Correlates of Excellence.* Ann Arbor: Center for the Study of Higher Education, University of Michigan, 1973.

Blackwell, James E. "Mentoring: An Action Strategy for Increasing Minority Faculty." *Academe* 75 (September/October, 1989): 8–14.

Blair, Dudley W., Cottle, Rex L., and Myles S. Wallace. "Faculty Ratings of Major Economics Departments by Citations: An Extension." *The American Economic Review* 76 (March, 1986): 264–267.

Blau, Peter M., and Rebecca Zames Margulies. "A Research Replication: The Reputations of American Professional Schools." *Change* 6 (December/January, 1974–75): 42–47.

Bloom, Allan. *The Closing of the American Mind: How Higher Education Has Failed Democracy and Impoverished the Souls of Today's Students.* New York: Simon and Schuster, 1987.

Bonwell, Charles C., and James A. Eison. *Active Learning: Creating Excitement in the Classroom* (ASHE-ERIC Higher Education Report no. 1). Washington D.C.: The George Washington University, School of Education and Human Development, 1991.

Bookstein, Abraham, and Mary Biggs. "Rating Higher Education Programs: The Case of the 1986 White Survey." *Library Quarterly* 57 (October, 1987): 351–399.

Bouton, Clark, and Russell Y. Garth. *Learning in Groups* (New Directions for Teaching and Learning, no. 14). San Francisco: Jossey-Bass, 1983.

Bowen, Howard R. *Investment in Learning.* San Francisco: Jossey-Bass, 1977.

Bowker, Albert H. "Quality and Quantity in Higher Education." *Journal of the American Statistical Association* 60 (March, 1965): 1–15.

Boyer, Ernest L. *College: The Undergraduate Experience in America.* New York: Harper and Row, 1987.

Boyer, Ernest L. *Scholarship Reconsidered: Priorities of the Professoriate.* Princeton, N.J.: Carnegie Foundation for the Advancement of Teaching, 1990.

Brookfield, Stephen D. *Developing Critical Thinkers: Challenging Adults to Explore Alternative Ways of Thinking and Acting.* San Francisco: Jossey-Bass, 1987.

Brown, Daniel Alan. "A Comparative Analysis of Bible College Quality." Los Angeles: University of California at Los Angeles, Ph.D. Dissertation, 1992.

Bruffee, Kenneth A. "The Art of Collaborative Learning." *Change* (March/April 1987): 42–27.

Bruffee, Kenneth A. *Collaborative Learning.* Baltimore: Johns Hopkins University Press, 1993.

Carnegie Foundation for the Advancement of Teaching. *Missions of the College Curriculum: A Contemporary Review with Suggestions.* San Francisco: Jossey-Bass, 1977.

Carnegie Foundation for the Advancement of Teaching. *A Classification of Institutions of Higher Education.* Princeton, N.J.: The Carnegie Foundation for the Advancement of Teaching, 1987.

Carnegie Foundation for the Advancement of Teaching. *Campus Life: In Search of Community.* Princeton, N.J.: Carnegie Foundation for the Advancement of Teaching, 1990.

Carpenter, Ray L., and Patricia A. Carpenter. "The Doctorate in Librarianship and an Assessment of Graduate Library Education." *Journal of Education for Librarianship* 11 (Summer, 1970): 3–45.

Cartter, Allan M. *An Assessment of Quality in Graduate Education.* Washington, D.C.: American Council on Education, 1966.

Cartter, Allan M., and Lewis C. Solmon. "The Cartter Report on the Leading Schools of Education, Law, and Business." *Change* (February, 1977): 44–48.

Centra, John. *Reflective Faculty Evaluation: Enhancing Teaching and Determining Faculty Effectiveness.* San Francisco: Jossey-Bass, 1993.

Chaffee, Ellen Earle, and William G. Tierney. *Collegiate Culture and Leadership Strategies.* New York: American Council on Education and Macmillan, 1988.

Chaffee, Ellen Earle, and Lawrence A. Sherr. *Quality: Transforming Postsecondary Education* (ASHE-ERIC Higher Education Report no. 3). Washington, D.C.: The George Washington University, School of Education and Human Development, 1992.

Chickering, Arthur W., and Zelda F. Gamson. "Seven Principles for Good Practice in Undergraduate Education." *AAHE Bulletin* 39 (March, 1987): 3–7.

Clark, Burton R. *The Academic Life: Small Worlds, Different Worlds.* Princeton, N.J.: Carnegie Foundation for the Advancement of Teaching, 1987.

Clark, Kenneth E. "The Issue of Quality in Master's Degree Programs." In *Proceedings on the Conference on the Assessment of Quality of Master's Programs,* by Council of Graduate Schools. College Park: University of Maryland, 1979.

Clark, Mary Jo. "The Meaning of Quality in Graduate and Professional Education." In *Scholars in the Making: The Development of Professional Students,* edited by Joseph Katz and Rodney T. Hartnett. Cambridge, Mass.: Ballinger, 1976.

Clark, Mary Jo, Hartnett, Rodney T., and Leonard L. Baird. *Assessing Dimensions of Quality in Doctoral Education: A Technical Report of a National Study in Three Fields.* Princeton, N.J: Educational Testing Service, 1976.

Clemente, Frank, and Richard B. Sturgis. "Quality of Departments of Doctoral Training and Research Productivity." *Sociology of Education* 47 (Spring, 1974): 287–299.

Conrad, Clifton F. *The Undergraduate Curriculum: A Guide to Innovation and Reform.* Boulder, Colo: Westview Press, 1978

Conrad, Clifton F. "Grounded Theory: An Alternative Approach to Research in Higher Education." *Review of Higher Education* 5 (Fall, 1982): 239–249.

Conrad, Clifton F. "Meditations on the Ideology of Inquiry in Higher Education: Exposition, Critique, and Conjecture." *Review of Higher Education* 12 (Spring, 1989): 199–220.

Conrad, Clifton F., and Robert T. Blackburn. "Correlates of Departmental Quality in Regional Colleges and Universities." *American Educational Research Journal* 22 (Summer, 1985a): 279–295.

Conrad, Clifton F., and Robert T. Blackburn. "Research on Program Quality: A Review and Critique of the Literature." In *Higher Education: Handbook of Theory and Research,* edited by John C. Smart, vol. 1. New York: Agathon Press, 1985b.

Conrad, Clifton F., and Robert T. Blackburn. "Current Views of Departmental Quality: An Empirical Examination." *Review of Higher Education* 9 (Fall, 1986): 249–265.

Conrad, Clifton F., and David J. Eagan. "Master's Degree Programs in American Higher Education." In *Higher Education: Handbook of Theory and Research,* edited by John C. Smart, vol. 6. New York: Agathon Press, 1990.

Conrad, Clifton F., and Anne M. Pratt. "Designing for Quality." *Journal of Higher Education* 56 (November/December, 1985): 601–622.

Conrad, Clifton F., and Richard F. Wilson. *Academic Program Reviews.* (ASHE-ERIC Higher Education Research Report no. 5). Washington, D.C.: American Association for Higher Education, 1985.

Conrad, Clifton F., Haworth, Jennifer Grant, and Susan Bolyard Millar. *A Silent Success: Master's Education in the United States.* Baltimore: Johns Hopkins University Press, 1993.

Cooper, James, and Randall Mueck. "Student Involvement in Learning: Cooperative Learning and College Instruction." *Journal of Excellence in College Teaching* 1 (1990): 68–76.

Council of Graduate Schools in the United States. *The Master's Degree: A Policy Statement.* Washington, D.C.: Council of Graduate Schools, 1981.

Courts, Patrick L., and Kathleen H. McInerney. *Assessment in Higher Education: Politics, Pedagogy, and Portfolios.* Westport, Conn: Praeger, 1993.

Cox, W. Miles, and Viola Catt. "Productivity Ratings of Graduate Programs in Psychology Based on Publication in the Journals of the American Psychological Association." *American Psychologist* 32 (October, 1977): 793–813.

Crane, Diana. "Scientists at Major and Minor Universities: A Study of Productivity and Recognition." *American Sociological Review* 30 (October, 1970): 699–714.

Cross, K. Patricia. "Teaching for Learning." *AAHE Bulletin* 39 (April, 1987): 3–7.

Davis, Barbara Gross. "Demystifying Assessment: Learning From the Field of Evaluation." In *Achieving Assessment Goals Using Evaluation Techniques* (New Directions for Higher Education no. 67), edited by Peter J. Gray. San Francisco: Jossey-Bass, 1989.

Dolan, W. Patrick. *The Ranking Game: The Power of the Academic Elite.* Lincoln, Neb.: University of Nebraska Printing and Duplicating Services, 1976.

Douglas, George H. *Education Without Impact: How Our Universities Fail the Young.* New York: Birch Lane Press, 1992.

Downey, Bernard J. "What is the Assessment of Quality?" In *Proceedings on the Conference on the Assessment of Quality of Master's Programs,* by Council of Graduate Schools. College Park: University of Maryland, 1979.

Drew, David E. *Science Development: An Evaluation Study.* Washington, D.C.: National Academy of Sciences, 1975.

Drew, David E., and Ronald Karpf. "Ranking Academic Departments: Empirical Findings and a Theoretical Perspective." *Research in Higher Education* 14 (June, 1981): 305–320.

D'Souza, Dinesh. *Illiberal Education: The Politics of Race and Sex on Campus.* New York: The Free Press, 1991.

Dube, W. F. "Undergraduate Origins of U.S. Medical Students." *Journal of Medical Education* 49 (1974): 1005–1010.

Eisenstat, Russell A., and Susan G. Cohen. "Summary: Top Management Group." In *Groups That Work (and Those that Don't): Creating Conditions for Effective Teamwork,* edited by J. Richard Hackman. San Francisco: Jossey-Bass, 1990.

Elton, Charles F., and Harriet A. Rose. "What are the Ratings Rating?" *American Psychologist* 27 (March, 1972): 197–201.

Epstein, Joyce L. "Quality Assessments of the Quality of Master's Programs." In *Proceedings on the Conference on the Assessment of Quality of Master's Programs,* by Council of Graduate Schools. College Park: University of Maryland, 1979.

Ewell, Peter T. "Assessment and TQM: In Search of Convergence." In *Total Quality Management in Higher Education* (New Directions for Institutional Research no. 71), edited by Lawrence A. Sherr and Deborah J. Teeter. San Francisco: Jossey-Bass, 1991.

Fairweather, James S. "Reputational Quality of Academic Programs: The Institutional Halo." *Research in Higher Education* 28 (June, 1988): 345–356.

Fairweather, James S., and Dennis F. Brown. "Dimensions of Academic Program Quality." *Review of Higher Education* 14 (Winter, 1991): 155–176.

Feldman, Kenneth A., and Theodore M. Newcomb. *The Impact of College on Students.* San Francisco: Jossey-Bass, 1969.

Fisher, Charles F. "Being There Vicariously By Case Studies." In *On College Teaching,* edited by Ohmer Milton. San Francisco: Jossey-Bass, 1978.

Fisher, James L. "Establishing Quality Criteria in Master's Programs." In *Proceedings on the Conference on the Assessment of Quality of Master's Programs,* by Council of Graduate Schools. *College Park: University of Maryland, 1979.*

Forrest, Aubrey. *Time Will Tell: Portfolio-Assisted Assessment of General Education.* Washington, D.C.: American Association for Higher Education/The AAHE Assessment Forum, 1990.

Freire, Paulo. *Pedagogy of the Oppressed.* New York: Seaview, 1970.

Fuller, Carol H. "Ph.D. Recipients: Where Did They Go to College?" *Change* 18 (November/December, 1986): 42–51.

Gabarro, John J. *The Dynamics of Taking Charge.* Boston: Harvard Business School Press, 1987.

Gabelnick, Faith, MacGregor, Jean, Matthews, Roberta F., and Barbara Leigh Smith. *Learning Communities: Creating Connections Among Students, Faculty, and Disciplines* (New Directions for Teaching and Learning, no. 41). San Francisco: Jossey-Bass, 1990.

Gaff, Jerry G. *New Life for the College Curriculum.* San Francisco: Jossey-Bass, 1991.

Gamson, Zelda F. "The Destruction and Re-creation of Academic Community: A Personal View." Keynote address presented at the Annual Meeting of the Association for the Study of Higher Education. Minneapolis, Minnesota, November 1, 1992.

Gamson, Zelda F. and Associates. *Liberating Education.* San Francisco: Jossey-Bass, 1984.

Geertz, Clifford. *The Interpretation of Cultures.* New York: Basic Books, 1974.

Geertz, Clifford. *Local Knowledge: Further Essays in Interpretive Anthropology.* New York: Basic Books, 1983.

Giroux, Henry. *Schooling and the Struggle for Public Life.* Minneapolis: University of Minnesota Press, 1988.

Glaser, Barney G. *Theoretical Sensitivity.* Mill Valley, Calif.: Sociology Press, 1978.

Glaser, Barney G., and Anselm L. Strauss. *The Discovery of Grounded Theory.* Chicago: Aldine, 1967.

Glazer, Judith S. *The Master's Degree: Tradition, Diversity, Innovation* (ASHE-ERIC Higher Education Research Report no. 6.). Washington, D.C.: Association for the Study of Higher Education, 1986.

Glenn, Novales D., and Wayne Villimez. "The Productivity of Sociologists at 45 American Universities." *American Sociologist* 5 (August, 1970): 244–252.

Glower, Donald G. "A Rational Method for Ranking Engineering Programs." *Engineering Education* 70 (1980): 788–794, 842.

Greene, David, and Jane L. David. "A Research Design for Generalizing from Multiple Case Studies." Palo Alto, Calif.: Bay Area Research Group, 1981.

Guba, Egon G., and Yvonna S. Lincoln. *Effective Evaluation.* San Francisco: Jossey-Bass, 1981.

Guskin, Alan. "Reducing Student Costs and Enhancing Student Learning: The University Challenge of the 1990s. *Change* 25 (July/August 1994): 23–29.

Hagstrom, Warren O. "Inputs, Outputs, and the Prestige of University Science Departments." *Sociology of Education* 44 (Fall, 1971): 375–397.

Harding, Sandra. *The Science Question in Feminism.* Ithaca, N.Y.: Cornell University Press, 1986.

Harding, Sandra. *Whose Science, Whose Knowledge: Thinking from Women's Lives.* Ithaca, N.Y.: Cornell University Press, 1991.

Hartnett, Rodney T., Clark, Mary Jo, and Leonard L. Baird. "Reputational Rankings of Doctoral Programs." *Science* 199 (1978): 1310-1314.

Hattendorf, Lynn C. "College and University Rankings: Part 4—An Annotated Bibliography of Analysis, Criticism, and Evaluation." *RQ* 28 (Spring, 1989): 340–367.

Haworth, Jennifer Grant. "A Grounded Theory of Program Quality in Master's Education." Ph.D. Dissertation, University of Wisconsin-Madison, 1993.

Hill, Patrick J. "The Rationale for Learning Communities." Paper presented at the Inaugural Conference of the Washington Center for Improving the Quality of Undergraduate Education. Olympia, Washington, October 22, 1985.

House, Donald R., and James H. Yeager, Jr. "The Distribution of Publication Success Within and Among Top Economics Departments: A Disaggregate View of Recent Evidence." *Economic Inquiry* 16 (October, 1978): 593–598.

Howard, George S., Cole, David A., and Scott E. Maxwell. "Research Productivity in Psychology Based on Publication in the Journals of the American Psychological Association." *American Psychologist* 86 (November 1987): 975–986.

Hoyte, Robert M., and Jonathan Collett. "'I Can Do It': Minority Undergraduate Science Experiences and the Professional Career Choice." In *Building A Diverse Faculty* (New Directions for Teaching and Learning no. 53), edited by Joanne Gainen and Robert Boice. San Francisco: Jossey-Bass, 1993.

Hughes, Raymond M. *A Study of Graduate Schools of America.* Oxford, Ohio: Miami University Press, 1925.

Hughes, Raymond M. "Report of the Committee on Graduate Instruction." *Educational Record* 15 (April, 1934): 192–234.

Hutchings, Pat. "Assessment and the Way We Work." In *Assessment 1990: Understanding the Implications* by the American Association for Higher Education Assessment Forum. Washington, D.C.: American Association for Higher Education, 1990.

Jacobi, Maryann. "Mentoring and Undergraduate Academic Success: A Literature Review." *Review of Educational Research,* 61 (Winter, 1991): 502–532.

Jacobs, Frederic, and Richard J. Allen, eds. *Expanding the Missions of Graduate and Professional Education* (New Directions for Experiential Learning, no. 15). San Francisco: Jossey-Bass, 1982.

Janes, R.W. "The Student Faculty Ratio in Graduate Programs of Selected Departments of Sociology." *American Sociologist* 4 (May, 1969): 123–127.

Johnson, David W., and Roger T. Johnson. *Cooperation and Competition: Theory and Research.* Edina, Minn: Interaction Book Company, 1989.

Johnson, David W., and Roger T. Johnson. *Learning Together and Alone: Cooperative,*

*Competitive, and Individualistic Learning.* Englewood Cliffs, N.J.: Prentice-Hall, 1991.

Johnson, David W., Johnson, Roger T., and Karl A. Smith. *Cooperative Learning: Increasing College Faculty Instructional Productivity* (ASHE-ERIC Higher Education Report no. 4). Washington D.C.: The George Washington University, School of Education and Human Development, 1991.

Johnson, David W., Maruyama, Geoffrey, Johnson, Roger T., Nelson, Deborah, and Linda Skon. "Effects of Cooperative, Competitive, and Individualistic Goal Structures on Achievements: A Meta-Analysis." *Psychological Bulletin* 89 (1981): 47–62.

Jones, Lyle V., Lindzey, Gardner, and Porter E. Coggeshall, eds. *An Assessment of Research-Doctorate Programs in the United States*, 5 vols. Washington, D.C.: National Academy Press, 1982.

Jordan, Robert T. "Library Characteristics of Colleges Ranking High in Academic Excellence." *College and Research Libraries* 24 (September, 1963): 369–376.

Kagan, Spencer. *Cooperative Learning.* San Juan Capistrano, Calif: Resources for Teachers, 1988.

Katz, Joseph, ed. *Teaching as Though Students Mattered* (New Directions for Teaching and Learning no. 21). San Francisco: Jossey-Bass, 1985.

Kaufman, George G. "Rankings of Finance Departments by Faculty Representation on Editorial Boards of Professional Journals: A Note." *Journal of Finance* 39 (September, 1984): 1189–1197.

Keeton, Morris T. *Defining and Assuring Quality in Experiential Learning.* San Francisco: Jossey-Bass, 1980.

Keeton, Morris T. *Experiential Learning.* San Francisco: Jossey-Bass, 1976.

Keeton, Morris T., and Pamela J. Tate. *Learning By Experience: What, Why, How* (New Directions for Teaching and Learning, no. 1). San Francisco: Jossey-Bass, 1978.

Kelso, Charles D. "How Does Your Law School Measure Up?" *Student Lawyer* 4 (1975): 20–24.

Keniston, Hayward. *Graduate Study in Research in the Arts and Sciences at the University of Pennsylvania.* Philadelphia: University of Pennsylvania Press, 1959.

King, Suzanne, and Lee Wolfe. "A Latent-Variable Causal Model of Faculty Reputational Ratings." *Research in Higher Education* 27 (1987): 99–106.

Kirkwood, Robert. "The Quest for Quality in Graduate Education." *Educational Record* 66 (Summer, 1985): 5–8.

Klein, Renate D. "The Dynamics of the Women's Studies Classroom: A Review Essay on the Teaching Practice of Women's Studies in Higher Education." *Women's Studies International Forum* 10 (2, 1987): 187–206.

Knight, Michael E., and Denise Gallaro, eds. *Portfolio Assessment: Application of Portfolio Analysis.* Lanham, MD: University Press of America, 1994.

Knudson, Dean D., and Ted R. Vaughan. "Quality in Graduate Education: A Reevaluation of the Rankings of Sociology Departments in the Cartter Report." *American Sociologist* 4 (February, 1969): 12–19.

Knapp, Robert H., and Hubert B. Goodrich. *Origins of American Scientists.* New York: Russell and Russell, 1952.

Knapp, Robert H., and Joseph J. Greenbaum. *The Younger American Scholar: His Collegiate Origins.* Chicago: University of Chicago Press, 1953.

Kolb, David A. *Experiential Learning: Experience as the Source of Learning and Development.* Englewood Cliffs, N.J.: Prentice-Hall, 1984.

Krause, Ervin, and Loretta Krause. The colleges that produce our best scientists: A study of the academic training grounds of a large group of distinguished American scientists. *Science Education* 54 (1970): 133–140.

Krueger, Richard A. *Focus Groups: A Practical Guide for Applied Research* (Second Edition). Thousand Oaks, Calif.: Sage Publications, 1994.

Kuh, George D. *Indices of Quality in the Undergraduate Experience* (AAHE-ERIC Higher Education Research Report no. 4). Washington, D.C.: American Association for Higher Education, 1981.

Kuh, George D. "What Do we Do Now? Implications for Educators of 'How College Affects Students.'" *Review of Higher Education* 15 (Spring, 1992): 349–363.

Kuh, George D. "In Their Own Words: What Students Learn Outside the Classroom." *American Educational Research Journal* 30 (Summer, 1993): 277–304.

Kuh, George, Schuh, John H., and Elizabeth J. Whitt. *Involving Colleges: Successful Approaches to Fostering Student Learning and Development Outside the Classroom.* San Francisco: Jossey-Bass, 1991.

Kurfiss, Joanne G. *Critical Thinking: Theory, Research, Practice, and Possibilities* (ASHE-ERIC Higher Education Report no. 2). Washington, D.C.: Association for the Study of Higher Education, 1988.

Lather, Patti. "Issues of Validity in Openly Ideological Research: Between a Rock and a Soft Place." *Interchange* 17 (Winter, 1986): 63–84.

Lavendar, Abraham D., Mathers, Richard A., and John Pease. "The Student Faculty Ratio in Graduate Programs of Selected Departments of Sociology: A Supplement to the Janes Report." *American Sociologist* 6 (February, 1971): 29–30.

Lawrence, Judith K., and Kenneth C. Green. *A Question of Quality: The Higher Education Ratings Game* (AAHE-ERIC/Higher Education Research Report no. 5). Washington, D.C.: American Association for Higher Education, 1980.

LeCompte, Margaret D., and Judith Preissle Goetz. "Problems of Reliability and Validity in Ethnographic Research." *Review of Educational Research* 52 (Spring, 1982): 31–60.

Leslie, Larry L., and Paul T. Brinkman. *The Economic Value of Higher Education.* New York: American Council on Education/Macmillan, 1988.

Lewis, Lionel S. "On Subjective and Objective Rankings of Sociology Departments." *American Sociologist* 3 (May, 1968): 129–131.

Light, Richard J. *The Harvard Assessment Seminars: First Report.* Cambridge, Mass: Harvard University Graduate School of Education and Kennedy School of Government, 1990.

Light, Richard J. *The Harvard Assessment Seminars: Second Report.* Cambridge, Mass: Harvard University Graduate School of Education and Kennedy School of Government, 1992.

Lincoln, Yvonna S. and Egon G. Guba. *Naturalistic Inquiry.* Beverly Hills, Calif.: Sage, 1985.

Lipschutz, Susan S. "Enhancing Success in Doctoral Education: From Policy to Practice." In *Increasing Graduate Student Retention and Degree Attainment* (New Directions For Institutional Research, no. 80), edited by Leonard L. Baird. San Francisco: Jossey-Bass, 1993.

Liu, Helen C. "Faculty Citation and Quality of Graduate Engineering Departments." *Engineering Education* 68 (April, 1978): 739–741.

Lowman, Joseph. *Mastering the Techniques of Teaching.* San Francisco: Jossey-Bass, 1984.

Lyons, William, Scroggins, Don, and Patra Bonham Rule. "The Mentor in Graduate Education." *Studies in Higher Education,* 15 (Fall, 1990): 277–185.

Macrorie, Ken. *Twenty Teachers.* New York: Oxford, 1984.

Maehl, William H. "The Graduate Tradition and Experiential Learning." In *Expanding the Missions of Graduate and Professional Education* (New Directions for Experiential Learning, no. 15), edited by Frederic Jacobs and Richard J. Allen. San Francisco: Jossey-Bass, 1982.

Marchese, Ted. "TQM: A Time for Ideas." *Change* 25 (May/June 1993): 10–13.

Mayhew, Lewis B., Ford, Patrick J., and Dean L. Hubbard. *The Quest for Quality.* San Francisco: Jossey-Bass, 1990.

McCarty, Donald J. "Issues in Quality Education and the Evaluation of Nontraditional Graduate Programs." *Alternative Higher Education* 4 (Fall, 1979): 61–69.

McKeachie, Wilbert J. *Teaching Tips: A Guidebook for the Beginning College Teacher.* Lexington, Mass: D.C. Heath and Company, 1969.

McKeachie, William J., Pintrich, Paul R., Yi-Guang, Lin, and David Smith. *Teaching and Learning in the College Classroom: A Review of the Research Literature.* Ann Arbor: University of Michigan, National Center for Research to Improve Postsecondary Teaching and Learning, 1986.

McLaren, Peter. *Life in Schools: An Introduction to Critical Pedagogy in the Foundations of Education.* White Plains, N.Y.: Longman, 1989.

Mentkowski, Marcia. "Creating A Context Where Institutional Assessment Yields Educational Improvement." *The Journal of General Education* 40 (1991): 255–283.

Merriam, Sharan. "Mentors and Proteges: A Critical Review of the Literature." *Adult Education Quarterly,* 33 (1983): 164–173.

Meyers, Chet and Thomas B. Jones. *Promoting Active Learning: Strategies for the College Classroom.* San Francisco: Jossey-Bass, 1993.

Millard, Richard M. "Assessing the Quality of Innovative Graduate Programs." In *Keeping Graduate Programs Responsive to National Needs* (New Directions for Higher Education, no. 46.), edited by Michael J. Pelczar, Jr., and Lewis C. Solmon. San Francisco: Jossey-Bass, 1984.

Millard, Richard M. *Today's Myths and Tomorrow's Realities: Overcoming Obstacles to Academic Leadership in the 21st Century.* San Francisco: Jossey-Bass, 1991.

Minkel, C.W., and Mary P. Richards. *Measures of Quality in Graduate Education.* Chattanooga, Tenn.: University of Tennessee at Chattanooga Graphic Services, 1981.

Minkel, C.W., and Mary P. Richards. *Components of Quality in Master's Degree Programs.* Knoxville, Tenn.: University of Tennessee at Knoxville Graphic Arts Service, 1986.

Minnich, Elizabeth K. *Transforming Knowledge.* Philadelphia: Temple University Press, 1990.

Moore, Lawrence J., and Bernard W. Taylor III. "A Study of Institutional Publications in Business-Related Academic Journals, 1972–1978." *Quarterly Review of Economics and Business* 20 (Spring, 1980): 87–97.

Morgan, David L. *Focus Groups as Qualitative Research.* Beverly Hills, Calif.: Sage Publications, 1988.

Morgan, David L., Kearney, Richard C., and James L. Regens. "Assessing Quality Among Graduate Institutions of Higher Education in the United States." *Social Science Quarterly* 57 (December, 1976): 670–679.

National Center for Education Statistics (NCES). U.S. Department of Education. *Digest of Education Statistics 1987.* Washington, D.C.: 1987.

National Center for Education Statistics (NCES). U.S. Department of Education. *Projections of Education Statistics to 2002.* Washington, D.C.: 1991.

Neumann, Anna, and Estela M. Bensimon. "Constructing the Presidency: College Presidents' Images of Their Leadership Roles, A Comparative Study." *Journal of Higher Education* 61 (July/August, 1990): 678–701.

Newman, Philip K., and Barbara M. Newman. "Identity Formation and the College Experience." *Adolescence* 13 (Summer, 1978): 311–326.

Oromaner, Mark J. "A Note on Analytical Properties and Prestige of Sociology Departments." *American Sociologist* 5 (August, 1970): 240–244.

Ory, John C., and Larry A. Braskamp. "Involvement and Growth of Students in Three Academic Programs." *Research in Higher Education* 28 (1988): 116–129.

Pace, C. Robert. "Measuring the Quality of Student Effort." *Current Issues in Higher Education: Improving Teaching and Institutional Quality.* Washington, D.C.: American Association for Higher Education, 1980.

Pace, C. Robert. *Measuring the Quality of College Student Experiences.* Los Angeles: Higher Education Research Institute, University of California, 1984.

Pace, C. Robert. *Student Effort: A New Key to Assessing Quality.* Project on the Study of Quality in Undergraduate Education. Los Angeles: Higher Education Research Institute, University of California, 1986.

Palmer, Parker J. *To Know as We Are Known: A Spirituality of Education.* San Francisco: HarperCollins, 1983.

Panel on Alternate Approaches to Graduate Education. *Scholarship for Society.* Princeton, N.J.: Educational Testing Service, 1973.

Parker, Clyde, and Janet Schmidt. "Effects of College Experience." In *Encyclopedia of Educational Research,* edited by Harold E. Mitzel. New York: Free Press, 1982.

Pascarella, Ernest T. "Student-Faculty Informal Contact and College Outcomes." *Review of Educational Research* 50 (Winter, 1980): 545–590.

Pascarella, Ernest T., and Patrick T. Terenzini. *How College Affects Students: Findings and Insights from Twenty Years of Research.* San Francisco: Jossey-Bass, 1991.

Pascarella, Ernest T., Ethington, Corinna A. and John C. Smart. "The Influence of College on Humanitarian/Civic Involvement Values." *Journal of Higher Education* 59 (July/August, 1988): 412–437.

Patton, Michael. *How to Use Qualitative Methods in Evaluation.* Newbury Park, Calif.: Sage Publications, 1987.

Perkins, Dexter, and John L. Snell. *The Education of Historians in the United States.* New York: McGraw-Hill, 1962.

Pirsig, Robert M. *Zen and the Art of Motorcycle Maintenance.* New York: William Morrow, 1974.

Prus, Joseph, and Reid A. Johnson. *A Critical Review of Student Assessment Options.* Rock Hill, S.C.: Winthrop College, 1992.

Roach, Deborah A., and Larry L. Barker. "An Evaluation of Master's Programs in Speech Communication by Region." *Association for Communication Administration Bulletin* 47 (January, 1984a): 67–74.

Roach, Deborah A., and Larry L. Barker. "An Evaluation of Master's Programs in the Speech Communication Discipline." *Communication Education* 33 (January, 1984b): 69–71.

Romer, Karen, ed. *CUE: Models of Collaboration in Undergraduate Education.* Providence, R.I.: Brown University Press, 1985.

Roose, Kenneth D., and Charles J. Anderson. *A Rating of Graduate Programs.* Washington, D.C.: American Council on Education, 1970.

Rosaldo, Renato. *Culture and Truth: The Remaking of Social Analysis.* Boston: Beacon Press, 1989.

Sanford, Nevitt. *Where Colleges Fail: A Study of the Student as a Person.* San Francisco: Jossey-Bass, 1968.

Schaefer, William D. *Education Without Compromise: From Chaos to Coherence in Higher Education.* San Francisco: Jossey-Bass, 1990.

Schilling, Karl, and Karen Maitland Schilling. "Descriptive Approaches to Assessment: Moving Beyond Meeting Requirements to Making A Difference." In *A Collection of Papers on Self-Study and Institutional Improvement,* by The Commission on Institutions of Higher Education, North Central Association of Colleges and Schools (98th Annual Meeting). Chicago: 1993.

Schniedewind, Nancy. "Teaching Feminist Process." *Women's Studies Quarterly* 15 (Fall/Winter, 1987): 15–31.

Schon, Donald A. *Educating the Reflective Practitioner.* San Francisco: Jossey-Bass, 1987.

Seidman, I.E. *Interviewing as Qualitative Research: A Guide for Researchers in Education and the Social Sciences.* New York: Teachers College Press, 1991.

Seldin, Peter. *Successful Use of Teaching Portfolios.* Bolton, Mass.: Anker Publishing, 1993.

Sell, G. Roger. "An Organizational Perspective for the Effective Practice of Assessment." In *Achieving Assessment Goals Using Evaluation Techniques* (New Directions for Higher Education no. 67), edited by Peter J. Gray. San Francisco: Jossey-Bass, 1989.

Senge, Peter M. *The Fifth Discipline: The Art and Practice of the Learning Organization.* New York: Currency/Doubleday, 1990.

Senge, Peter M., Roberts, Charlotte, Ross, Richard B., Smith, Bryan J., and Art Kleiner. *The Fifth Discipline Fieldbook: Strategies and Tools for Building A Learning Organization.* New York: Currency/Doubleday, 1994.

Seymour, Daniel T. *On Q: Causing Quality in Higher Education.* New York: American Council on Education and Macmillan Publishing Company, 1992.

Sherr, Lawrence A., and Deborah J. Teeter. *Total Quality Management in Higher Education* (New Directions for Institutional Research, no. 71). San Francisco: Jossey-Bass, 1991.

Shor, Ira. *Critical Teaching and Everyday Life.* Boston: South End Press, 1980.

Shor, Ira, ed. *Freire for the Classroom: A Sourcebook for Liberatory Teaching.* Portsmouth, N.H.: Heinemann Educational Books, 1987.

Shrewsbury, Carolyn M. "What is Feminist Pedagogy?" *Women's Studies Quarterly* 15 (Fall/Winter, 1987): 6–13.

Slavin, Robert E. "Cooperative Learning." *Review of Educational Research* 50 (Summer, 1980): 315–42.

Slavin, Robert E. *Cooperative Learning.* New York: Longman, 1983.

Slavin, Robert E. *Cooperative Learning: Theory, Research, and Practice.* Englewood Cliffs, N.J.: Prentice-Hall, 1990.

Smith, Dorothy E. *The Conceptual Practices of Power: A Feminist Sociology of Knowledge*. Boston: Northeastern University Press, 1990.

Smith, Page. *Killing the Spirit: Higher Education in America*. New York: Viking Penguin, 1990.

Snow, Susan G. "Correlates of Faculty-Student Interaction." *Sociology of Education* 46 (Fall, 1973): 489-498.

Snyder, Mary Elisabeth. "An Assessment of Quality in Undergraduate Education." Los Angeles: University of California at Los Angeles, Ph.D. Dissertation, 1993.

Solmon, Lewis C., and Alexander W. Astin. "Departments Without Distinguished Graduate Programs." *Change* 13 (September, 1981): 23-28.

Somit, Alfred, and Joseph Tanenhaus. *American Political Science: A Profile of a Discipline*. New York: Atherton Press, 1964.

Sorcinelli, Mary Deane. "Research Findings on the Seven Principles." In *Applying the Seven Principles for Good Practice in Undergraduate Education* (New Directions for Teaching and Learning, no. 47), edited by Arthur W. Chickering and Zelda F. Gamson. San Francisco: Jossey-Bass, 1991.

Southern Association of Colleges and Schools. *Criteria for Accreditation (Proposed)*. Atlanta: Commmission on Colleges, Southern Association of Colleges and Schools, 1982.

Spitzberg, Irving J., Jr., and Virginia V. Thorndike. *Creating Community on College Campuses*. Albany, N.Y.: State University of New York Press, 1992.

Strauss, Anselm. *Qualitative Analysis for Social Scientists*. New York: Cambridge University Press, 1987.

Strauss, Anselm, and Juliet Corbin. *Basics of Qualitative Research: Grounded Theory Procedures and Techniques*. Newbury Park, Calif.: Sage, 1990.

Student Task Force on Education at Stanford. *The Other Stanford*. Palo Alto, Calif: Stanford Workshop on Political and Social Issues, 1973.

Study Group on the Conditions of Excellence in American Higher Education. *Involvement in Learning: Realizing the Potential of American Higher Education*. Washington, D.C.: National Institute of Education, 1984.

Sykes, Charles J. *Profscam: Professors and the Demise of Higher Education*. Washington, D.C.: Regnery Gateway, 1988.

Tan, David L. "The Assessment of Quality in Higher Education: A Critical View of the Literature and Research." *Research in Higher Education* 24 (November, 1986): 223-265.

Terenzini, Patrick T. "Assessment With Open Eyes: Pitfalls In Studying Student Outcomes." *Journal of Higher Education* 60 (November/December, 1989): 644-664.

Terenzini, Patrick T., Pascarella, Ernest T., and Wendell Lorang. "An Assessment of the Academic and Social Influences on Freshman Year Educational Outcomes." *Review of Higher Education* 5 (Winter, 1982): 86-110.

Thomas, Alice M. "Consideration of the Resources Needed in an Assessment Program." *NCA Quarterly* 66 (1991): 430-443.

Tierney, William G. "Cultural Politics and the Curriculum in Postsecondary Education." *Journal of Education* 171 (Fall, 1989a): 72-88.

Tierney, William G. *Curricular Landscapes, Democratic Vistas: Transformative Leadership in Higher Education*. New York: Praeger Publishers, 1989b.

Toombs, William, and William G. Tierney. *Meeting the Mandate: Renewing the College and Departmental Curriculum*. (ASHE-ERIC/Higher Education Research Report no. 6). Washington, D.C.: Association for the Study of Higher Education, 1992.

Trott, Darlene, Barker, Deborah Roach, and Larry L. Barker. "Evaluation of Master's Programs in the Speech Communication Discipline." *Communication in Education* 37 (October, 1988): 257-262.

Vonnegut, Kurt. *Slaughterhouse Five*. New York: Delacorte Press, 1969.

Webster, David S. "Advantages and Disadvantages of Methods of Assessing Quality." *Change* 13 (October, 1981): 20-24.

Webster, David S. *Academic Quality Rankings of American Colleges and Universities*. Springfield, Ill.: Charles C. Thomas, 1986a.

Webster, David S. "Ranking Academic Quality." *Change* 18 (November/December, 1986b): 34-41.

Webster, David S., and Clifton F. Conrad. "Using Faculty Research Performance for Academic Quality Rankings." In *Measuring Faculty Research Performance* (New Directions for Institutional Research, no. 50), edited by John Creswell. San Francisco: Jossey-Bass, 1986.

Webster, David S., Conrad, Clifton F., and Eric L. Jensen. "Objective and Reputational Rankings of Ph.D.-Granting Departments of Sociology." *Sociological Focus* 21 (April, 1988): 177-198.

Weis, Lois. *Between Two Worlds: Black Students in an Urban Community College*. Boston: Routledge and Kegan Paul, 1985.

White, Herbert S. "Perceptions by Educators and Administrators of the Ranking of Library School Programs: An Update and Analysis." *Library Quarterly* 57 (Summer, 1987): 252-268.

Wilson, Everett K. "The Entering Student: Attributes and Agents of Change." In *College Peer Groups*, edited by Theodore Newcomb and Everett K. Wilson. Chicago: Aldine, 1966.

Wilson, Robert C., Gaff, Jerry G., Dienst, Evelyn R., Wood, Lynn, and James L. Bavry. *College Professors and Their Impact on Students*. New York: Wiley, 1975.

Wispe, Lauren G. "The Bigger the Better: Productivity, Size, and Turnover in a Sample of Psychology Departments." *American Psychologist* 24 (1969): 662-668.

Worthen, Blaine R., and James R. Sanders. *Educational Evaluation: Alternative Approaches and Practical Guidelines*. New York: Longman, 1987.

Wright, Barbara. "So How Do We Know It Will Work: An Assessment Memoir." *AAHE Bulletin* (April 1990); 14-17.

Wulff, Donald, and Jody Nyquist. "Using Field Methods as an Instructional Tool." In *To Improve the Academy*, vol. 7, edited by Joanne Kurfiss, Linda Hilsen, Susan Kahn, Mary Deane Sorcinelli, and Richard Tiberius. Stillwater, Okla: POD/New Forums Press, 1988.

Young, Denise L., Blackburn, Robert T., and Clifton F. Conrad. "Research Note: Dimensions of Program Quality in Regional Universities." *American Educational Research Journal* 24 (Summer, 1987): 319-323.

Young, Denise L., Blackburn, Robert T., Conrad, Clifton F., and Kim S. Cameron. "Relationships Between Leadership, Student Effort, and Departmental Program Quality: An Exploration of Quality Across Levels of Analysis." *Review of Higher Education* 12 (Spring, 1989): 265-277.

Young, Kenneth E., Chambers, Charles M., and H.R. Kells and Associates. *Understanding Accreditation*. San Francisco: Jossey-Bass, 1983.

# Index